LOVE & DEATH IN RENAISS

❧ ❦

Thomas V. Cohen

❧❧

LOVE & DEATH IN
RENAISSANCE
ITALY

THE UNIVERSITY OF CHICAGO PRESS · *Chicago & London*

THOMAS V. COHEN is professor of history at York University. He is
coauthor, with his wife, Elizabeth Cohen, of *Words and Deeds in Renaissance
Rome: Trials before the Papal Magistrates* and *Daily Life in Renaissance Italy.*

❀

The University of Chicago Press, Chicago 60637
The University of Chicago Press, Ltd., London
© 2004 by The University of Chicago
All rights reserved. Published 2004
Printed in the United States of America

13 12 11 10 09 08 07 06 05 04   5 4 3 2 1

ISBN (cloth): 0-226-11258-6

Library of Congress Cataloging-in-Publication Data

Cohen, Thomas V. (Thomas Vance), 1942–
    Love & death in Renaissance Italy / Thomas V. Cohen.
      p.   cm.
    Includes bibliographical references and index.
    ISBN 0-226-11258-6 (cloth : alk paper)
      1. Italy—Social life and customs—To 1500—Sources.
    2. Renaissance—Italy—Sources.   I. Title: Love and death
    in Renaissance Italy.   II. Title.
      DG445.C64   2004
      945'.05—dc22

                                    2004001458

CONTENTS

ACKNOWLEDGMENTS

A BOOK LONG IN GESTATING OWES MANY thanks. Mine would have been impossible without the counsel and support of friends and colleagues in Italy and elsewhere. An Italian list should go on and on. Let me single out Claudio and Daniela Gori-Giorgi for endless Roman hospitality and help; Paolo Grandi for Pallantieri adventures in Castel Bolognese; architect Giorgio Tarquini, curator-doctor Fiora Bellini, and the late Père Jean Coste for help with the mysteries of Cretone castle; and doctors Laura Venditelli and Daniele Manacorda for the enthusiastic good offices of the Crypta Balbi/Santa Caterina museum and dig. I must also salute Giampiero Brunelli for generous data on the military career of Pompeo Giustini. Professoressa Irene Fosi of Rome and Chieti has been a wonderful colleague for two decades of Roman work. I must also thank the entire staff, from top to bottom, of the Archivio di Stato di Roma, and especially Annalia Bonella, for unfailing support and infinite patience with *"quelli canadesi,"* us two Cohens, with our many needs and queries. Among the many who have offered hearty guidance, I will single out some scholars: Renata Ago, Anna Esposito, Anna Foa, Massimo Miglio,

Elisje and Peter Van Kessel, and, for her warmth, wisdom, and amazing roof looking down on Rome at dusk, Angiolina Arrù.

Outside Italy, I have benefited from the counsel and the patience of too many experts to name. I will single out Jane Bestor, Charles Burroughs, Kathleen Christian, Bill Found, David Gentilcore, Elliot Horowitz, Laurie Nussdorfer, John and Meg Pinto, Susanne Pohl, Nancy Siraisi, and Roni Weinstein, all for special efforts on my behalf, and Thomas Kuehn for a thorough and characteristically hard-hitting critique. I owe special gratitude to my colleagues in my own department, a truly bracing institution, and to the lively members of York's faculty seminar on social history and anthropology, who heard many of my chapters as early drafts. Over the years, I had institutional support and funding from the American Council of Learned Societies, the National Endowment for the Humanities in association with the American Academy in Rome, the Social Sciences and Humanities Research Council of Canada, and my own Faculty of Arts, which granted me a year free of teaching to finish the book. And I cannot forget the contributions of my students, especially the undergraduates. Special credit goes to Linda Traverso Girardo and Raffaele Girardo for finding, transcribing, and translating the Innocentia trial, and to Deborah Hicks and all the first-year students of History 1000B (year 2000/2001), my Cretone detective crew, and especially to Jennifer Johnson and her grandmother, too old to come downstairs but who, unbeknownst to me, from the blueprints built a giant cutaway model of the Savelli castle for the class.

Last of all, I want to thank three generations of my own family for endless contributions. The youngsters, Will and Julie, abandoned familiar haunts to take on Italian schools, no mean task, and to plunge into Roman life and, years later, reviewed chapters as they rolled out. Richard and Virginia Storr, my wife's parents, read too, with canny and sympathetic eyes. My wife, Elizabeth, colleague and delightful companion in so much Roman work and life, as always helped keep my feet on solid intellectual ground.

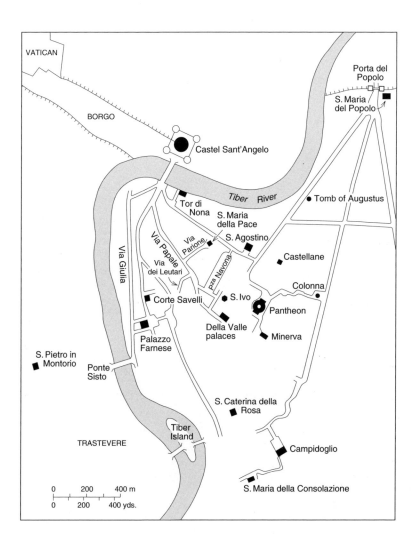

VATICAN

Porta del
Popolo

S. Maria
del Popolo

BORGO

Castel Sant'Angelo

Tiber River

Tor di
Nona
S. Maria
della Pace

S. Agostino

Tomb of Augustus

Via Papale

Via
Parione

Via
dei Leutari

Castellane

Via Giulia

pza Navona

Colonna

Corte Savelli

S. Ivo

S. Pietro in
Montorio

Palazzo
Farnese

Della Valle
palaces

Pantheon

Minerva

Ponte
Sisto

S. Caterina della
Rosa

Tiber
Island

TRASTEVERE

Campidoglio

0   200   400 m

0   200   400 yds.

S. Maria della Consolazione

Rome ca. 1560, with a few major landmarks and some of the places that figure in the stories in this book.

INTRODUCTION

IT IS HARD TO IMAGINE A MORE CONGENIAL place to study history than the State Archive—the Archivio di Stato—in Rome. First is the location, for the archive, with reading room, library, and vast shelves of ancient papers, inhabits the old buildings of the papal university, the Sapienza, in the very heart of town. Two blocks west is lovely Piazza Navona, with its tourists, good ice cream, vendors of kitschy art, and young men on the lookout for young, blond naiveté. Two blocks east is the Pantheon and the cafe with good granita. Three blocks south is the Campo di Fiori, after five centuries still a working market where vendors keep me posted on the birth of grandchildren and where the bakery in the corner, if ever you fight your way to the counter, will sell you a succulent bread full of big green olives.

Then there is the atmosphere. The state archive is a friendly, informal place. It has none of the rectitude and taut routine of Florence or the august officiousness of the Vatican. Everyone, from the director and the scholars who staff the study room, to the photographers and the clerks who fetch out dusty volumes, is quick to smile, lend a hand, help solve a problem. We foreigners who come

I

and go are assured a welcome on our return. And among the schol-ars there is real camaraderie; it is often easy to look over a stu-diously bent shoulder and inquire what a tome or a cluttered page contains, to strike up acquaintances, to make alliances. Rome is so immensely important to historians—of politics, religion, society, painting, architecture, sculpture, music, higher learning, and ur-ban form—that it draws fascinating scholars. Over the years, I have learned from many, not least from young Italian students who have mastered archival tricks. One can whisper at the desk or, for longer talk, retreat outdoors to the wide arcade overlooking the courtyard or duck into the second cafe just down the street, the friendly, honest one.

The old university itself is a splendid piece of architecture. A composite, it was built over many decades by several popes, who left their rival emblems in crazy plenty. Still, on three sides, it is de-ceptively uniform: two stories of severe arcades and one of modest windows around an oblong courtyard. The fourth side, however, is all caprice and fantasy, a library hidden on the left and, straight ahead, a billowing church, Sant'Ivo, both works of that brilliant, mysterious genius Borromini. Of all his pieces, the church may be his most eccentric, most beguiling, and most playful. Certainly, Rome has nothing else remotely like it. The ground plan is mod-eled on a six-point star. The walls, imprisoned at their base by the floor plan, sway and lunge as they rise and then, imperceptibly, brilliantly, somehow make peace with one another, smooth down their differences, and blend into a perfect dome. Atop the whole, outside, a central steeple rises, a tight corkscrew or mini-ziggurat, spiraling steeply to an iron crown. Sant'Ivo, the chapel for the uni-versity, seems to play, as if to amuse clever seventeenth-century minds. Long largely closed, it is now generously open to earnest German tourists, sober guidebook in hand, and to troops of flirta-tious high school students half-heedful of their *professoressa's* lec-ture on one more Roman wonder. Meanwhile, archive workers still use the church's upstairs balcony as a shortcut to their stacks, library, and administrative offices. Once in a while, as a courtesy, an employee has led me across to speed an errand; a door opens off a humdrum little corridor; one strides, briefly bedazzled, through sudden beauty.

For the past thirty-five years I have returned to Rome whenever possible to wallow in old friendships, fine architecture, good food, and archival papers. Among the papers, my favorites are the records of the criminal court of an official called the governor of Rome. This officer, usually a bishop, was a potent man with several jobs: papal bureaucrat, judge of a major criminal court, master of the biggest police force. His court had sufficient jurisdiction that no other tribunal could overturn its verdicts. His judges dealt with the gravest crimes: fraud, counterfeiting, homicide, lèse majesté, and treason; but, at the same time, they oversaw as well myriad minor brawls, slanging matches, and infractions of the decrees on bearing arms or taking whores to wine shops. Great crimes and lesser misdemeanors left an exuberant trail of judicial paper, much of which, by good luck, survives. These documents run in assorted series, bound and dated separately: denunciations, suspects' initial testimony, surgeons' reports on victims' wounds, logbooks of court transactions, backers' oaths and promises on behalf of prisoners, sentences. Thus, a single trial often meanders across several separate records; only the historian's skill or luck can reconstruct its story.

Of all these archival series, the richest, and best inventoried, are the *processi*. The term's easiest translation is "trials," but the word needs explaining, for, as proceedings, *processi* in form and spirit are far from trials in the Anglo-Saxon tradition we know by heart from film and television. The governor's tribunal, like many in Catholic Europe, followed the procedures of *inquisitio*, rooted in ancient and medieval Roman law. Unlike jury trials, rather public events where laity and a judge heard competing tales and oaths from witnesses, trials by *inquisitio* were closed affairs that relied on judicial expertise. There, it fell to the court to gather evidence by careful method, weigh it systematically, and pass trained judgment. Accordingly, its magistrates investigated suspects meticulously, kept faithful records of all words exchanged, and furnished a transcript to both defense and prosecution lawyers. *Inquisitio*'s evidentiary doctrine preferred confessions or, in their absence, the incontrovertible evidence of two good witnesses. But lesser evidence still could help a case; there was a whole calculus for weighing hints and clues. In a *processo,* and in all other exchanges with informants, courts hewed methodically to procedures designed to extort truth from reluctant witnesses. Secrecy reigned; in theory,

suspects at the outset did not know the reasons for their arraign-
ment. The court astutely veiled its information, tipping its hand
only to frame questions or trip or shock a witness. Thus, witnesses
testified in camera, in the suspect's absence, unless the court
staged a dramatic confrontation gauged to shake confession loose.
Mostly, suspects and witnesses stood alone before the judge and
notary, and sometimes before a prosecutor too, with neither counsel nor the support of friends. The court's great trump was torture;
prized midwife of confessions, it often accosted suspects of low
status or shady morals. Thus, in its traits, a *processo* fell somewhere
between an inquest and a trial; it passed no judgment; that came
later, after the lawyers' written briefs. But it was this preliminary
hearing, often, that sealed a suspect's fate.

What makes *processi* so fascinating to historians is the nature of
the papers they produced. In theory, the court notary was bound
to take down everything, verbatim—indeed, not only words but
even blushes, sighs, shrugs, and tears. For all his scribal skills, it is
unlikely the notary succeeded. On paper, depositions lack some of
the jerky quality of real speech, with its false starts, hesitations, and
repetitions. And assorted Italian dialects all come out looking like
the homogenized, semi-Tuscan language understood up and down
the Boot. Nevertheless, clearly the notary came close; his record
retains much of the tang of actual speech. Witnesses and suspects
have very distinct, very personal voices; their recorded talk often
conserves its metaphor and lilt. The scribal hand, it seems, was
light, and the ear was true. Consequently, these court papers are
marvelous cultural documents; they open windows onto modes of
thought and speech and tell precious stories about how sixteenth-
century Italy worked. Often, early in a deposition, the court ordered a witness to "tell the whole story, *ab initio usque ad finem* [from
beginning to end]." Then, the judge almost always held his tongue
for many minutes and long pages of unbroken monologue, while
his witness lapsed into the swing of narrative, with its cadences
and devices of fireside yarn or tavern storytelling. At other times,
the court fired serried, aggressive questions. Then, in terms and
structure, a witness's replies often echoed legal terminology. As
historians who work with tribunals' records are quick to admit or
warn, all court talk, even when the leash is long and lax, heels to
forensic circumstances. Witnesses always, in some measure, con-

form their rhetoric and diction to the law's peculiar thought and language. So no trial utters pure vox populi. Nevertheless, the populace is still nicely audible.

A good trial is a little world; it draws the reader in. Still, not all trials are equally enthralling. I have read homicide cases featuring a long procession of villagers who saw poor Antonio on the ground, his brains bashed out through his ears. Then, my curiosity sates far faster than does a sixteenth-century magistrate's. But most trials are thicker and more tangled; they have meandering lines of twisting plot and unexpected knots where several fates entwined and snarled. At the center, often, is some mishap or catastrophe, the corpus delicti that spurred the trial. And all around the crisis lie the fragments of many lives, some tightly bound and others linked only by the caprice of connection to the crime. A trial is two stories, and two dramas, quite distinct. The second went on in court; the first out in the world. The historian, gliding through the forensic story, watches the earlier tale of grief and mishap gradually emerge, as witness follows witness and as the judge, like a restless helmsman, tacks back and forth across their memories. Sometimes insight comes with reading. Eureka strikes. Often, however, the whole picture comes much more slowly, especially if a trial is long. I keep lists: of names, of places, of themes. Most useful of all, I find, are the timelines, great tapeworms of queries, charges, allegations, and concessions, sometimes concordant and sometimes wildly contradictory, each tagged by speaker, folio, forensic circumstance, and date. Working up a trial can take weeks or months. Ever so slowly, a picture emerges.

No historian just renders truth. It is a truism of our art and science that any history must bear the stamp of its writer's time, place, class, gender, professional position, private tastes and obsessions, and habitual mood and voice. A history is an interpretation, always, by necessity. But, I suspect, few historical enterprises make this fact more salient than does work with trials. For trials are at once intensely vivid and maddeningly incomplete. They remind me of those wonderful Chinese paintings, often applied to folding screens, that display in minute detail scenes from daily life—a market, jugglers, sedan chairs, children's games—but with thick white clouds masking half the scene. So trials, by their nature, force the scholar to fill in the gaps. And at the same time, very often, a trial brings the historian face-to-face with intense pain and searing passion. It is strange, reading these faded documents, with their bled-through ink and crumbling edges, to meet such feelings from persons now 450 years dead and to reflect that, almost always, no one in all those years has heeded them. It can be very moving. Not long ago, I read a little trial where one Federico, an old-clothes dealer in Campo di Fiori market, had been hauled to jail as suspect in the killing of a prostitute. Clearly, the man was innocent; I hope he convinced the judge. He had been called by frantic neighbors, he said, because his friend, Hortensia the prostitute, was wounded. He came running madly, only to find her dead. He told the court:

> I began to cry, and I found her sprawled at the foot of the bed,
> naked, on the floor. She had on a sheet that had been laid over
> her. And then I said, "Hortensia mine! I told you so many times,
> when you were alive, not to trust him, for he would kill you."[1]

Hortensia and Federico had planned to marry come next Easter; she had been saving her earnings, pooled with his, toward a nest egg for a family. A jealous fellow lover, chagrined at losing her, killed her. To read this tale of broken love and failed redemption is both very sad and oddly sweet. It lures the inner writer.

Distance, famously, has pathos; persons far away and long ago stir us because they seem to let us conquer space and time. Folk long gone, if we can see them well, at once defy mortality and remind us of its finality. They are so lively but also so very dead and gone. And when they lived as far back as 1550, they tease us, for they seem at once so knowable and so mysteriously alien, for the past, as I tell my students, is indeed a foreign country. That is the vivid paradox in reading trials: the sharp tension between intimacy and strangeness. To cite stories in this book, what did it really feel like to a man of twenty to snuggle in bed with the wet nurse of his infancy? How did a girl of twenty weigh the risks of wedding the stranger at her window against a lifetime shut inside her nunnery? With what mix of guile and passion did a husband entrap and kill his unfaithful wife? We can imagine but never know. For understanding, the best we can do is heap up "local knowledge." But, unlike the anthropologist out in the field, eating, conversing, bargaining, trading stories with the inhabitants and scratching the local fleas, we historians must scrounge our local knowledge secondhand, from papers.

It is the pathos of distance that invites art, for a shapely story, by its very artfulness, proclaims its artificiality. History told as story, with its literary devices—frame, flashback, metaphor, analogy, apostrophe, for instance—and with its evocation of the tricks of film and stage, reminds the reader that historical knowledge is self-conscious, is made, not just given. An artful story imposes its own order and, by doing so, at once evokes and subverts orders in the world it purports to depict. A story, then, can serve as a *figura* for the historian's crafty task: to take raw experience, in its turbulent confusion, and force it into a plausible and pleasing shape.

That, precisely, is what this book's stories do. "The Last Will of Vittoria Giustini" appears as a soap opera; the "The Lady Lives, the Pigeon Dies" launches as an epistolary novelette. The other four aspire to masquerade as short stories for an upscale literary magazine. The chapters mull on genre matters: the Cretone murder story meditates on fairy tales; the story of Innocentia and Vespasiano explores poetry as testimony in court; the pigeon tale anatomizes the textual schemes of a rare old lab report; the handkerchief tale of Alessio the amorous beadle starts by evoking ghosts. And, like Borromini's athletic, sly Sant'Ivo church, I aim for transformation; my stories change shape as they go along, gliding from one to another literary model.

In my first-year humanities course (great books—medieval and Renaissance), I tell the students that I have two chief lessons, easy to recite but hard to take to heart. The first is the pastness of the past; the second, the textuality of text. In this book, I hew to the same lessons: the more clearly textual my own texts, the more manifestly the past will seem the past and the more deliberate, strained, and passionate will seem our yearning to know it and depict it.

Ever since I first studied trials, I have taught with them. My students who know Italian have transcribed them from the crabbed originals and translated them, as training, for the use of classmates. An especially talented undergraduate, Linda Traverso, went all the way to the Roman state archive and found for me, among other things, the trial about Innocentia and Vespasiano. She and her friend and later husband, Raffaele Girardo, did the first transcription and an English version. Usually, however, my students have to start in English. The tasks are various: to annotate a trial, to lay out the persons, times, and spaces of the story, to give a canny interpretation, and to retell the events as a coherent story. I often assign such jobs to teams, for the work is hard and several minds and points of view often help see clearly. With the Cretone murder case, I gave my first-year students the modern blueprints of the castle and made them follow textual clues to find the corpses and all the other places of the tale—and, having found them, to contrive a space-conscious telling of the story. Since my students have better instincts for the big and little screen than for the printed page, our discussion turned to cinematic techniques: flashback, cross-cutting, zooming, panning, tracking, all camera tricks with parallels in prose. We also fantasized our casting. "I'll be the wife, and Tom Cruise will be my lover," a willowy student volunteered. As for the death of poor Vittoria Giustini, the class enacted it, right through the fraternal sword fight.

The pedagogy has many charms. The subjects of the trials—sex and violence, greed and sacrifice, love and death, youth and age, rebellion and authority—catch the student eye, heart, and mind. So vivid are the trials that it is hard not to identify with the men and women who inhabit them. At the same time, that very ease of identification opens the way to the usual lessons: pastness and textuality. For all their vividness, the old Italians elude us; their choices, whims, and yearnings remain firmly in the past, half unknowable. The very debate about which movie stars to hire to play the characters drives home the artfulness and artifice of any modern exposition—or, to rephrase, the textuality of any history we produce. But there is another textual lesson, more crucial to a course in historians' methods. That second lesson is the very textual nature of the documents themselves, for a trial, like any document, is a subtle intersection of many genres. Habits of vernacular speech and homespun narrative collide with the more formal languages of deposition and interrogation. Under these constraints and influences, the witness's mouth speaks, but we hear it only through the ear, mind, and hand of the notary. And every witness has motives and reasons to reshape a story. Moreover, the

events themselves often took cues from old Italian narratives; seduction, betrayal, and revenge were life genres that echoed an
abundant literature. In class discussion, every attempt to puzzle
out "what really happened" must confront this array of subtle
lenses refracting events into words on paper.

Why the particular stories in this book? Why these trials and
not others of the extant thousands? Mostly, because they feel like
good stories. Some trials are flat, others fragmentary, or just too
huge. And others, though full and shapely, are still baffling. Assorted traits might invite a storyteller. Voice matters, as does
depth of feeling. Every trial in this book has a streak of pain, grief,
or anger. And most have tenderness as well. Also, as a writer, I like
trials with irony: odd twists of fate, cruel reversals of fortune, and
incongruous juxtapositions of actions, desires, and states of heart
and mind. Then add a whiff of enigma; in the end, reader—and
writer—should still hear questions nagging.

These criteria are personal, a quirk of taste. No great science
here, no argument or lesson. Nevertheless, my choice of stories
does evoke my understanding of the Italy of the time. There are
several ways. Take cruelty. My stories are often cruel. So was Italy
in the Renaissance. It seems uncharitable and smug to say this as
we exit the twentieth century and its litany of horrors. But our
public culture is averse to cruelty; we exalt gentleness—to children, to the poor and weak, to animals. Renaissance Italians, when
in the Christian mode, could also cultivate compassion. But their
cruelties were far less abashed than ours—toward enemies foreign
and domestic, toward underlings and outcasts, and certainly toward beasts. Hierarchic social structures, customs of vendetta,
fractious local politics, and ferocious rites of justice all permitted
or exalted cruelty. And my taste for irony evokes the tensions of a
society that hewed to contradictory codes of ethics. Italians lived
with local loyalties to family and kin and patron, imperatives in
fierce tension with their ideals—Christian, legal, and communal—of the larger public good. They hearkened both to honor
(vindictive, combative, and particularistic) and to religion (merciful, irenic, and loyal to the brotherhood and sisterhood of all
Christendom).

When several competing codes and principles collide, in dramatic, ironic clash, they often help uncover the conditions that shaped life. As always, rules of conduct mattered not because they governed every action but because they set the price for choices. In any place and time, persons have a wealth of options, each with its costs and benefits. Some of these are material; others, legal, ethical, emotional, or even otherworldly, as when God is angry or the Virgin coddles a supplicant. Choice, therefore, often juggles a bewildering array of options. The great French sociologist Pierre Bourdieu offers what seems a very subtle way of framing the nature and limits of freedom and of rational calculation; I come back to it in reflecting on the wry love story of Innocentia and Vespasiano. Having himself played rugby, Bourdieu conjures up the mind of a player amid the swift and swirling action on the playing field. By instinct or well-honed habit, a skilled athlete takes in the movement of the game and plots his steps and dodges. But he lacks the time to place all the players' moves or map out the web of consequences; the game is just too swift and complicated. On the field of life, Bourdieu argues, we do the same. We strategize, we play to win, but we seldom sit back, like perspicacious Machiavelli at his desk, and work out long chains of choices. The tactic barely works for rule-bound, finite chess; for life, it cannot work at all. Even rugby has rules—a standard field, a standard ball, sidelines, goals, and a gentlemen's agreement not to shoot or stab the other team. It is just a game, and the rules and penalties thus have artificial simplicity and clarity. Life too is a game of sorts, Bourdieu has argued, but the rules are fuzzy and the players scramble on many fields at once.

My short stories, themselves playful, try to evoke the sixteenth-century Italian play of life. As historian, I am especially drawn to moments where the fields of play meet in dramatic, crazy, ironic ways. Choice, and that semifreedom-amid-constraint we call agency, are often best illustrated when the choices themselves are sharp and strange. A trial itself makes for hard choices, as witnesses are often caught between their yen for safety from the law of perjury and their loyalties to social allies who need lies. Many a witness plays risky forensic games. My stories themselves, behind the trials, offer many moments where imperatives clash. Silvia Giustini juggles compassion for her dying sister, loyalty to her black-sheep brother Ascanio, and family solidarity with the other brothers. Francesca the wet nurse, though obliged as governess to protect teenaged Innocentia, aches to help her erstwhile milk-son seduce the girl. Prosecutor Alessandro Pallantieri, serial rapist of adolescent girls, plays doting father to the children his cruel liaisons engender. Nimble Lelio Perleoni, amid protestations of passionate devotion, betrays everyone in sight. Lucretia Casasanta is humble nun in the monastery parlor and giggling flirt at the nuns' back window. Such old hard choices and madcap compromises teach good new lessons, for they help chart the edges of fields of social play and suggest the rewards and penalties at stake.

Nevertheless, life is never simply play, and history is not fiction. Our push toward fiction's modes of writing helps lay bare the differences. Historians have two problems: the world is full; their knowledge is largely empty. Let us take the first. An unsigned article in the *New Yorker* in 1986 put the matter beautifully. The author mused that he or she could never in good conscience write fiction, because one could not add anything true—a Caribbean island, a new apartment in New York, a housewife (the author remembered the days of housewives)—to a world already full. Historical novelists and dramatists have few such compunctions; their craft allows them to implant imaginary persons and to graft onto real ones new words, thoughts, dreams, and, often, thrilling imaginary loves. Meanwhile, we historians, reined in by conscience, science, and our colleagues' watchful gaze, cannot vent a lover's sigh, affix a blossom to a cherry tree, or bounce the glimmer of moonlight off a puddle without footnotes to prove them real. Nothing added and, meanwhile, so much taken away! Almost all the past is lost; even yesterday is largely gone, and from centuries back all we have is a flimsy gauze of hints of memory. This fact is at once the bane and the blessing of our craft, bane in that it frustrates, blessing in that it invites and liberates the speculation in which we revel.

History's shape and shapeliness are also different. Fiction can set the scene and lay the climax and the resolution in accordance with the conventions and skills of art. History, on the other hand, is almost always messy. As I writer, I find beginnings easy, mostly because one can start with a handsome scene and then flash back to fetch its origins. Endings are another matter, much less bang than whimper. Very often, handsome tales just unravel as the participants trail off on their separate ways. Eventually, death finishes them off, but seldom neatly. The executioner finally caught up with Alessandro Pallantieri, but it took thirteen years and the ax came down for crimes other than mine to tell. Most of my other protagonists died far offstage, out of sight and mind. In histories based on trials, readers, like the audience for television's *Law and Order*, yearn for the final gavel-thumping sentence of the court. Sadly, many sentences are lost, and others, like Vespasiano's, probably never happened. A sixteenth-century trial was not freestanding. Rather, it was the tip of a larger iceberg of contest and negotiation, and its aim, quite often, was not a sentence but a solution to a conflict. Courts mediated and brokered settlements. Closure, such as it was, could be social, as when Vespasiano caved in and married Innocentia. Generally, such reckonings happened outside the courtroom; we can only guess their presence.

Thus, loose ends abound. Did Giovanni Battista Savelli get back his confiscated castle? Probably. Did Cintia Antelma suffer for the poison plot? Maybe. Did the beadle Alessio ever marry his beloved, the reluctant nun? Unlikely. Did the Giustini ever accept Laodomia, ex-courtesan, their brother's widow? I have not the faintest idea. And so on, at length. One problem with trials on paper is that hindsight soundly trumps foresight; origins are far clearer than are fates. So, as writer, I often invite my readers in, bringing them into almost tender intimacy with my characters, and then rudely drop them with no time or literary space for parting and resolution—an emotional one-night stand, but little can repair it. The abruptness of the loss at a microhistory's end evokes once more that familiar lesson, the finality of the past's pastness.

❦❧

What follows in chapter 1, the story of the Savelli double murder, is by design no less formal than a sixteenth-century castle garden, with its thyme and marjoram, dill and sage, arugula and mint, in tidy plots inside geometric little hedges. In my story, both space and time, as I lay them out, have shapely boundaries. Though I traverse by flashback, time divides, stage by stage, as in a play or film. First there is a secret love affair, slow and furtive, cream-smooth at the outset and later curdled by suspicion and anxiety. Second comes an awful killing, swift and furious. Third comes a frozen time, with everyone locked in by fear, confusion, and blocked grief, until stage four, the sudden thaw, a spate of social resolution that is set moving by the arrival of a grieving prince and that lets all actors, both dead and living, resume their ordained courses. Space too has its elegant, evanescent geometry of concentric circles around the bodies of the unquiet dead.

Neat. Perhaps far too neat! Why force something so tremendous, passionate, painful, and mournful as this murder tale into so strait an esthetic jacket? What lessons have I here? I have two.

Lesson one: Life itself had art. It had story lines and actors, who followed—not to the word, but loosely—scripts from experience, from stories told aloud, and from plays and books. Italians improvised, as in fact we all do, from well-honed roles; the temper of their acting, often, was the measure of their agency. To be a surreptitious lover, an outraged husband, a faithful maidservant, a grieving brother, a peasant subject of a feudal lord, all these things had their customary attitudes, acts, words, and feelings. That is why, in what follows, readers will sometimes feel as if they have strayed into a story by Boccaccio, Sercambi, Bandello, or some other Italian short-story writer. The old novelle imitated life. Meanwhile, life itself, at some remove, aped novelle.

Lesson two: My push for narrative, I hope, alerts us to the frailty of our knowledge. The harder we try, as readers or writers, to lay a handsome shape upon the past, the more aware we grow that our story grasps in vain to clasp its subjects—real people, with real passions, very long ago. What tenderness, what zest, what longing provoked a lover to dangle, for the sake of sex, from a castle wall? What heartsickness and delight led a wife to let him into her room and bed and belly? What mix of rage and cunning shaped the husband's plot? And so on with the others. We can never truly know. Unlike the lover, unlike the husband's dagger, we can, for all our wistful longing, never enter poor Vittoria Savelli. The more artful the telling, the more alert we become to the teller and the chasm between the telling and the told, and the more alive we grow to the sad, sweet alienation of doing history.

In chapter 1, suffering sears the heart. Watch the women, especially the peasant wives who wash the bodies. But, swiftly, the village, the castle, and the Savelli clan resurrect a semblance of the normal. So keep an eye as well to all the words and ceremonies that channel pain and convert catastrophe into something that is, because encoded, bearable. Observe the edgy parleys with the victim's brother, designed to chart a route to reconciliation. And note how peasant reasons and moral judgments smooth roiled feelings. And, finally, ponder the visiting magistrate, who transforms a murder into transcript and legal process, yet one more resurrection of routine, yet one more closure ritual.

❧❧

Chapter 1

DOUBLE MURDER
IN
CRETONE CASTLE

ON THE LAST NIGHT OF HER LIFE VITTORIA
Savelli wore an old shift. She lay in her bed, in her quirky little bedroom cut concave by the ballooning indoor wall of the old round
tower of her husband's castle. Now, on the last night of his life,
Troiano Savelli wore nothing at all. He lay in the same room and
bed, atop Vittoria. One can only surmise what tenderness or ela-
tion mingled with the thrills of their sexual union. Alongside good
feelings, there may have been as well a wary undertow of fear, for
Troiano, despite his surname, was not Vittoria's husband. This
then was adultery. That was already bad enough, but to make matters worse, the act took place inside the husband's house. To make
things graver yet, Troiano was neither wholly noble nor even legitimate, for he had sprung of a union between the local lord and a
peasant woman. But, worst of all, Vittoria and Troiano, in their
bed, wallowed in incest, for Troiano, son of the husband's father,
was his half-brother. None of this deterred the lovers from their
reckless union.[1]

Archival and published records tell us little about the three
principals to this tale: lord, lady, and lover. There is an eighteenth-
century history of the Savelli family,[2] but it passes over Vittoria's

17

husband, Giovanni Battista, one of the less illustrious Savelli to bear that traditional family name. He and Vittoria do figure in modern genealogies, and they have left a few notarial footprints, most notably a record of their marriage. The events of July 1563 recounted here may have also left their traces in the weekly *avvisi,* newsletters mailed out from Rome; it is hard to say, for the Vatican collection has a month-long, midsummer lacuna. We know the following. The cuckold, Giovanni Battista, as a Savelli belonged to one of the few surviving great baronial families of the Papal State.[3] In 1563, the Savelli had three main branches, each with its ancestral lands. To the north were the Savelli of the Sabine foothills and, across the Tiber, around the lonely stump of Monte Soratte. To the south, below Rome, were those of the Alban hills. Giovanni Battista belonged to the Palombara branch, in the middle. They held castles, fiefs, and lands at the foot of Monte Gennaro, east of Rome, north of Tivoli. It was pretty country, a rolling hill zone of orchards, vineyards, and grain. There were also Savelli palaces in Rome, hereditary military offices in the Papal State, and ancestral rights to the revenues of the pope's main urban court and jails. Although the Savelli were doomed to eclipse in the early seventeenth century, when their ancestral holdings fell to newly noble members of ascending curial elites, in the 1560s they still mattered; they even had a cardinal.[4] Our Giovanni Battista, however, was no magnate. He had a single fief and petty castle, at Cretone, a tiny village in the shadow of Monte Gennaro, just down the hill from the main stronghold of the local Savelli branch, Palombara, a conical hilltop village with massive fortress and soaring medieval tower, perched a few miles to the east.[5]

Unlike the usual cuckolds of Boccaccio and other *novellisti,* Giovanni Battista was no doddering graybeard. In the summer of 1563, he was just past youth, between twenty-two and twenty-six years of age.[6] For a Renaissance Italian man, he had married young, four years back. A notarial document of 19 March 1559 records how his bride and he pledged their faith and notes their exchange of rings. It preserves the futile invocation: "What God has put together let no man sunder."[7] As for Vittoria, she was a distant cousin, daughter to Antonello Savelli, of the Albano branch. We know neither her age nor her dowry, though the generous 12,000 scudi Giovanni Battista dowered his sister Hieronima (2,000 of it trousseau and spending money) suggests its measure.[8] But whatever money Vittoria brought with her did not suffice to float the payments to Hieronima's in-laws, the noble Massimi. Although he farmed out a portion of his Cretone lands to jobbers, Giovanni Battista fell into arrears. His in-laws collected interest in the usual way until at last he coughed up back payments.[9]

Giovanni Battista's castle, as castles went, was modest. For a lord, he kept a small household: a page, two servants, a head maid/ governess, and four maids to dress and serve his wife.[10] If there were others, they do not turn up in the stories we are told. His village, too, was a mean affair. By 1563, Cretone was in steep decline; in subsequent years, it shriveled to a hamlet and then almost melted away.[11] Indeed, by the end of the nineteenth century, many inhabitants had carved modest apartments out of the castle itself. Nevertheless, the town survived; Cretone today still feels like a place of substance. It has its hillside piazza with a fine view, its clubs of fans for the two Roman soccer teams, its cafe with tables where the men play cards. The castle itself, newly restored, still raises its shoulders, now freshly stuccoed, above the jumble of slipshod rural houses at its skirts. So far as I can tell, nobody remembers what happened to the lovers.

The story of Troiano and Vittoria's intrigue is hard to reconstruct. By the time the inquisitive magistrates arrived on the scene, the pair were in no state to give their version. The serving women, many of whom did speak to the court, probably knew a lot but had good reason to play dumb, for the more they confessed to knowing, the better they demonstrated their infidelity to their lord and master, Giovanni Battista. Nevertheless, hints slipped by villagers and servants make clear that July's passion was no sudden thing. The lovers had long cozied in the public eye.[12] As far back as Christmas, one villager, husband of Troiano's peasant half sister, Gentilesca, had seen such hints of dalliance that he warned the young man to watch his step.

> Mario, my husband, told this Signor Troiano in my presence several times, and in particular last Christmas, that he had noticed certain acts and joking that he [Troiano] was doing with Signora Vittoria, and then he warned him, telling him that he should be

careful not to fall into something with the Signora that was not right. And Troiano took it ill that he should say such words to him, and since then I do not believe he has come into our house more than two or three times.[13]

This warning, clearly, did little good. By then, or not long after, the lovers had found their way into a common bed; Diamante, one of Vittoria's young attendants, had, she reported, known of the affair since Christmas.[14] The older women, she claimed, had told her. The affair was also common knowledge in the village.[15]

THE LAYOUT OF THE CASTLE

Though close-quarters trysts are never easy, Cretone's architecture lent the lovers a hand. For Vittoria's room stood at the end of the castle's piano nobile, at its northwest point. Part of the westward sixteenth-century annex, it was beyond the sturdy old round tower that once had reinforced the corner of the original castle nucleus.[16] The Renaissance addition, swallowing up half the tower, had afforded the piano nobile three new rooms, the smallest being hers. Below Vittoria were two floors of vaulted storerooms, on ground level and lower, and, above her, just a gently sloping roof. The older, taller part of the castle had a small mezzanine—on the north side only—with access to the tower stairs and, above that, an attic that ran its length and breadth.

These details mattered to the lovers, for castle geometry connived at their perilous trysts. At first glance, for adultery, Vittoria's room was an awkward rendezvous. It had only a single door, opening onto the chamber with the two beds where slept four maidservants (damigelle)—the two sisters Diamante and Temperanza, Attilia, and Ottavia—and also the senior female servant (massara), Silea, an old widow who served Vittoria's daughter as governess.[17] The antechamber where the servants slept had two other doors. One led east, toward the main stairway and the sala, the great eastern hall with its noble frieze of swirling acanthus garlands, its carved beams, its splendid mantelpiece, and its fine Renaissance windows, with their sweeping view of fields, orchards, and the wooded slopes of Monte Gennaro. It was there that Troiano usually slept.

The second door of the servants' room opened southward to the husband's bedroom in the southwest corner, where Giovanni Battista slept, at least these days, while his wife—she had told him—was a bit sick.[18] The master had a well-lit chamber. One window looked out over a small walled garden, on the sunny south side; the other, westerly, overlooked one of Cretone's streets. All these details matter for our story. The servant women, by virtue of their location between master and mistress, should have been privy to all traffic in and out of Vittoria's room and, most likely, to her every passage from her bed to her husband's. How, then, had Troiano come undetected into Vittoria's room, bed, and arms?

The lover had come by air. More precisely, he had come dangling, on cloth bands anchored by a bolt affixed to a higher window; Vittoria had helped him clamber in. The tower clinched the trick. Its narrow twisting stairway spiraled to the castle's top, lit by little windows some fourteen inches wide, just big enough to wriggle out if one were lithe and nimble. The topmost window of the tower opened just south of westward, over the annex's gentle roof. From there, Troiano, strips in hand, could work his way to the north face and lower himself to Vittoria's chamber. The castle's principal stairway, far more commodious and better lit, was farther east. It rose in steady, ample flights from the only external doorway, in the north façade, just to the east of middle. On his midnight forays, Troiano most likely used to creep from his bed in the sala, climb the main stairs to the mezzanine, tiptoe softly across to the tower and its obscure stairway to nowhere, and affix his climbing rig to the topmost window.[19]

That then was how Troiano made his final tryst, as he had at least once before and probably far more often. As Bandello wrote, in one of his *novelle* that, as often, ends in tragedy, when the way is blocked, love is ingenious. It borrows eyes from Argus.[20] But, as in that *novella,* so in Cretone on 26 July 1563, ingenuity fell short, for suddenly, in the midst of sex, the bedroom door crashed open, and there, in the flickering glare of a page's torch, stood the husband. Giovanni Battista strode in, a dagger in his hand. With him came a second servant, also armed. At their backs, in alarm and horror, the serving women gathered. What happened next was swift and ghastly.

But wait! First, watch the lord build and spring his trap.

Cretone castle in 2001, north façade, tower at center, annex to the right. Vittoria's window is the one with two panes. Photo by the author.

SETTING AND SPRINGING THE TRAP

All the moves and devices that conspired to doom the lovers involved the castle's males. As in many households, serving women and men wove separate networks and alliances. Male servants looked to their master, females to their mistress. In Cretone, for seven months, female solidarity of some kind had kept Vittoria's intrigue a secret. How much of this discretion connived and how much cowered is hard to say. After the fact, when the court came through, the serving women strove to shuck off complicity. They therefore cited fear. Young Diamante told the visiting magistrate that, once the maids had caught scent of the affair, they had—oh yes!—wanted to tell their master. "We wanted to tell the signore, but the signora threatened us, saying she would hit us, so we were afraid."[21] An unlikely story. Tattling would surely have heaped catastrophe on the patroness. What master's reward could make good the loss of a mistress's protection and employment and offset the opprobrium, largely female, that would befall the woman who betrayed her?

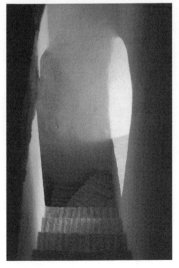

The male servants, on the other hand, owed their mistress little. They were the lord's, and served his interests. There were

(above) Cretone castle, tower, Troiano's window above, Vittoria's below. Photo by the author. (below) Cretone castle, Troiano's stairway in the tower. Photo by the author.

several on the scene. One was Giacobo, born Jacques, a French-man and thus an outsider; he was something of a gossip. Another, Stefano, had married a village woman. He was by birth a local, for his father's name traced to Nerola, a few miles away. A third, Domenico, as a page was probably too young to marry. All three men helped lay the lovers' trap.

There had been hints in plenty: cozy embraces, perhaps frater-nal, perhaps less innocent.[22] Giacobo claimed afterward to have had his doubts.[23] But it was page Domenico who played spy. At his master's orders, the maid Silea told the court, he had kept an eye on the pair; they seemed too familiar for the husband's comfort.[24] One night, we know not when, while lying in his trundle cot below the master's bed, the page saw Vittoria pass through the hall, head-ing for the sala.[25] He then went there himself and touched the bedclothes on Troiano's bed. According to the story (we have it via Giacobo, who, before he fled, told the village headman, Loreto), when Troiano felt Domenico's hand on the bed, he protested, "What are you doing? Don't you see that it is my cape?"[26] The page then returned to his master's room. We do not know whether he reported at once on what he had found, but we doubt he long stayed silent.

It may have been Domenico's spying that persuaded the lovers to resort to Vittoria's bedroom. We cannot tell how often Troiano scrambled down the roof tiles. Nor do we know how much the serving women knew about the trick. It would have been hard not to catch wind of what went on in Vittoria's room. Even if the lovers were discreetly quiet, it was strange of the mistress to ask to sleep not with servants but alone. This was not the normal way a lady spent the night. She claimed to be indisposed, they reported, per-haps truthfully, and she shut the door.[27] Eventually, Domenico fer-reted out Troiano's window trick. It was Sunday evening, 25 July. Perhaps the heat made Giovanni Battista thirsty. The lord was dressed for bed, most likely in his chamber. He sent his page over to the sala to fetch a little jug of water. A light in the great hall re-vealed Troiano's empty bed. Suspicious already, Domenico went snooping. The tower stairs had a doorway near the entrance to the maids' bedroom. Hearing a noise above, the page crept up the nar-row, winding steps until he saw the bastard at the topmost window affixing his bar and bands of cloth. Domenico slipped down to alert his master.[28] From Silea, the head serving woman, we hear what happened next.

> And the signore rose in his shift and went to the door of the room and he said that he saw them, but, because he was not armed and was alone, he was afraid and did not want to do anything. And he also said to me, "Let them enjoy this night, for another evening will go another way."[29]

Contemplate Silea's quandary. She had two bonds, one to her mistress, the other to her master. Whatever she did, she would betray one of them. On his side, Giovanni Battista had male power, local connections, and the code of honor. On hers, presumably, Vittoria had affection and female loyalty. Silea chose the more prudent path, kept silent, and sealed her mistress's doom. A quiet word the next morning might have spared at least one life and even, perhaps, two, for Giovanni Battista was intent on well-timed revenge.

Both law and family politics argued that, were the lovers to die, they should do so on adulterous sheets. Legal doctrines tracing back to ancient Rome often pardoned a vengeful husband, especially if he acted in hot passion, killing wife and lover when he caught them in the act.[30] But Giovanni Battista had a problem; his passionate moment of discovery found him unarmed and wavering. He needed a second occasion, equally flagrant, when, better prepared and thus less startled but still sufficiently aroused, he might strike sure and yet appease the law and justify the carnage to his in-law Savelli cousins. Accordingly, he set his trap and waited. The next night, as if to sleep, with Domenico the page he retired to his usual room. He stationed Giacobo in a facing house and Stefano in the street below, to the north or west, whence they could spy on the windows of the tower and of Vittoria's chamber.[31] Giacobo carried a long gun to finish Troiano off should he make a bold long leap for safety.[32] The trap sprang true. Around midnight, Troiano once more crept to the tower window and rappelled into Vittoria's helping arms and window.[33] The spies, having seen her ease him in, went into action. One of the servants threw a stone in the master's western window. Domenico heard its rattle and said, "Signore, it's time."[34] Soon, Stefano came up and joined them. Giacobo and his musket stayed in ambush below.

Unaware of the impending crisis, Temperanza, one of the young maidservants, chose this moment to go pee. The close stool must have been a flight or two above, for Giovanni Battista heard her retreating steps upon the castle's stairs. Misprising the sound, he dashed up after her, dagger drawn, shouting, "Ah traitress, you are fleeing!" In the nick of time, her sister, Diamante, tells us, Domenico called him off: "Don't do it, Signore! It's not the signora! It's Temperanza!"[35]

The vengeful trio, torch in hand, then entered the maids' quarters. In Temperanza's bed lay her sister, Diamante, just dozing off.[36] Silea was already asleep, with Helena, the Savelli daughter, a child of two. When the men came in, Helena, startled, began to cry, awakening her governess.[37] Diamante was awake enough to see the three men move toward the closed door.[38] At the portal, the trio may have paused to listen for sounds of sex, but not long, for as they shoved it open, Diamante could see Troiano still atop her mistress.[39]

Despite the heat of the moment, Giovanni Battista observed vendetta's proprieties. These matters had their script; amid the carnage, he followed it. He may have first addressed his bastard brother. Cecco, a villager who heard from Giacobo, who still in ambush was never there, told the court that Savelli said, "O brother, traitor, this is the benevolence I bore to you [and yet you do] this to me!"[40] Hearsay! A fitting speech but corroborated by no witness on the scene. Silea, who was there indeed, reported a much simpler exclamation: "Oh, I have brought you this for my sake!"[41] Giovanni Battista almost certainly did address his brother. Whatever he said, all agree that he gave Troiano a quick dagger blow to the forehead and then at once commanded Stefano: "You kill him, and I don't want anybody to lay a hand on the signora." Silea, though slower than Diamante to her feet, was at the door to hear these words.[42] While the servant butchered Troiano with a dagger, cutting him everywhere, Giovanni Battista addressed his wife.[43] On essentials, the several versions of what he said agree. Silea reported the most interesting, on her first interrogation, just as malarial delirium began to fog her mind: "Ah, traitress, you have cut off the nose—to me, to Signor Ludovico, and to the Savelli house." The next day, fever abated, Silea instead retailed the simpler: "Ah, traitress, this is the honor that you do the Savelli house. You have cut off the nose of the Savelli house!"[44] The earlier, delirium-tainted version is the more interesting. It is worth unwrapping its poetics, even if the servant and her fever may have shared in authorship. Nose cutting, in Renaissance Italy, was a gesture of extreme contempt, a permanent disfigurement penalized in law codes and signaled in local speech and custom. As act, as notion, it often attached to adultery and cuckoldry.[45] In grammar and in bloody deed, it took the dative; it was "to" persons and collectivities that one cut off noses. In Silea's first rendering, Giovanni Battista's speech moved outward, from self to the larger sphere of aggrieved victims in whose name he struck. The ordering reflected a gradient, not of importance, but of location, outward. Vittoria's treason had afflicted her husband, her brother, and the whole Savelli house. Ludovico, then, was the conduit to a wider thirst for blood. Giovanni Battista would slake it.

Hardly any assault story in the Italian courts lacks its defiant speech. Like paladins in the *Song of Roland,* ancient foe, casual rivals, and even hired strangers often roared out insults before bringing down the blade. The victim seldom had much time to answer. Vittoria was no exception. On her back, helpless, all she could muster was three cries: "Ah, Signore! You do this to me!" "Yes, to you, traitress!" her assassin bellowed. He first hit her forehead and then slit her throat, cutting her head half off, slicing as he did so three fingers from a sheltering hand vainly risen. Giovanni Battista then stabbed Vittoria in the head and, finally, sank his dagger deep into her breast.[46] Instrumental or expressive butchery? Hard to say. Slicing the neck, *scannare* in Italian, typically was the method used to dispatch livestock. I have encountered it in another honor killing of a girl.[47] And Vittoria's head and heart had contrived adultery. But no local glossator affirms this reading. In the midst of murder, Giovanni Battista looked up and descried the servants huddled in the doorway. "Get out of here or I will kill both of you. Go, take care of that little girl."[48]

This slaughter cannot have taken long. When it was over, Giovanni Battista, though still raging, nevertheless knew the moves revenge required. Dripping dagger still in hand, he turned from the blood-smeared little room to confront the clutch of terrified serving women. "All of you, go to bed!"[49] "And we went to bed," as Diamante later said.[50] What else could they do? As Silea later told it:

> Then we left and went to bed. Soon afterward, the signore, Stefano, and the page came out of the signora's bedchamber, and they locked the door of the room where the two corpses were, and when they were in the *anticamera* of the signora, where we others were sleeping, Signor Giovanni Battista said, turning toward me and that little girl, his daughter, who was in the bed, with his unsheathed dagger in his hand, all covered with blood, "If I saw that this little girl didn't look just like me, as she resembles me at this very moment, I would kill her too."[51]

THE GEOMETRY OF SUSPENSE

As his rage abated, Giovanni Battista began to dispose his castle and his village to absorb the murders. It was crucial that he, not others, control how the word got out. The first step, already accomplished, was to lock the room and keep it sealed and undisturbed. The second was to corral gossip. Accordingly, he commanded the women to keep silent and not leave the castle, lest the villagers find out.[52] He then retired to his room.[53]

Next morning, Tuesday, 27 July, Giovanni Battista took more ambitious steps to seal his secret from the world. He sent his servant Giacobo to Loreto, a middle-aged *massaro* (headman) of Cretone. It was very early; Loreto still lay in bed. On his master's behalf, Giacobo inquired who stood guard at the village gate. Loreto did not know. "Don't leave the village, because Signor Giovanni Battista does not want you to leave," said the servant.[54] He then ordered that the gate stay locked. Shut in for an entire summer's day, the peasants traded anxious rumors. Meanwhile, the lord sent a rider with a hasty summons to Vittoria's brother Ludovico. We cannot say how much the messenger told him, but it was urgent enough to fetch him the next morning.

Note the cultural logic of Giovanni Battista's moves. His commands had staked a triple circle around the corpses of his wife and brother. Behind the locked door, the fatal room enclosed them

from the castle, barring molestation, observation, and due obsequies. The castle walls themselves formed the second circle, en-
forcing silence toward outsiders and barring traffic, and inquiry,
from the village. The third circle was the ring of walls that cut off
the villagers from their fields and the outside world. Both castle
folk and peasants, then, were sealed both inward and outward.
Around the corpses, they formed two anxious, concentric rings,
awaiting clarity and action. Giovanni Battista's three closures produced in everyone an almost uncanny state of agitated foreboding
and expectancy. Work stopped. Time almost froze. Cretone, from
top to bottom, from lord to servants to rural tenants, was immo-
bilized in deepest liminality. The two deaths, a tremendous fact,
required heavy emotional and ritual work. They needed digesting,
both personal and collective. But, until someone broke through
the circles, there was no way to begin those actions. Cretone, all of
it, held its breath, awaiting, sometimes unwittingly, the arrival of
Ludovico. Like a fairy-tale prince, only he could pierce the en-
chanted circles to unleash a castle's love. But, this time, the charm
lacked magic, the princess was dead, and, as we shall see, the loves
in question, once set in motion, were to be nuanced, guarded, and
laced with darker passions.

Still, the castle did not keep entirely mum. Within its walls, the
inhabitants busily absorbed, and judged, the night's event. One
villager, caught inside its walls by chance, heard an account of what
had happened. Cecco, a peasant, had spent Monday night in a
vaulted ground-floor room, sleeping off a bout of malaria. He
awoke to find the castle in an uproar, "some people going up, others going down." Asking Domenico what was afoot, he learned of
the killings. Cecco also spoke to Giacobo, who reported a declaration by Giovanni Battista, at once macabre and, in its stark double
parallels, nicely aligned with honor's usual fine sense of balances:
"Say that now they are lying together. The friendly things I have
done for my brother, and then he betrays me in this manner!"[55]
Note the ironic reversals and explicit pairings behind this phrase:
'the bodies lay in sex, now justly reversed, for they lie in death; I
once did Troiano good, first reversed by his treason, then re-
reversed by the condign death I inflicted.' The lord's moralizing
version, spread as gossip, helped the castle gloss the deed. It was
not only to Giacobo that Giovanni Battista unburdened himself.

To Silea, on Tuesday morning, he unraveled all the workings of his trap.[56] Such easy talk about so sensitive an affair illustrates Renaissance masters' habitual intimacy with their dependents.[57]

Despite these indiscretions within the walls, with the villagers outside, the castle, so far as we can tell, kept its secret to the end. "No one told about that room," Diamante told the court.[58] We should not doubt her; *massaro* Loreto, despite his visits to the castle, never pierced the veil of silence.[59] And, early Wednesday morning, Silea appeared on the doorstep of a peasant called Caterina, carrying little Helena and clearly bursting to unburden herself—but she held herself in. Like an oracle, she said only, "This Signora Vittoria, with this Signor Troiano, I hope to God that they are doing the right thing!" Caterina, aware of the sealed door and agitated spirits of the castle folk, divined a death.[60] But nothing was sure until a little later, when, at the village gate, riding attended, Ludovico Savelli appeared.[61]

CEREMONIES OF CLOSURE

Ludovico's arrival opened all three doors and dispelled the horrid irresolution that gripped the castle and the village. When he came, *massaro* Loreto was there.

> I was walking with Giacobo outside the palace. I asked him, "What does this mean, that the signore does not want us to leave?" Then Giacobo answered me, "Before night you will know." At that moment, Signor Ludovico Savelli of Albano arrived, the brother-in-law of Signor Giovanni Battista, with two other horses, and when he was near me, he put his hand to his head, asking me, "What's the news of Signor Giovanni Battista?" I answered him, "He is well!" And then he asked me about Signora Vittoria, his sister and the wife of Signor Giovanni Battista, and I said that I did not know anything and that I had not seen her since last Monday evening.
>
> Signor Ludovico dismounted from his horse and went up into the palace, and I went on foot with him, together with those other two whom he had brought with him. As soon as he arrived in the sala, he asked for Signor Giovanni Battista and was given the answer that he had not yet risen from bed. So, after we had

stayed for a little while in the hall, Signor Giovanni Battista came
out of his bedroom.

Signor Ludovico went to meet him, and both of them went
into the room [*la camera;* this, probably, was the lord's bedroom, or
else the room between the sala and where he slept; certainly, it
was not the scene of the crime], and I heard Signor Ludovico say,
"Well, who killed her?" And Signor Giovanni Battista answered,
"It was I who killed her, Signore, both of them." Then Signor
Ludovico said, "You did the right thing, and you have honored the
Casa Savelli, and if you had not done it, I would have done it."[62]

This last sentence, clause by weighty clause, was what all Giovanni
Battista's plot and later preparations had aimed at. Read it again;
ponder it, step-by-step!

Ludovico's parley with Giovanni Battista cannot have been easy
for either man. As for Ludovico, whatever love and loyalty he bore
his sister yielded to the proprieties of honor and clan cohesion, but
surely at painful cost. As for Giovanni Battista, to keep the peace
with kindred, he had to extract the blessings of his wife's protector. He succeeded, winning Ludovico's sanguinary declaration,
whether sincere or merely proper, so necessary for Savelli harmony. He had crafted well his mise-en-scène: let the surprise be
great, let the evidence of Vittoria's guilt be overwhelming, leave
the corpses together on their adulterous sheets. Leave also every
relic of the killing, every stain and crusted pool, banishing any
hint of sham. Once he had extracted Ludovico's reassuring words,
Giovanni Battista led him to the grisly scene itself. Some underlings came too, Loreto among them. The *massaro* later told the
court that he almost fainted with terror at the sight.[63]

Loreto's narrative of the bedroom ceremony left out further
niceties. We know from Silea that several servitors also found
their way to the death-scene colloquy. Ludovico's own two men
were there. So were Silea herself, another serving woman, and
Stefano. Given the words exchanged, they probably attended at
their master's behest, for, as he should, Ludovico interrogated
them sharply. Silea later reported:

And Signor Ludovico turned to me, asking, "Why did you not
take care of Vittoria?" I answered that the signora told me to take

care of the little girl, because she knew how to take care of herself.
Then Signor Ludovico turned to Signor Giovanni Battista, asking
him who killed the signora. Signor Giovanni Battista answered,
"I killed her myself with my own hands." Then Signor Ludovico
answered, "If you had not killed her yourself, I would kill all three
of you." At this point, this Stefano, who was present, said to
Signor Ludovico, "Signore, nobody laid a hand on the signora
except Signor Giovanni Battista, but as for Troiano, I'm the one
who killed him because I loved Your Lordship and because Signor
Giovanni Battista commanded me to."[64]

In all this colloquy, probably only the husband spoke the simple
truth. Ludovico and two servitors said what the situation demanded. Silea's partial fib shifted blame from the castle onto Vittoria; there had been no negligence. Stefano's improbable declaration of love reached out to make Ludovico complicit, a putative
advocate of killings done on his behalf. Here, Stefano's *amore* was
of the instrumental variety, not expressive passion but social obligation, tagged in the language of affect. In the Renaissance, this
usage was rife. As for Ludovico's blood-curdling declaration, it at
once sanctioned and hedged the double murder. The weight of his
mock threat gave the killing gravitas and underlined its propriety.
Here, as so often in Renaissance lay culture, risk or its semblance
gave words or actions weight.[65] But this message was double-
bladed, for it also served to underline how much to heart the
Albano Savelli still took Vittoria's purity and safety. Ludovico
would have protected her, he averred, from any derogation of her
honor. He thus became a retrospective guarantor of the propriety
of her death; he reattached Vittoria to his family. While doing so,
he helped Giovanni Battista ennoble and purify not only his
killing but also his wife's demise.
Ludovico's visit brought the broken Savelli household back out
of its suspended liminality. Having reintegrated his brother-in-
law into a familial love of sorts, Savelli unity laced with obligation,
he could now fetch back his sister. He, not Giovanni Battista, ordered that she be buried, as was proper, for, having betrayed her
husband, she had in a sense reverted to her natal house. The command that she be readied for the grave released another sort of
love and duty. His words set in motion the obsequies that would

permit the commoners of Cretone to take up the familiar rites of closure.

Meanwhile, Ludovico himself was not yet done. More witnessing remained. He had already held in his hands the bands by which Troiano had slid down the castle wall. Now he had to climb the turret to inspect the little window with its furtive crossbar still in place. That accomplished, the two Savelli men left castle and village and walked, conversing, in the fields.[66]

As soon as the news was out and the funeral set in motion, the villagers began the work of digesting and accepting what had passed. Testimony in court gives the merest hints of what people really felt and said. It seems that men and women differed. Males quaked, marveled, and condemned. Women grieved and recoiled.[67] It fell to Silea, as the castle's senior woman, to marshal the females, as was customary, for a burial. She summoned assorted village wives to come help wash the bodies. A Caterina came and even brought Antonia, wife of Stefano, the stabber.[68] Antonia fetched one Maddalena, still unwitting, who, upon arrival, heard the news from Silea: "Walk fast, for the signora is dead!" The maids then told her why. As she later informed the court, she learned "the lord had found that the two of them were sleeping together."[69] These village women found their task almost too much to bear. In the little room, in the July heat, the corpses and gore stank so much that the washers could barely stand it. "Unable to dress the signora because of the great stench that was there, we wrapped her in a sheet and we sewed it up," Maddalena later said.[70] Notice how, in these words, their mistress was still a person; clearly, Maddalena regretted her hasty, nearly naked burial. The women's repugnance mingled with shock and mourning. Maddalena later told the court that she had never observed Troiano's wounds, "on account of the great grief [dolore] I had."[71]

We see the men less well. Loreto, having been taken by surprise, reported shock and dread:

> For I, who knew not a thing, saw Signora Vittoria in the
> bed, dead, together with Signor Troiano, and I saw the whole
> room full of blood, and then I could have fallen to the ground
> from fear, seeing the signora dead and not knowing who had
> killed her.[72]

Likewise, the laborer Bernardino told the court, "I was amazed."

More than the women, the men reduced the story to its raw physical circumstances and, sometimes, their honor implications. Bernardino added, "Signor Giovanni Battista found them together in the bed, naked."[73] Another villager, Cocorzotto (Little Gourd), recounted:

> When my wife came to find me as I was plowing the fallow, to bring me bread, she told me that throughout the village they said that Signora Vittoria and Signor Troiano had been killed, and they said that Signor Giovanni Battista, the husband of Signora Vittoria, had killed the two of them because they were screwing.[74]

Note how the drama of the news marked in memory the telling's place, time, and circumstances. Cocorzotto, like Bernardino, remarked on the physical circumstances; the man had been nude and the woman in her shift. At least in court, Cocorzotto distilled the moral of the story to its stark, physical essentials. He evoked no passion or principle. His choice of verb hardly translates into modern English; we lack anything quite so neutral as *chiavare*. It was and is the usual blunt term for sexual congress. It neither smirked nor sneered. Bernardino, likewise, though more delicate in his choice of verbs, focused on the physical. "Talking with the other people of the village the way one does, I learned in public [that the lord] found them to be sleeping together, for Signor Giovanni Battista found them together in the bed naked."[75]

Unlike these two compatriots, Loreto in his testimony endowed the deaths with a moral, psychological, and social meaning: "I asked that Giacobo and the others of the house. They said that Signor Giovanni Battista had killed her for his honor."[76] He later said that he had told the servant, "It is an ugly affair [*una cosa brutta*] that a brother, even though he is a bastard, should try to take away another brother's honor."[77] Giacobo, of course, had good reason to evoke the morality of his own bloody actions. Note how, by the *massaro's* moral calculus, as reported, Troiano's bastardy mitigated the affront. It may as well, however, have exposed the perpetrator to the husband's vengeance. Garrulous Giacobo's apologia—the betrayal theme—extended also to Cecco, the fever sufferer. The villager relayed the servant's gloss of the event via the lord's purported words: "I cannot believe that my blood brother is casting such shame upon me [*mi facci tal vergogna*]." And then, at the moment of discovery, "O brother, traitor, this is the benevolence I bore to you [and yet you do] this to me!"[78] In all this male talk, as reported, there was not one Christian word: no "sin," no "incest." All terms lodged in the lexicon of honor. Such would be expected of a killing of this sort, far more easily squared with honor than with Christian mercy.

While the women did their best to prepare the corpses for burial, Ludovico and Giovanni Battista took their morning meal. They then rode off together, Ludovico with his escort, and Giovanni Battista with "all his household." Witnesses specified that Stefano was among the departers.[79] Giacobo's and Domenico's names are absent from the escort list. But they do not figure as witnesses in the court's surviving papers, nor, given their lord's flight, their guilt, and the law's imminence, are they likely to have dallied.

As Ludovico left, the villagers interred the corpses, apart. Vittoria lay inside the village, at a church called San Nicola. Troiano's cadaver, fittingly, came to rest several hundred yards outside the walls, at the church of San Vito.[80]

Two days later, on 29 July, Alessandro Pallantieri, the governor and chief judge of Rome—himself a very twisted man—sent a roving judge under a letter patent. This *commissario* had "the usual powers of subpoena, examination, judicial torture, confiscation, imprisonment, and so on."[81] The better to prosecute this uxoricide and fratricide, the judge, the letter patent said, should confiscate the Savelli property. Not until a week later, so far as we can tell, did the envoy, a prominent lawyer, Francesco Coltello, begin his interrogations. From 5 August to 9 August, he heard witnesses, first in Cretone and then in two nearby villages. So far as we can tell, despite his patent he arrested and tortured no one. The villagers must have used his presence to rearrange their thoughts and feelings; the process, though, is not easily deciphered.

Of all the testimonies, the last, Silea's, is most interesting. She had retreated to Sabellico, another village, perhaps to assuage her distress, perhaps to duck interrogation, perhaps to nurse malaria.

When, on the evening of 8 August, the court quizzed her, a mounting fever clouded her testimony. She could not name for sure the second killer. "'With the signore there was Giacobo.' Then she said, 'There was Stefano.'"[82] As delirium and fever rose, the judge halted the interrogation, but unstoppable as a brook, Silea still babbled:

"That poor signore has had good cause to kill her, and he killed her, and I saw. . . ."

And his lordship said that she should answer the question "Was it Giacobo or Stefano?"

She answered: "I couldn't tell you more. He was justified in hitting her. The devil! If you find the two of them together, wasn't he right?"

And his lordship replied that she should answer the question "Was it Giacobo or Stefano?" and she should not answer questions that have not been asked her.

She answered: "It seemed to me Stefano, it seemed to me Giacobo. Whatever Diamante told you, that other serving woman, he's the one and I didn't see anything except the signora dead."[83]

Even delirium has its guile. Silea's condemnation of Vittoria and espousal of her master's actions may have been strategic. Giovanni Battista might suspect her of passive complicity or worse. She may have used the judge as a sounding board, hoping that her erstwhile master would someday hear the purr of loyalty.

The next morning, the court tried again. This time, despite the lingering malady, Silea was quite coherent:

Signore, yesterday morning I had a great cold fever, and last evening, when your lordship examined me, I had the hot fever and I wasn't too much in my wits. And this morning I feel a bit better and, to tell you the matter of Signor Giovanni Battista, I will tell you everything that I saw and heard said the night that the signora was killed.[84]

She went on to give a rich account. Without her, this tale would be far sparer.

After Silea's deposition, we lose all trace of the story. By the time she spoke, the drama had much dissipated. The breaking of the weird silence, the revelation of the secret, Ludovico's careful acceptance of the deed, and the burial of the dead had released Cretone from its suspended, liminal condition. The arrival of the court probably gave a focus to what had to follow: quiet lobbying by the Savelli to get Cretone back. As almost always with noble contumely, sooner or later they would have their way, and Cretone would remain theirs until, decades later, the upstart Borghese bought it. Nothing in the records of the court suggests the case went far; the whole thing disappears. There is no trace of a sentence or a pardon.[85] Giovanni Battista, according to nineteenth-century genealogy, lived on to take a second wife, presumably impeccably faithful, and have children with her. He may well have married down, for the genealogist knew neither hers nor her children's names.[86] By 1569, however, the man was dead. The offspring of both marriages fell under the guardianship of one Camillo Savelli; so did Cretone, and, soon after, Camillo had the title too.[87] Little Helena lived on until 1573. When she died, she was only about twelve years old.

AFTERWORD

I first saw Cretone in the spring of 1999. I was in the district to prowl another village that figures in a book of mine, where I shot my last scrap of film. It was after lunch, sacred naptime. I scoured outer Palombara in vain for another roll of film, and then descended to Cretone, curious to see the castle where Vittoria and Troiano died. I knew that the place still stood, for a scholar friend had told me that it belonged to a childhood acquaintance's cousin, who was renovating it. True enough. My wife and I found the workers on the site. I asked them, pointing at the semiemergent tower, if it still contained a stairway, and told them why. They pointed me to the site architect, who smiled at the tale of ancient mayhem—"Ah, those old signori!"—and offered to take us around. Amid plaster dust and rubble, we toured with him, cursing the lack of film and sleuthing, as best we could, to find the fatal chamber. In vain.

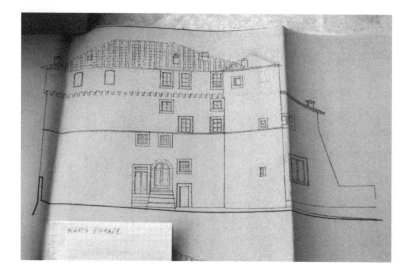

Cretone castle, ca. 1900, elevation of the north façade with portal, tower, and western annex. Troiano's window is invisible, but Vittoria's window appears just to the tower's right, near the roof. Photo by the author.

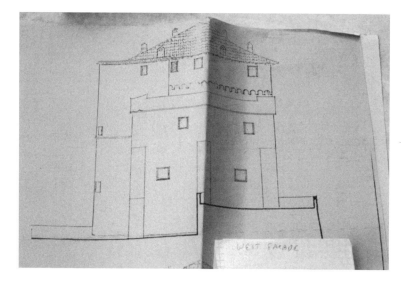

Cretone castle, ca. 1900, elevation of the west façade. The Tower stands to the left and Troiano's exit window is visible, high on its façade. Below the roof, to the right, is the husband's window, portal for the servant's flung stone. Photo by the author.

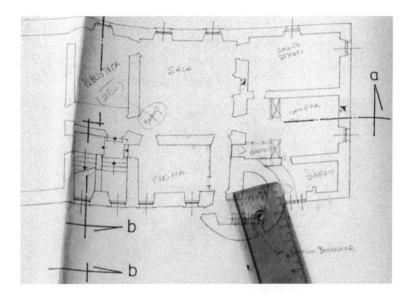

Cretone castle, ca. 1900, floor plan of the piano nobile, the ceremonial main floor above the ground-floor storage chambers. The sala lies to the left (partly beyond this picture's edge) and, to the right, lie the three rooms of the Renaissance annex: the husband's (top), the servant women's (center), and the wife's (bottom). The ruler lies across the old tower; the main stairway appears at some remove, to its left.

One year later, we were back in Rome. We contacted our friend's friend, Dottoressa Fiora Bellini, a curator at Castel Sant' Angelo and expert on baroque art. She lent a generous hand, dredged up some early-twentieth-century blueprints reused in the recent restoration, cleared things with her cousin, and tracked down the head architect, Giorgio Tarquini, who had overseen the project. A few days later, by appointment, Signor Tarquini drove down from Bracciano to meet us at the castle, where, we then found out, he had a small apartment of his own. He entered sympathetically into our inquiry and took us around the building, pointing out many clues to the evolution of the fabric. We were just about everywhere, from vaulted ground-floor storage chambers to the western upstairs terrace where Troiano's handy roof had been. But we found out later that, ironically, only our grown daughter wandered into the obscure chamber, now a quirky en

suite bathroom, where the couple had died. On the site, the four
of us proposed half a dozen solutions to the mystery, but each one
shattered on some stubborn reef of architecture.

The answer hit later. Like Archimedes in his tub, I had my mind
on other things. It was our last day in Rome. I had laid the blueprints out on the table on our apartment's terrace to take pictures
of them before I restored them to Fiora Bellini, at her museum
castle. Just before the end, through my viewfinder, I noticed a forgotten window on the tower, too far south of west to be seen from
the castle's north front, and not too far above the vanished roof of
the annex, still figured on the blueprints of the castle before, not
after, the 1900 restoration. Eureka, indeed! Once I had the window, the whole plot fell into focus.

Two years ago, my first-year students had the lot: trial, notaries,
genealogy, blueprints, and slides. But not the answer. Their mission: find the corpses. The teacher's goal: to show what historians
really do and, in particular, how often, as the ancient sculptor
Praxiteles and his admirers have said, God is in the details.

To be useful to the profession, the essays we historians write are
obliged to have a larger meaning. But this story has no single
weighty point. It shows some things about the intimacy of lords and
their dependents and about the subtle shadings of ceremonious
speech and action in the zone where honor figured. It opens, as well,
a tiny window, no larger than Troiano's secret exit, into the moral
universe of villagers. In the end, however, I have written it because
the tale wants telling. It is at once too bitter and too oddly sweet.

*In Greek tragedy, heroic characters hurtle to destruction in the face of quirky gods
and iron codes of conduct. What of the several Savelli? There were no gods but*

codes in plenty. Of these, the sternest was male honor, a retributive ethic that proclaimed a cuckolded husband's right and duty to avenge his manhood's affront. Other codes also shaped the story: a code of love and loving; a code of faithful service binding maids to their mistress and menservants to their master; a code of family solidarity compelling Ludovico to make peace; a peasant code of subservient respect owed to the feudal lord. None of these codes were Christian; this is a tale with few pieties, except the compassion, deeply felt but still encoded, of the village women. Nevertheless, in real life, not Greek tragedy, codes are often placable. Did Giovanni Battista have to kill his wife and bastard brother? Not quite. But the code, as codes do, eased the deed; in hindsight, it gave his dire action a reason, name, and patina of right and law.

Why then the opprobrious judge? Not clear. The pope could have blinked and winked at marital revenge, as in the past popes often had. Perhaps Pallantieri, the governor who signed the warrant, our villain of chapter 4, was behind the judicial moves. As we shall see, as state attorney, he had served the present pope, Pius IV, three years earlier by destroying the Carafa, the nephews of Pope Paul IV, in a scandalously trumped-up trial. The prosecution had hinged on a noble husband's murder of a wife suspected of adultery. Moral and legal consistency, both pope's and prosecutor's, may have conjured up the Savelli inquest.

Codes, by nature, seldom line up neatly, with just one for every circumstance. Rather, most often, several apply at once, with imperatives crazily askew. Should a maidservant heed loyalty to mistress or to lord? Should a brother avenge his sister or embrace his kinsman, her killer? For that matter, should a lover betray his brother, lord, and host, the rightful husband of a woman whom, by the shifty code of love, he woos and conquers? Moral discord gives stories tension and the characters a pinch of liberty.

In chapter 2, the plot is looser than with the Savelli killings. Rather than confine the tale with geometric conceits, I relax my hand and let the story sprawl and ramble. The shape, if such there is, is monologue, interpolated with yet further monologue, as my character, Alessio the beadle, has his garrulous days in court. Anti-art and lower tension. It is a slipshod tale of a courtship's gradual unraveling. What attracted me, in the first place, was not high drama but Alessio's quirks. Seldom do we see such devotion to a girl, at great expense, in so grown a man, who knows her by needlework alone. So Alessio is a mystery, wrapped in a handkerchief, as, under her nun's headkerchief, is the girl, who says yes and no at once, who takes the veil and giggles behind it at the monastery window.

For social historians the tale is useful. It shows courtship and attitudes toward both marriage and religion among the urban working class. It also illustrates the *machinery of a house of discipline and confinement, the* conservatorio, *one of the many totalizing institutions that spread far and wide in early modern Europe.*

As with the Savelli story, the building itself is a protagonist. Its layout, as with the castle, helps shape the tale. Chapter 2, like chapter 1, practices and preaches spatial history.

Chapter 2

LOST LOVE
AND
A HANDKERCHIEF

THERE IS A FAMOUS PHOTOGRAPH, AN ICON
of a dubious time. It shows Mussolini, sledgehammer in hand, demolishing a piece of Rome. Mussolini adored his capital. Indeed,
he probably loved it far too much, for it offered him a splendid
backdrop for parades and pomp. Accordingly, many neighbor-
hoods felt Il Duce's hammer blows as he smashed pieces of his
capital's medieval and Renaissance fabric to feed his twin manias
for baring ancient monuments and for laying avenues for troops
and tanks. The lovely oval of Piazza Navona escaped demolition by
the merest hair's breadth, saved by the unsuspected travertine
bleachers of a Roman stadium found inside some houses in the
way. War, disastrous in so many ways, brought a tiny blessing in its
wake, for with the regime's debacle it halted the juggernaut of Fascist urban renewal.

The collapse of Il Duce's regime caught at least one project still
busily demolishing. Mussolini had already widened the once intimate Via delle Botteghe Oscure, later famous as the Communists'
home address and today still desolate with raucous traffic. At the
corner where the short, broad avenue meets the narrow Via Caetani, a national institute for international exchange chose to build

itself an ungainly Fascist palace.[1] As usual with such projects, it had to smash a lot of past. The sledgehammers did their work, reducing much of a city block to rubble, but then the war froze everything, for decades. For almost forty years, until 1981, many tons of this new rubble and ancient detritus sat under a flourishing thicket of volunteer trees behind the remaining old walls and buildings. Then a team of archeologists began to sift the wreckage, for many seasons digging patiently and precisely down toward an ancient Roman theater, the Crypt of Balbus, two dozen feet below.[2] As Jane Jacobs might have observed, no archeological dig ever enlivens a nocturnal street. Nor does a heavy palace across the way when its ground floor lacks shops. Thus, in 1978, the Red Brigadisti who killed Aldo Moro found Via Caetani a fine place to park the car in which they left the famous politician's corpse, a mere two blocks from the headquarters of not only the Communists but also Moro's own Christian Democrats. A mournful plaque now marks the historic spot.

Thus, like so much of Rome, the neighborhood is full of ghosts, from those of the great (of dead regimes and empires—Caesar died just two blocks west, under the new streetcar tracks at Largo Argentina) to those of fading hegemonic parties (Partito Communista, Democrazia Cristiana) and down to wraiths of countless lesser beings. One tantalizing local ghost among so many is the elusive, wistful specter of a flimsy love, unconsummated on this now desolate city block. This tale is a wispy trace of that baffled yearning.

What the wreckers pulverized in 1943 had been a monastic complex, the cloister, refectory, dormitory, service buildings, and garden of the Augustinian nuns of a rather pretty church still standing at the block's southeastern corner. The church goes by two names: Santa Caterina della Rosa and Santa Caterina dei Funari. The first name picks up the title of an earlier, smaller church, Santa Maria Dominae Rosae, once elsewhere on the property and now vanished.[3] The second hearkens to the neighborhood's sixteenth-century vocation, rope (*fune*) spinning. The present monastic church, still with iron nun-grills at altar level but now without its convent, stands on the site of earlier houses and rope walks of *fune* makers; their profession had long worshiped Catherine of

Alexandria, for she, as emblem of her martyrdom, had a wheel, as had they for spinning cable.[4]

Santa Caterina, like many early modern Roman convents, did more than harbor some dozen nuns.[5] It had as well a modest house for poor widows and for *malmaritate,* women who had fled unhappy marriages. And it owned a fair-sized residence and school for cloistered girls awaiting marriage. This was what Italians call a *conservatorio,* an institution designed for conserving maidens' maidenheads and reputations. All over Italy, the Catholic Reformation sprouted such institutions by the dozen; Santa Caterina's was among the first. It owed its existence to no less a founder than Saint Ignatius Loyola, who in 1542 helped set up a refuge for the daughters of prostitutes and for other girls whose virtue seemed at risk.[6] The early years are poorly documented; still, clearly, by 1548, the institute was taking in *zitelle* (maidens). It prospered and grew; by 1580, it housed 180 unmarried wards.

Like most *conservatori,* Santa Caterina's was under lay administration. The nuns who supervised and fed the girls offered a service but did not govern. Rather, policy, administration, finances, and fund-raising all fell to a pious confraternity of both men and women, some clerics, many laity, mostly tied to Rome's elites.[7] The wellborn women had no voice in council; the men decided on admission, screened suitors, allocated dowries, policed recipients' marital morals, and disbursed the funds. The organization's women, however, did have a real role to play, because by virtue of their sex, they had a better eye for female character and readier access to girls in *clausura* (seclusion).[8]

Santa Caterina, like most other Catholic Reformation shelters for girls at risk, soon diluted its strenuous social mission to fall back on helping daughters of solid artisans await a decent match.[9] By the later 1550s, it seems, few children of prostitutes resided there. In the 1570s, the house would try again to foster girls from women in the trade, even kidnapping them or using police raids and judicial coercion to snatch them from dens of vice and danger.[10] But in the 1550s, it seems, most inmates suffered lesser handicaps: a parent had died or left or the family had hit hard times. Before she joined, two members of the organization appraised a girl at home, and before she entered the *conservatorio,* to vouch for her virginity, two midwives inspected her hymen. Then, custom was, the maiden entered fast, lest she lose it in the interval.[11] To avoid the taint of sex, by the statutes, the *conservatorio* took girls at childhood's end, aged nine to twelve. Thirteen seemed risky; to enter, a girl so old needed dispensation, and also, by the rules, she was easy to expel.[12] Once in, most girls stayed about seven or eight years, locked away from the world and from their parents' influence and love.[13] The house was vigilant lest mothers hover by the *rota*—the blind-communication wheel between world and cloister. By statute, families could contact daughters only four times yearly.[14] On Saint Catherine's Day, 25 November, however, the maidens came out from behind their walls for a single annual outing. They marched in procession to a nearby church, the Gesù or the Minerva. A few went costumed as biblical figures, but most marched along in plain tan smocks under white aprons, their heads draped in white cloths.[15] In the city, this parade was an event to watch; bachelors came wife-shopping. In 1611, after kinsmen abducted a girl, the processions stopped for almost three anxious decades; then they resumed, for as the diarist Gigli, a neighbor on Via delle Botteghe Oscure, noted, girls, unseen in cloister, were languishing unmarried.[16]

The *conservatorio* helped prepare its maidens for marriage. Not only did it separate them from abusive men and worldly women, but it also taught some skills, especially embroidery. Many *conservatori* put their girls to work; long hours of spinning and stitching, often for a jobber, helped fund dowries.[17] Some work supervision fell to nuns and some to senior *zitelle*. There may have been light instruction in reading and writing. But to marry, along with virtue and domestic skills, a girl needed the all-important dowry. This the *conservatorio* often furnished, either in a lump sum or in serial small payments designed to keep recipients in line. In the sixteenth century, the usual dowry was fifty or a hundred scudi, not sumptuous but, for artisans, respectable.[18] The conservators not only aimed to keep their graduates from vice but were also vigilant against callous men who took a girl for cash and then abused or abandoned her. Dowries were not automatic; each marriage entailed negotiations, where interested parties scrounged for cash to pad the payment and sweeten prospects for a match.[19]

Most girls finally married. Some, however, went into domestic

A modern image of the annual procession of the maidens of Santa Caterina della Rosa. Courtesy of Dottoressa Venditelli and the Museo Nazionale Romano Crypta Balbi.

service, often to earn a later dowry. A few boarders stayed on with the nuns for life. The album of the *zitelle,* now in the Archivio di Stato di Roma, suggests that only a few became real nuns, usually at Santa Caterina.[20]

Despite the nunnery's destruction, the archeologists have deciphered much of the place's history. Besides the data from the dig, old site plans and notarial records of real estate transactions furnish foundation lines and purchase dates. At the end of the 1550s, the time of our love story, the nunnery was growing fast. In 1555, Cardinal Cesi, the house's official protector, made a grant that let the nuns expand their operations.[21] In 1560, in the southwest corner of the block, the new, surviving church would start to rise, and before long its predecessor, halfway up the west side, would vanish. Today, recycled masonry in later walls and a few foundations unearthed by archeologists under the new cloister are all that remains of Santa Maria Dominae Rosae.[22] With Cesi's funds, the nunnery began to creep south- and northward, buying houses along the western edge and gardens in the center of the block. Nevertheless, on the northern boundary, facing Via delle Botteghe Oscure, a row of modest houses, mostly two rooms wide, remained in private hands. As for the *conservatorio* girls themselves, they seem at this time of rapid building to have dwelt in some old houses and rooms outside the cloister proper. These dwellings, rented by the nuns or guardians, lay to the north of the evolving cloister complex.[23] In the 1550s, these properties were not yet well walled in against intruding eyes; after 1579, having bought more property in the middle of the block, the nunnery threw up a high wall to protect enclosure.[24] Just where the maidens lodged should be remembered; it matters for what happens in our story.

Was a *zitella*'s lot a happy one? There are conflicting schools of thought. Historians have noted that, in many ways, the Counter-Reformation houses for enclosed laywomen were one laboratory for later totalizing institutions: the poorhouse, the madhouse, the penitentiary.[25] Enclosure, surveillance, isolation, routine, thin intellectual gruel, and restricted agency, therefore, may have dampened spirits and stunted intellectual or emotional maturation. Even without Foucault's help, one could construe the *conservatorio* as a dreary, impoverished place, a laboratory for surveillance and punishment. Some historians, however, offer less bleak a reading. For one thing, the lives of young women outside the *conservatorio* might be little less confining; postpubescent girls in sixteenth-century Rome had little freedom of movement.[26] On the other hand, the world did sometimes come to uncloistered girls, for, at home or in service, they could often mingle with visitors. There might be more talk and news, more chance to flirt with men. As for the long hours of toil in the *conservatorio,* the same was often true outside. Then there was the matter of safety. We moderns

tend to scoff or marvel at sixteenth-century obsessions with female sexual purity, for our values are so different. But historians
point out the risks that sixteenth-century women ran—to their
reputations, their marriage prospects, and their safety. An unpro-
tected young woman with few resources and few male kinsmen to
ward off trouble fell easy victim to bad sexual bargains with callous
men.[27] As for the notion that the *conservatorio* infantilized its inmates, some historians have argued to the contrary that, in the
search for marriages, young women and their families were far
from passive. Together, they scoured the city for money and mates.
With or without their families, the young women took steps to secure their futures, often by building networks inside and outside
the institution. And some subverted, resisted, or fled.[28]

The archeologists unearthed clues to the material life of Santa
Caterina. The garden's soil yielded up assorted knives, scissors,
pins, belt ornaments, bottles,[29] keys,[30] thimbles,[31] sacred medal-
lions, and counters for board games.[32] It also disgorged many
pounds of sixteenth-century majolica, little of it as fine as a museum piece but much of it cheerfully decorated with bright geometric designs and flowers, snails, birds, rabbits, dragons, lions,
putti, houses, and landscapes, all hand-painted in broad strokes
on a pink, cream, or white background.[33] Clearly, not all this ware
was for the nuns, for some pieces have inmates' names written
crudely on the bottom. Agnese, Amelia, Carolina, Caterina, Claudia, Emma, Fausta, and so on down to Vera, Virginia, and Vittoria
each had a decorated dish, now unearthed and catalogued, she
called her own.[34] We also know something about the food that
filled these dishes, for the garden's soil was packed with the cooks'
discarded bones of cattle, pigs, goats, and sheep. The nuns, at least,
seem to have eaten lots of meat, beef in summer and fall and, after
Lent, lamb in spring and Romans' beloved *porchetta* when the piglets
were still suckling.[35] The girls themselves probably ate well too.

Whether the *conservatorio* was grim or pleasant, most young
women, clearly, preferred a husband and motherhood to growing
old inside. Not only did most survivors marry, but the records of
the institution show that, for their sakes and their families', many
played hard the endgame that would bring them out. This, clearly,
could be complicated, as all the parties, the congregation included,
had complex stakes in play. The guardians wanted their money

well invested, and carefully disbursed, to guarantee the couple's solvency and good behavior. And, to spare their capital, they tried to maximize outside cash. Meanwhile, grooms wanted a good match, with good money attached. The campaign to arrange a marriage therefore pitted the girls and their allies against prospective husbands, on the one hand, and against the conservators, on the other. Our evanescent love story played out against a background of such match strategies.

ALESSIO'S STORY

Alessio Lorenziano was thirty-five—more than old enough to be a married man.[36] He was the beadle of the university, a doorkeeper and factotum, seemingly literate, not rich; his friends, it seems, were often artisans. On Saturday, 4 February 1559, a prisoner, he appeared before a judge at Corte Savelli jail and related a story so strange, and so well told, that I intend to let him have the floor, with only a few interruptions for modern thoughts and comments. Three days later, Alessio returned and, under more aggressive questioning, clarified some points. At that session's end, the magistrate sent him back to his solitary cell, "with the intention of continuing." But there is no apparent continuation, no further papers, nor can I find a trace of sentencing. Most likely, as often happened, the court dropped the case or brokered a settlement that brought the whole story to a close.

This is what Alessio, on Saturday, told the magistrate, verbatim and entire.

> I am here because I desired to have a poor maiden [*zitella*; Alessio will use the term throughout to signal the convent's maiden wards], a young one of good family, as wife.

Alessio's story carries him back to 1556, almost three years before the trial at which he is now testifying.

> There was proposed to me a maiden called Lucretia Casasanta, the daughter of Maestro Giovanni Pietro, a goldsmith from Vicovaro [in the mountains east of Rome]. It was my intent to take a poor youngster as wife and to live in Christian fashion

upon the small labors God grants me. The person who proposed
this maiden to me was Madonna Livia, the wife of one Maestro
Pietro, a carpenter; she said it to me in the presence of an aunt of
mine. When I learned that this maiden was of good stock, I said,
"Well, I'll take her!"

And since she did not have a penny to her name, I wanted to
know first if she knew how to work. And since she was staying at
the monastery of Santa Caterina of the Virgins, I went to the pri-
oress [of the *conservatorio*] and asked her if she could please show
me a little of Lucretia's handwork, but I told her neither why nor
what for. She showed me a little of her work, and I liked it. And
then I inquired of various people to know if Lucretia were born
of legitimate matrimony. I was told that it was so, and that she
was born of a good father and a good mother. Then, I thought to
myself: there are two things that bring a Christian to salvation—
the monastic life and marriage. "Make up your mind, Alessio," I
said to myself, "either to be a monk or to take a wife and live in a
Christian way as the Holy Mother Church commands."

Is Alessio deeply pious? Perhaps! Or is he cutting his rhetorical
cloth to fit his suit and legal plight? More likely!

I was told that a Maestro Giacomino from Piacenza, a setter of
gems, was this maiden's guardian. So I went to find him with one
hundred scudi in my purse, for I wanted to donate the dowry for
this maiden, through him. And I asked him to let me have this
maiden as my wife. He told me that he wanted to give her to
me, but that I should go slow and easy, for he wanted to make
inquiries about my condition. In short, Signore, on account
of "good tongues" [Alessio is sarcastic here] or other words,
Giacomino let me be told via some other person—I don't remember who—that he did not want to give her to me, and that
I should think of something else.

I went about my business. A year later, this Giacomino took
sick. His womenfolk told him, "You could have married off that
poor maiden Lucretia, and you didn't want to!" He said, "If I escape this sickness, I promise to marry her [off]. Send for him, for
I want to promise him now to give her to him." I was called at his
request. He told me to be of good cheer, for he wanted to content

me. So he got well, and I went to the guardians of Santa Caterina
to ask them if they were willing to give me that maiden. Giacomino did the same, and the guardians were Monsignor [the
bishop of] Mondovì and Monsignor Lomellino, and the cham-
berlain was Battista Maratta.

The bishop of Mondovì, Bartolomeo Piperi, was to die in 1559,
leaving Santa Caterina as his heir. He would be buried in the new
church.[37] Monsignor Benedetto Lomellino, a noble Genoese
churchman in his early forties, was rising fast in Paul IV's administration. He was a companion to Cardinal Carafa, chief man of
state, and legate to King Philip in Flanders. In 1565, he would become a cardinal.[38]

They told me that they were pleased that I had come to ask them
for one of their *zitelle,* and that they wanted to make inquiries
about me here and there, and that then they would give her to
me. About fifteen days later I came back to hear what they had
done. They told me that they gave her to me willingly, for they
had found out about me, and that they owed her to me, for they
knew that I was the beadle, and cheerful, with an eye to making a
little extra money. And they gave me their faith that she would be
my wife, clasping my hand and embracing me. And they made a
decree for me—I am certain they put it in writing—that ruled
that Lucretia Casasanta was to be Alessio's wife.

Not only did *conservatori* vet the girls for virtue (and, often, for
pulchritude) before they took them in, but they also usually vetted
the men who wanted them as wives. It was all part of making a
solid match.[39]

Holy Saturday [at Easter, 1557], I gave orders to take the measure
for a ring. I sent an amount—I don't know how much—as a gift,
and the poor maiden took it, and she made the model for the
ring, and I gave the gold to Madonna Isabetta, the wife of this
Maestro Giacomino, to make the girl's ring. She [Lucretia] said,
they tell me, when they made the model, "If you have given me a
husband, may it be in the name of God!"

Later, Alessio tells the court that, along with the money, his gift to Lucretia was wine and (he thought) two kids, presumably to eat.[40]

> And since I had had expenses and had no more than forty scudi, and Giacomino had a wholesaler living in his house, and he wanted to give her to that merchant, he let me understand that he no longer wanted to give me Lucretia as a wife because I had not kept to what I had promised about the hundred scudi. And, likewise, the Company [Confraternity] of Santa Caterina said that they did not want to give her to me because I had not kept the promise about the one hundred scudi.
>
> And, from the beginning, they said that she wanted to become a nun, God willing. And so all that summer I was immensely anxious—that is, the summer of 1557. So I tried to find out what Lucretia's intentions were. In short, some people inside the company told me that if I brought the hundred scudi, they would give her to me.
>
> This past summer of '58, a friend of Lucretia's called Sigismonda came out of the convent [i.e., the *conservatorio*]. She is a good *zitella*.

Alessio, at first, had not known of Sigismonda. We learn from Alessio's later testimony that "Sigismonda was married this past May [of 1558] to a prosperous baker named Giacomo who runs a bakery in Trastevere at the Ponte di Quattro Capi" and that she "is the niece of the mother abbess of the convent of Santa Caterina."[41] "I learned of her from other maidens who have come out of the convent, that is, Elena, who is married to a schoolmaster in Campo di Fiori, Messer Giovanni, who is a friend of mine, and Chiara, who is married to a German baker at the Trevi Fountain."[42]

To return to Alessio's first deposition:

> I asked her [Sigismonda] if Lucretia was aware of me and had ever asked about my affairs, and if she thought about me. She said yes, that she had been unhappy and that, when she heard mention of me, she would cry. And I made more inquiries from another maiden, a companion of hers, who had left that place. She told me the same and added that Lucretia had washed her hair and her

whole body, hoping to come out. And I said, "Since it is God's will that this maiden be mine, and he has made her ready, I intend to take steps to have her."

It was not every day a woman took a bath. All through this passage, Alessio's story aims for the judge's respect and sympathy. Accordingly, the beadle takes pains to freight his narrative with signs, divine and human, to give his love suit weight and sanction. So far, the material signs have nothing holy to them: the ring, the head-and-body bath. But Lucretia's imputed words, as she lends her finger to make the measure for the ring, invoke God's will, as do Alessio's own. Was the actual negotiation in this pious spirit? It is impossible to say; we have no second witness, just Alessio.

And I took a hundred scudi, in cash, to the company this past summer [1558], and I told the guardians that they had to give Lucretia in marriage. And that I was giving the hundred scudi and that I desired that they remain attached to the altar of Santa Caterina in the event that I and she died without heirs. And they answered me that they wanted to hear the desires of the maiden. So they sent in Giacomino, Alemanno Alemanni, a Suor Angela di Casasanta, and Battista Maratta to hear the will of the young woman. But they did not go inside but sent in Suor Angela to hear Lucretia's intentions. And I was told that Suor Angela suborned her. So Lucretia, not knowing that I wanted her, also said that she wanted to become a nun, and the guardians told me that she wanted to be a nun and did not want a husband.

I went back to that Sigismonda, her companion, and asked her if she was sure that Lucretia wanted to be a nun. She answered me that Lucretia was a nun on account of me. And another time I asked her to find her, and she told me that Lucretia had commissioned her please to find out my intentions, did I want her or not? And Sigismonda had told her, "I cannot get the word to you on account of the guardians." And that Lucretia had told her, "Unless you let me know, I will become a nun."

The arrangement that the dowry return in absence of issue, described by Alessio as an act of piety, was in fact just the normal practice whenever funds came from the company itself.[43]

Between them, they agreed that Sigismonda would speak to me and that she [Sigismonda] would give her a striped shawl if I desired to have her. And when Sigismonda told me about this shawl, I bought her three to take to Lucretia. And, in the end, she took one of them to her and kept the other two.

So I went to see the datary and argued that he should please make them give me that young woman, whom they had promised to me, for I knew for certain that she wanted me. And the bishop of Verona came by and asked, "How is it that you know that she wants you?" And I said, "If I can make it evident that she wants me, give me your faith as gentlemen to give her to me afterward." He told me that he would have it done. So I told the bishop of Verona that the young woman had asked Sigismonda, her companion, to find out if I wanted her and that I should give her a sign, and Sigismonda had promised her a shawl if I wanted her as wife, and that, afterward, when [Sigismonda] had spoken with me and heard that I wanted her, I had given her that shawl and she [Lucretia] had accepted it.

The datary, Bishop Francesco Bacodio, was a high papal official who, among other jobs, oversaw religious congregations.[44] I do not know if this particular datary belonged to Santa Caterina. The bishop of Verona, Luigi Lippomano, definitely had very close ties with the congregation. A wellborn Venetian, learned, pious, and well connected in spiritual circles, Lippomano had a long career in papal service, as nuncio in Germany (1548–50) and Poland (1555–56) and as co-president of the second conciliar session at Trent. He had close ties with the Jesuits. At the time of Alessio's courtship campaign, Lippomano was particularly well placed to help, for in the spring of 1557 he became private secretary to Pope Paul IV. The job had pull. Lippomano was to die on 15 August 1559, just three days before his master and a few months after Alessio's trial. His body would rest in Santa Caterina; the tomb sits there still.[45]

After the bishop had heard this, a few days later, Sigismonda brought me back that shawl. She told me that I had made it public knowledge, and that she did not want to get mixed up in it anymore. And, indeed, if I told what she had said to me, she would deny it and call me liar.

Alessio later told the court that Sigismonda told him that the abbess, her aunt, had chewed her out.[46] Despite her kinship with the abbess, Sigismonda had good reason to tread lightly. Once married, Santa Caterina's alumnae were hardly free of the *conservatorio*'s earnest surveillance. Follow-up visits policed their good behavior, and the guardians could always suspend installments of the dowry payments or, worse, could move to repocket the disbursed capital.[47]

> And before Sigismonda told me about this and came out of the convent, I sometimes went into the church of Santa Caterina—to say my paternosters and also because of the love I bore this Lucretia—and I heard a great sigh in the choir, and I believed it was Lucretia. And I saw a person at the grill, and I believe it was she, though I did not recognize her for sure. And one morning I saw her at a corner of the grill, and she gave an enormous sigh. And I, who knew that Lucretia wanted me, became even firmer in my opinion on account of the words Sigismonda later told me. Sometimes I went to the church only for the love I bore her, and I turned toward the grill, but I could not make her out.

Santa Caterina served both a convent and a parish. Like many other nunnery churches, it had an altar out in public space, where a priest said Mass. The nuns and maidens, locked in, could not enter the public nave. Rather, to assist at Mass, they gathered in a room near the sanctuary, separated from it by an iron grill through which they watched the service. Such a grill survives in the present Santa Caterina, to the altar's left; Alessio, however, sucked up sighs in the old church, leveled soon after.

> And at the end of last June [1558] or thereabouts—I do not remember for sure—I was in Botteghe Oscure, in the house of Ottaviano Mancino, who lives across the way from the convent. There is a little courtyard in the middle, between Ottaviano's windows and those of the convent. So I was there, at that window, around the twenty-second hour [around 7 P.M.]. I said to myself, "Oh God, couldn't I see her!" And so, a maiden came to the window, and then two others came to the window of the convent that overlooked that little courtyard. And I said to myself, "How is it

possible that these *zitelle* came to the window like that!" So I waved to those three maidens and said, "Do you want me?" And they waved back, to say yes. But one of them turned and made a sign to the others. And then she said yes. And when the maidens had waved to me like that, I called the wife of Ottaviano Mancino, who makes woolen blankets—her name is Panta—and I said to her, "Look at this!" And she told me, "It is a great shame. You see that these maidens want you, and you don't fetch them out." And so I continued to go there for about a month. That is, I went there fifteen or twenty times to wave to those maidens, asking if they wanted me as a husband. And I showed them the ring. They said yes to me. The last time, I asked them to show me Lucretia Casasanta. And a girl came—it seemed to me that she was one of those three. And I asked, "Which is Lucretia Casasanta?" And one of them made a sign, "I am she!" touching her breast with her hand. And I showed her the ring, asking, "Do you want it?" And she made a sign that she did. And so I told all three girls that I intended to send in a person to whom Lucretia could tell her wishes. And I arranged that Abbot Martinenghi go in to talk. And the abbot said that she wished to become a nun.[48]

Did Alessio really intend to marry all three girls at the window? Of course not. He and they were flirting, all four playing with their fantasies. For bored girls, with little to do but sew, embroider, weave, and pray, Alessio must have offered a welcome diversion from the usual round.[49] That they succeeded so long in their parleys is a puzzle. It certainly suggests that they were lodged in a house on Via Caetani, at the northern edge of the monastic compound, not yet walled up in the usual way. However small the courtyard, the line of sight between Ottaviano's back window and the girls' own must have been difficult, for Alessio was unsure as to whether Lucretia, when she appeared to his summons, had been one of his three usual flirting companions. Ottaviano's own shop, clearly, was one of the modest houses on the northern fringe of the city block, facing the Via delle Botteghe Oscure. Site maps and archeological charts do not allow us to pin down just where Alessio stood, cajoling maidens for joint amusement. We do know the names of the houses' owners, but Ottaviano does not appear among them. Most likely, like many Romans, he rented premises.

Was the Lucretia at the window real, or was she a cruel hoax perpetrated by the girls to ease their tedium? The latter notion has a delicious tinge of intrigue and irony, but many details of Alessio's tale will prove that, whoever did lean out the window—probably it was Lucretia herself—the girl's mixed feelings indeed were real.

> I returned to the house of Ottaviano Mancino all desperate and went to that window. With me was Ottaviano's wife, who told me that it was a great sin not to bring the maiden out. And she also said that it was a great sin that they did not marry her off. And so those three maidens came to the window. And I asked if anyone had been in to parley. They said no. And I had the wife of Otta-viano ask them, but she did it secretly, lest anyone notice. And so I remained almost half-desperate and never went back again— except sometimes. And still those maidens kept coming to that window, and they asked me to get them out quickly. And I told them that I wanted one of them for me, and that I would have also married another of them off.

Alessio later told the court that he had thought of marrying off one of the girls to a brother of his. "I had already planned to give one of them to a brother of mine, and they made signs that they agreed. And so I talked with them and made signs to them two or three times, to help them get married, for maidens who are twenty or twenty-three years old want a husband."[50]

At some point in the summer, Alessio's importunities came to the attention of the governor of Rome, the city's most potent mag-istrate. As Alessio said in later testimony, "And he [the governor] prohibited me [from contact], in his house, before Lucretia took vesture, and he told me to let things go because they did not want to give her to me, for she wished to become a nun, and that if I had wanted a different one, they would have given her to me."[51]

Meanwhile, Alessio kept enlisting members of the company as allies. He brought to Panta's house a Messer Giacomo Vipera. "Panta said to Messer Giacomo that he should try to get Lucretia out of the convent as soon as possible and to marry her off, for it was a great sin to hold her when she wished to marry, and that it was wrong not to marry off young women and then to keep them locked up inside."[52]

Then came October [1558], and they [greeted me as a guest, not as a husband: difficult passage]. They vested her [Lucretia] as a nun and [four words difficult to make out]. And I passed by there, because my heart told me to and because those maidens had told me to be quick to get them out. And when I was there, one Sunday morning, I was arrested and put in jail.

We learn from Alessio's later testimony that the day before his arrest, the congregation had forbidden him to approach the convent.[53]

And she really cried when she was vested, so they told me. And the very day that I was put in jail, two maidens came to those windows. And Ottaviano's wife said, "Go away, you scamps. Look how you played tricks on us! Go mind your own business! Don't break my neck!" And they made signs that they wanted to come out. And I didn't want to go there anymore.

And after I got out of jail—I was there for a day and a night— Ottaviano's wife came to find me at my house and told me that those maidens kept coming back to talk at the window, and that the one in the habit wanted to tear it up and did not want to stay. And, doubting that it was true, I told her not to break my neck. She told me, "Come. You have to come. They want to see you." And she told me to bring with me a man who belonged to the company, to see the whole thing, for she did not want any more of this affair. So I went; it was Saint Andrew's Day [30 November 1558].

Alessio was to see Lucretia four times once she had put on a sister's habit. The first two times he waved but did not speak, as he was not sure if it were she.[54] And then, when they did communicate, Lucretia sent Alessio a flagrant signal of her desires.

So Lucretia came alone, dressed as a nun. I asked her if she wanted me and she said yes, with a nod, for I saw her incline her head. And she threw down from that window a lovely handkerchief, close by, in the corner, for she threw it into the courtyard, and I sent Ottaviano's wife to fetch it. And since Ottaviano's wife had urged me to find a worthy man who belonged to the company to see these things, since it was a great sin to me and to the company to let her stay there, I found Maestro Ippolito the physician. I told him, "Maestro Ippolito, so many times have I told you that that young woman wanted me. And that she did not wish to be a nun. If I made you see it, what would you say?" And he said, "Make me see this thing one time, and I will have her given to you, but watch out that they don't make us look like fools!" And I showed him that handkerchief, asking him, "If she gave me this handkerchief, what would you say about it?" He told me that it seemed to him a serious matter, and that if it were true, he would have her given to me.

When Shakespeare had Othello kill his wife for a dropped handkerchief, the playwright made good Renaissance sense because such a gift was not a symbol but a sign, a pledge, with all the solidity the culture of the time invested in things given. Maestro Ippolito's reaction thus reflects his times. Ippolito himself, in the absence of a surname, remains untraced. To judge by Alessio's account, the physician had the clout inside the company to sway decisions.

The company, for all its piety, may not have shared the nuns' desires to vest Lucretia. The guardians were in the business of finding girls good futures, be they in marriage, in service, or in a nunnery. They may have had in mind not only a tidy ending for the girl but also the drain on their capital. While the rich saw nunneries as a cheap dumping ground for excess daughters, the poor did not; a nun's dowry at Santa Caterina ran to 200 scudi, twice a *zitella's* marriage portion. Unless Lucretia, like some novices, had a subsidy, the company would be out of pocket.[55]

So that woman [Panta] kept asking me to bring that worthy man, and to be quick about it. So one evening I brought Maestro Ippolito to Ottaviano's house. We waited for a little bit, until Lucretia came to the window. And I had Panta ask her if she wanted me. Lucretia said she did and nodded. And she also made me a sign to ask if I had had the handkerchief. And after Maestro Ippolito saw this, he said, "Well, leave it to me! For I want to make sure that you have her. It is a great sin to have made her an imprisoned nun."

Maestro Ippolito and I went to the bishop of Verona. And he told the story, and the bishop said that if it were true, he would have given me a dowry. So Maestro Ippolito had me give the handkerchief to him. And then, with him [or "with it"], they held a meeting and resolved that, if it were true that she had given me that handkerchief, it was their intention to give her to me. They went into the monastery—Maestro Ippolito, the bishop of Verona, Monsignor Lomellino, Giovanni Battista Maratta, and Alemanno Alemanni—and they talked to that young woman, telling her that they knew she did not want to be a nun. And Maestro Ippolito said, "It is not proper for you to deny it, for I saw you with my very eyes talking with the beadle." And then she was all [quiet?] and Maestro Ippolito showed her the orange and the handkerchief. And she said that it was true that she had given them to me, but that the devil had tempted her. And they gave her three days to think her affairs over.

Here we have more proof of the power of the handkerchief. The orange, only mentioned this once, however, is a puzzle. Early winter was orange season, but why would Lucretia have dropped one?

We have already met some of these high churchmen. I have not been able to trace Alemanni. In his later testimony, Alessio added the names of other members of the company whom he had enlisted for his campaign. He cited a Messer Simone Firenzuola, "who knows well that this is a trick and that Lucretia is a sister by force."[56] He also mentioned the bishop of Pesaro, soon to succeed the present datary and then become a cardinal.[57]

Then they sent Signora [Vittoria] Sanguigni to speak to Lucretia. So I believe, but first the bishop of Verona talked with her [Vittoria Sanguigni], and I also spoke with Signora Vittoria, telling her about the affair, how it had happened, and Signora Vittoria also reported that Lucretia had said that she wanted to be a nun. Then the countess of Carpi talked to her, to satisfy me, and Lucretia said to that lady that she wanted to be a nun. And in the end she said, "If they have to marry me off, let them marry me off, but that is not what I want." And Signora Costanza Salviati also went, to whom Lucretia, in tears and with her eyes to the ground, said with her voice all quiet that she wanted to be a nun.

Finally, Signora Giulia Colonna went, and to her Lucretia said
that she wanted to be a nun, but she kept looking at the ground.
Signora Giulia told me that, so far as she can tell, Lucretia does
not want to be a nun.

These four ladies all belonged to Rome's elite. The Sanguigni
were civic nobles with fourteenth-century roots. The Pio di Carpi
were a great Lombard house, lately lords of Carpi. Costanza
Salviati was the wife of Alemanno Salviati, son and secular heir to
the wealthy papal banker Giacopo, a brother of two cardinals. Her
Florentine family of marriage was swiftly turning Roman, landed,
and noble. Giulia Colonna, of venerable baronial stock, was the
wife of the magnate Giuliano Cesarini, hereditary standard-
bearer of Rome, rich and influential but in the pope's bad graces.
All four surely belonged to the female wing of the Santa Caterina
confraternity; in visiting Lucretia, they were upholding, as aristocratic women in the Catholic Reformation often did, the informal, diplomatic side of a charity's social work.[58] Note how easily, if
Alessio was telling the truth, an underling could make use of the
good offices of the city's great, male and female.[59]

After these ladies had talked to her, Lucretia returned one day to
that window and gestured to Panta, meaning to say yes. [This
would have been in January 1559.][60] Now, not this Sunday, but
the one before [22 January 1559], I went to a meeting and said,
"Signore, do me a favor. Let it be judged for me by the church if
she is mine or not. And, for my sake, put her in another monastery so that it be seen by the church if she be mine or not." And
the company decided that it should be left to Lucretia to judge,
and, if she would be mine, they would have her given, and if not,
I should go about my affairs. And after that, Monsignor the governor had me arrested and put in jail, and that is why I am now
in jail.

Here ends Alessio's unbroken narrative, unprompted by the
court's questions. In the court's ensuing interrogation, some
things become a bit clearer.

Did Ottaviano know about the facing windows? Indeed he did,

and he shared his wife's opinions and advised Alessio to get help from a worthy of the company.

Did Alessio pay the couple for the use of their house and court-yard? Yes, a little—he bought a cape and jacket and a pair of hose for their little boy. "He was almost naked." "And I promised both of them to do them good, if God ever gave me the means, and I promised to hold the child at his anointment and to be a good godfather." Beyond that, he had also given Panta some small change to buy dinner. He did all this not only for the use of the house but also just because of his friendship with those "good poor folk who live by their labors." In this testimony, Alessio is careful to protect his hosts from charges of complicity.

Had the governor prohibited him from contact with the convent? He had indeed, at the datary's house. And Alessio had, he claimed, agreed to let the church be judge in the affair.

Given the prohibition, why had he kept going? "I did not do it to displease the governor. Indeed, I regard him as my lord. But that she should know that I desire her and not fall into despera-tion. And not for any other cause. And I spoke with Monsignor Governor after last Christmas [1558], and I showed him the de-cree and made him speak with Maestro Ippolito. And he said, 'If I had known these things! Why did you not tell me sooner?'"

Asked at his second session three days later about why he did not heed the governor's prohibitions and penalties, Alessio of-fered a curiously ingenuous excuse: "I do not remember the pre-cise penalty, but he [the governor] gave me a dressing down several times and told me not to go there and not to get mixed up in any such affairs, but I disobeyed because I saw him as speaking, not as the governor, but in a fatherly way, as an honored friend, for he is a member of the company."[61] The governor of Rome, exalted friend indeed, was a functionary with great power in the state, ow-ing his office to his larger role as vice-chamberlain. He was always a prelate and in 1559 was bishop of Chiusi.[62]

Had Alessio given Lucretia anything? Only the shawl. Since her vesture, he had given nothing.

After that question, the court remanded the beadle to solitary confinement, the usual place for suspects still under examination.

When Alessio came back, on Tuesday, three days later, the court

asked if he wished to add anything to what he had said and confessed, as they put it, the time before. His answer, at the outset, was
a curious tale.

> Signore, yes, it occurs to me to say that just recently I passed by
> Santa Caterina. And I found a chaplain at the door of the church,
> with a serving lad, to keep me from going in. I told the chaplain
> to tell Lucretia that she should speak her mind freely, that she
> should not be ashamed to. And I asked him, "Chaplain, who is in-
> side now?" He said that inside there was a servant of the bishop
> of Bergamo, and I went away about my business. And when I was
> in Piazza Mattei [a block away], I turned back to see who that
> servant of the bishop was, thinking that it was he who was teach-
> ing Lucretia to play music. And incidentally, to see if he were old
> or young, I went into the courtyard, and I saw inside Battista
> Maratta, who threatened me for going in. And I told him that
> I had come in to see what they were doing, and at that moment
> I saw coming out of the parlor room where they teach singing
> that servant of the bishop of Bergamo carrying a songbook and a
> baton. He could have been my age, that is, about thirty-five, and
> it was he who was teaching Lucretia to sing. I told him, "I can
> sing well too!" And then I left and went about my business.[63]

AFTERWORD

This odd story distills Alessio's strangeness. A well-seasoned man
of thirty-five has been haunting the convent like a love-struck
puppy, sucking up sighs and pouting at the sight of a music teacher
young enough to be a sentimental rival. And all this for a girl he
knows best by her embroidery and with whom his only conversation has been a few strained words and gestures from windows
across a courtyard. All the while, he has known that, for the *conservatorio,* any other girl would do as wife, just not this one. Was
Alessio an obsessive stalker or just a very stubborn man? What
ideal, what fantasy, what feeling drove him to such efforts, so costly
to himself and her?

Alessio, of course, is not our only puzzle. Lucretia too is
baffling, the girl who can say neither yes nor no to Alessio, and to
religion. Of course, she was far younger than he and far less an-

nealed by life. Her wavering, perhaps, was only natural in a sheltered young woman who feared the world, all the while it tempted
her, and who, even after vesture, had second thoughts about her
vocation. Alessio suspected that she had two voices: one, at liberty,
through the window, and the other, constrained by pressure, in the
parlor rooms, as visitors came by to test her will. He may well have
judged her correctly, whence his canny play for her removal to a
neutral place.

Historians know little about the emotional lives of premodern
commoners. Those who study *conservatori* have suggested that
many grooms took girls as a way to pocket money, and historians
in general have viewed marriage in this old regime as more pragmatic, less romantic, than we wish and fancy it today. Alessio's behavior, by such lights, is curious: such a bloom of feelings, so little
fertilizer. A mystery. As so often, a Roman trial leaves room for
many modern readings.

Yet there are some firmer lessons about the nature of their
world. If Alessio's story has any truth in it, women seem, as so often, to have had far more informal power and agency than the formal structures—laws, institutions, doctrines—would lead us to expect. In this story, almost all initiative, except Alessio's, is female.[64]
It was Livia, a carpenter's wife, who, in front of Alessio's aunt, first
suggested a marriage. It was not the ailing goldsmith, Giacomino,
who reopened the subject of the Lucretia match, but his womenfolk. And it was Giacomino's wife, Isabetta, who contrived the
making of the wedding ring. It was not Ottaviano who arranged,
and glossed, the courtyard meetings, but Panta, his wife. And it
was she who fetched Alessio after his release from jail to see the
girls at her window, and she who pushed him to bring a worthy
member of the company as witness. And, of course, it was Sigismonda who carried messages, as no man could, and who told
Alessio to back off when he spilled the beans.

Let us return to where we started, among so many ghosts. The
work I do ensnares me in a web of stories. I have lived in central
Rome; indeed, not long ago I perched and wrote all year four
flights above where Caesar's startled corpse once lay and in easy
sight of Santa Caterina. I walked to work, shopped, and talked
with lively Roman friends and neighbors amid the specters of my
vanished subjects. Their exploits and misadventures haunt almost

every corner, alleyway, and courtyard; as I wander throughout the city, I often cannot brush their memories off.

One intoxication, for us historians, is the pathos of distance. We strive to reach the people we describe, but time and oblivion just tease us. We yearn for them, but, like Alessio and perhaps like, in her odd way, Lucretia, we writers can never clasp the persons whom we seek. So the story of a baffled love neatly doubles our own pathos and desire. And a story with a missing ending teases us the more, sharpening the feeling. Did boy get girl, and vice versa? Unlikely, but not impossible.

In the summer of 2000, I was back in Rome, visiting friends and chasing loose archival ends. The pretty Museo Nazionale Romano Crypta Balbi, with its mixed display of on-site archeology, medieval life, and history of the later monument, had just opened. Most of the museum resides in resuscitated remnants of the monastic complex. Meanwhile, the center of the block is still littered with the tools, grids, trenches, and other disheveled arcana of archeology. The museum's director, Doctor Venditelli, treated me with the suavest Roman courtesy and introduced me to Professor Manacorda, the veteran chief of two decades of digging at the site. I related to them the story of Alessio and promised a copy of the transcript of his trial. In exchange, the two scholars gave me what turned out to be a very useful gift: two of the volumes of the publication of the archeologists' results. There I learned, among much else, that the garden excavations have served the history of everyday sixteenth-century Italian ceramics. There are thousands of shards from workshops all over the peninsula. Among them, as I have said already, are bowls on which the maidens or their keepers painted and scratched their names.[65] Lucretia has proven elusive. In the Archivio di Stato is an album of the Santa Caterina *zitelle* that gives their origins and fates; it is alphabetical, but the letters *I* and *L* have fallen out.[66] But in the archeological publication, in the middle of page 427 of volume 3, part 2, among other images, appears a drawing of the bottom of a *scodella,* an eating bowl of a Tuscan type, that dates from the middle third of the sixteenth century. It was one of those on which girls affixed their names. It had belonged to a *zitella* called Lavinia. But someone crossed the name Lavinia out. Curious! There are 155 pottery fragments with names, and only this one has a crossed-out name. Did Lavinia sin? Or die?

Underneath the canceled name, in a steady hand, appear the block letters LVCRRTI//A (the last letter is below the rest). Was this Alessio's Lucretia? Did she write it? It would be nice to think so, but we have no way to tell; the classicizing name was popular in sixteenth-century Rome, as was the famous legend of the virtuous Roman wife violated by the seventh and last ancient king, Tarquin the Proud, who then killed herself to guard her pure repute. It is a story that exalts both matrimony and chastity. And Casasanta, the girl's surname, evokes a church or monastery. In her bouts of wavering, did Lucretia Casasanta ever ponder the several meanings woven through her name?

If the chapter about the beadle wrote itself, with barely a touch by me, what comes next took far more carpentry. For Alessio, we have a single document, in a single voice. For the Giustini family of our next chapter, we have several trials, a bundle of notarial records, a printed libel, a sheaf of family letters, published family trees, and a patriarchal statue on a pillar in a church. And, on paper, there are voices by the dozens: male and female, noble and commoner, master and servant, insider and passerby. Silvia, the eldest sister, passionately defying her brothers by poor Vittoria's bedside, first drew me in. To make sense of her, and the whole story, I played my usual tricks, building a list of characters, with their assembled traits, and filling out a time-line of speeches, entreaties, curses, and blows. But, this time, so many were the witnesses that description thickened to the point that, for much that happened, my time-line acquired long strings of dialogue. It is a soap opera, I thought, and presented it that way, speaking in some two dozen voices, for a seminar.

I had planned to slide my whole running commentary into the stage directions. But since I knew too much, observations spilled over into a prologue, an epilogue, and two entr'actes. I tried my draft on a solid journal. Two assessors opined, firmly and unhappily, that, clearly, this was a beginner's lame effort. A sobering day for me! Clearly, I fumed, follies such as mine should be a sign of longer aging. I gnashed my teeth, lamented with my colleagues, and gamely tried another learned publication. The assessor's word came back: good stuff, but I wager the board will never have it. Prophetic! And it is too long; why not, the reader asked, make a book of it? But by itself, I thought, the story is too short; it needs more tales. So, to keep it company, I wrote this book.

As in chapter 1, artistry itself here aims at a lesson. The soap opera form at once subtracts and adds the author. Dialogue, by convention, removes the historian; he or she steps back. But the stage directions reinsert the modern commentator and remind us that the very conceit that presents the past as if it were unmediated in fact does just the very opposite. The story here, though seemingly raw, is in fact cooked, and cooked up, by sleuthing, by judgment, by choices, by argument, by all those quirks of sentiment and voice and vision that anchor the teller to a modern time and place.

We readers are prisoners of our present. The past, here, comes down to us through a long train of lenses of sixteenth-century experience, perception, and memory in the Giustini house and garden, and then through narrative and scribal hearing and transcription in court, followed at great remove by twenty-first-century reading, understanding, translation, and interpretation, at last to make its way onto the pages here. Refraction, all the way! A lovely way to teach this lesson, if one has a class, is to perform the Giustini story. Students learn at once that every inflection of the voice, every movement of the limbs, and every expression of the face is a dialogue between now and very long ago. History, all history, is interpretation.

Chapter 3

THE LAST WILL
OF
VITTORIA GIUSTINI

WHEN WE HISTORIANS QUOTE PAST VOICES, it is our wont and fate to lodge them in narratives of our own design.[1] The records of times gone by are so sparse, so fragmentary, that they rarely render up, on their own, a story that speaks for itself; the scholar must plaster in the ample gaps with modern prose. This chapter, however, tries to awaken the dead, that is, to let a Roman family of 445 years ago speak for itself, indeed, not only speak, but even reenact two sad and stressful days, all on its own. The historian, here, becomes a mere stage director, reduced to setting the time and place and to letting the past strut and fret again, as indeed the men did strut and the women fretted on two July days in 1557.[2]

This artifice of Clio's and mine relies on the happy conjunction of three sets of documents. Of these, the liveliest is a trial before the criminal court of the governor of Rome. There, the heart of the matter is the charge that a nobleman, Pompeo Giustini, coerced his dying sister to make a will that, because extorted, lacked validity. This central legal issue tangles with other alleged crimes: a proscribed fraternal sword fight, a rumored fraternal poisoning, and a purported wily exploitation of a seemingly talking corpse.

All these accusations, some bizarre, all passionate, sprang from within Pompeo's own tempestuous family. While sixteenth-century Roman trials vary enormously in richness, this one versus Pompeo and his brother Ascanio is a rare gem, a description of domestic life so thick that it lets the historian resuscitate the very rhythm of conversations, plots, and heated parleys. The magistrates and their assiduous notaries took down verbatim many long depositions from servants, friends, bystanders, and Giustini kin and siblings. By dint of patient, wily reconstruction, the scholar can thus withdraw a bit to let the past speak for itself. By unsnarling the chronology and warily choosing versions with an eye to bias and seeming veracity, the modern author can line up plausible quotations from the manuscripts themselves, like so many gleaming beads upon time's thread. Clio, as dramaturge, thus judiciously picks the dialogue and sets the scene and then lets the past speak its lines.

This chapter stretches the conventions of scholarly narrative to evoke the feel and texture of a lost event. The very effort alerts the reader to history's limitations, for what we recapture, in the end, is of course not the past exactly as it happened; myriad things are missing: the tones of voices, the rhythm of speech, the movements of bodies, heads, and hands, not to mention the smells—of cooking, of sickness, of death. We lack as well the precise spaces, with their light, their heat, their furnishings, their drafts, their sharp or muffled acoustics. Indeed, we still lack the precise words themselves, for no recollected quotation is ever exact. We are in the zone, not of fact, but of drama-as-hypothesis. But it is drama—by virtue of patient, cautious archeology in texts—far more faithful to the cadences of sixteenth-century Roman family life than is any historical fiction.

As for other documents, the second set, less dramatic but a precious supplement to court testimony, consists of the many notarial acts of the Giustini. These furnish details about lands, houses, offices, rents, dowries, bequests, settlements, and other exchanges both inside the family and with other Roman houses, noble and commoner. The third set is a trove of lively family letters, mostly by Silvia, sister and feisty protagonist in this whole affair. Together, trial, protocols, and epistles weave a tale.

But why bother? Standing alone, a story such as this is only yet one more microhistory, swelling a genre now sometimes lambasted as neo-antiquarian.[3] No story, however lively, serves historians unless it teaches a lesson. A tale about any mere two days in the life of one family cannot undertake the inductive reasoning that forges historical generalizations. Furthermore, these two days in the Giustini house were far from normal. Nevertheless, as always, even extreme moments are built of myriad ordinary pieces, albeit sometimes joined at unwonted angles. Furthermore, the extraordinary always illumines the boundaries of the ordinary. The story of the sad death of Vittoria Giustini thus offers many lessons about how families worked. Of these, some of the most interesting bear on female solidarity and on the many political devices by which women could thwart male intentions, impulses, and values. The thesis here is not that women had agency; that of course we already know. Rather, I argue that, inside the family, despite all the obvious male advantages, women's moral, emotional, rhetorical, and political resources were manifold, that they fit very female strategies and tactics, and that they fostered female coalitions.

The Giustini story, though it shows women's agency, nevertheless chronicles a female defeat. In the end, the men achieved all their ends, but not before the women had made the going rough. The victory of the male coalition is not hard to fathom, for the men had the bigger battalions. Theirs were the prestige, the habit of command, the stronger arms, the dagger at the belt. Theirs too were the connections to state and courts and the formal training in the law. Theirs, as well, in a world defined by lineage, were the stronger kinship ties. Nevertheless, the women put up a concerted, effective resistance. Inside a household, where politics turns as much on speech and gesture as on formal institutions, the women could bring to bear their *volgar'eloquentia* and their instincts for collaboration. We will several times pause in the midst of this drama of gendered politics to weigh the competing coalitions and to untangle single contestants' motives, motifs, metaphors, and ploys.

So the purpose here is first to retrieve real conversations and then to parse their rhetorical strategies. This, then, is a history of the spoken word, in domestic politics, where gender, station, age, and power all shape speech. Yet we lack the precise words spoken. Rather, all that remains is recollection, retrieved as judicial testimony shaped to slip into judges' ears. No testimony is ever neutral.

Since all witnesses are partisan, we must untangle one political moment, the act of testifying, itself fraught with purposes and shaped by linguistic habits, both legal and narrative, to dig down to an earlier moment, no less fraught and molded: the actual dialogue in the Giustini house. Thus, for caution's sake, the notes name the witness who proffered each quoted phrase.[4]

PROLOGUE: SETTING THE SCENE

A spoken reenactment of a family crisis requires first a well-painted backdrop. Who, then, were the Giustini? At midcentury, they were new to Rome. Amayden's gossipy old history of Roman families traces the local branch of the family, immigrants influential in Città di Castello, back only to Geronimo, the family patriarch, a doctor of both canon and civil law and noted lawyer.[5] By the 1540s, Geronimo had dwelt long enough in Rome to amass a goodly fortune and to weave alliances with the civic nobility.[6] He had married Geronima, a daughter of the Fabii, a well-rooted clan.[7] He had also won a coveted papal title, "advocate of the Consistory."[8]

Like most prosperous Romans, Geronimo had put his resources in offices, rents, and much real estate. He possessed vineyards to the south and north.[9] One of these, just outside Rome's northern gate, was fit to receive the pope for an hour or so as guest; in 1538, between prolix ceremonies of his pompous return from Nice, Paul III rested there.[10] More substantial were three *casali* (large farms).[11] Geronimo also had various holdings inside the city, including three grain storage pits below the Capitoline Hill.[12] He had owned a modest house in the thick of town, by the Cancelleria palace, but in his lifetime sold it.[13] With his wife's dowry had come a house behind the busy commercial street of the Banchi.[14] These properties Geronimo rented out, as he did a palace near the Tiber.[15] Besides these scattered urban dwellings, Geronimo had a substantial residence of his own,[16] with shops on the ground floor, facing west, at the south end of Via di Parione, a short street running north from the old procession route, the Via Papale (now Governo Vecchio).

When next in Rome, pay the man a call. To find where his house once sat, walk two blocks west from Pasquino, the famous talking statue just outside Piazza Navona, turn to the right at the

The neighborhood of the Giustini family and of Pallantieri and the Gramar family, looking east. Piazza Navona (Agonis) is toward the top of the view. Pasquino, the talking statue, is in the little triangular piazza below it and to its right. For Pallantieri and Via dei Leutari, take the street to the right of the statue's image. For the Giustini and Via di Parione, take the second street below it, to the left, just before the dome that cuts the view of the Via Papale. Two blocks along Via di Parione is the Pace church. Tempesta map, 1593, courtesy of the Biblioteca Apostolica Vaticana.

bottom of Via di Parioni, and then, immediately, at your right hand imagine his door, ensconced among the shops he rented out.[17] Across the street, though the façade is new, the church of San Tommaso still stands. This central location was the core of the family's Roman settlement. A very short block up the street, at the next corner, also to your right, stood a second house (with three ground-floor shops), where Geronimo's sister Lucretia lived and finally died, in 1554.[18] The Giustini were thus a local family; they always held public office in their home ward, Rione Parione. Now go two blocks more, to the monastery of Santa Maria della Pace. There the Giustini buried their dead and, for convenience, stored their marble busts and valuables. The famous façade is a later work, as is the apse. But Bramante's lovely cloister tucked around the back is early Renaissance, as are the first chapels in the nave with their fine Raphael and Peruzzi frescoes. They were there long before Geronimo made his will, dictated his epitaph, and laid out money for his portrait statue.[19] You still can visit the man himself, first pillar to your left. He looks out from his niche, stately, composed, handsomely intelligent. Quiz his placid features; can you detect the headaches his family cost him?

We know little more. No complete catalogue of Geronimo's rents and papal offices survives. We do know the value of some of them, and we learn from his will that he believed that they yielded enough income to furnish fat dowries for his two unmarried daughters.[20] One last thing: Geronimo intended his epitaph, says his will, to boast of his profession and his diligence in its

The funeral bust of Geronimo Giustini in Santa Maria della Pace. Photo by the author.

pursuit: "Here lies Geronimo di Giustini of Città di Castello, consistorial advocate, who took care of himself and of his affairs."[21] His heirs engraved the title but just concluded with a plainer claim: "He lived 55 years, 9 months. He died on 20 June 1548."

Fortunate Geronimo Giustini not only increased but multiplied; he was rich in not only goods but progeny. When he died, eight offspring survived him: five boys, three girls. The youngest, our Vittoria, was then only five, while the two eldest sons were in their legal majority, and Silvia, his firstborn, had already wed five years earlier.[22] Fecund parenthood, however, had proven bittersweet, for Geronimo's will thunders against the two eldest sons, Ascanio and Pompeo, disinheriting them as "ingrates and unworthy of their paternal inheritance, both because of the insulting and vile words against their mother and their father and because of their extreme disobedience and other unworthy deeds perpetrated against them."[23] For reasons unknown, Geronimo's ire ebbed with his health, for six months later, shortly before his death, he annulled this drastic will. He nevertheless hedged his pardon, dangling his old testament over his sons' heads and commissioning three trustees—his sister Lucretia; Orazio Lancellotti, a prominent physician and business associate; and Bernardino del Conte, the family's perennial and deeply trusted notary, later central to this tale—to verify the probity of his offspring and ascertain whether they should escape his first will's dire provisions and inherit.[24] As, indeed, they did.

We know not just what had kindled or quenched Geronimo's paternal wrath, but subsequent events confirm that the senior sons spelled trouble. Neither the elder, Ascanio, nor the second, Pompeo, followed their father's placid footsteps into law and high office.[25] Rather, both took to the spendthrift, violent aristocratic life. Evidence for this ominous turn comes not from notarial records but from their testimony before the magistrates, first in 1555 and then in the summer and fall of 1557. Both had gambled in noble houses. Ascanio told the court he had risked his assets in the very best baronial and official company: "I have gambled with Signor Francesco Colonna and with Signor Giulio Orsini and in the house of Signor Alessandro Colonna, with a hundred gentlemen, and with Francesco d'Aspra, the past [state] treasurer." He also played with, among others, a noble cousin, the soldier Cencio Capizucchi, an ally we will see again.[26] Ascanio claimed to be a big loser. "Ask if, between Tivoli and Rome, I have not lost more than three thousand scudi."[27] Sometimes, in a single session, the brothers won or lost hundreds of scudi, the price of a substantial Roman house.[28]

Ascanio's sporting reputation was shabby. In summer 1555, after skinning Pompeo at *primiera,* a game like poker, he was accused the next morning of holding five cards in what by the rules should have been a four-card hand. The ensuing recriminations sparked a falling out, as Pompeo helped round up court witnesses to Ascanio's perfidy.[29] Between the brothers blood already ran bad; earlier, Pompeo had ambushed Ascanio in the streets one night and drawn blood.[30] When word of this fracas came to Rome's governor, he imposed a formal peace forbidding combat, under pain of a 1,000-scudi fine.[31] Ascanio's bad odor wafted well beyond his family; his card trick against Pompeo was no odd slip; the incident brought a cascade of denunciations before the governor himself, as men of note whom Ascanio had stung at cards or gulled with his infamous loaded dice lined up to vent their spleen.[32] One victim, Cencio Dolce, spread wide the word; some three years later, Ascanio finally gave him the lie and demanded a duel. Dolce assembled notables in the house of a Colonna prince, gathered witnesses to his challenger's infamy, and published a scathing pamphlet refusing the fight in light of Ascanio's alleged perfidy at the gaming table and notorious cowardice.[33] Ascanio, clearly, had forfeited for good the respect of his peers, for after holding the minor post of *maresciallo* in 1546, he never again held the public offices that routinely fell to respected men of Rome's elite. As for Dolce, he would suffer for his affront to Giustini honor, but, as we shall see, not at Ascanio's hand.

In the eyes of the Giustini, however, what crowned Ascanio's disgrace was not his scams at dice and cards but his marriage to "that whore, Laodomia." To the magistrates, Ascanio himself conceded her past profession but, in serpentine testimony, declined to confirm the marriage.[34] Yet a notarial act on her behalf makes clear that by September 1552 Laodomia, who had invested her dowry in Ascanio's real estate, was indeed his legal wife.[35] The liaison, notorious in the city, was trumpeted in the same damning broadside

that decried his cheats.[36] Although Roman notables did sometimes marry courtesans, clearly, as here, the step could cost them
dearly.[37] In the eyes of his family, Ascanio was a sheep so black that,
a familial pariah, he forfeited to the next son in line his leadership
of the younger generation.

Pompeo, despite his heavy gambling, stood in much better light.
In the 1560s, he three times held public office, including the prestigious post of *caporione,* or chief magistrate of his *rione* (district).[38]
By 1557, he had usurped Ascanio's post as the *primo di tutti,* the first
of all the brothers. And, unlike Ascanio, he married respectably;
his wife, Califurnia, was an Alberini of civic noble lineage.[39] Yet
Pompeo's reputation had pimples. Though married, he frequented
famous courtesans.[40] In the bellicose summer of 1557, someone,
possibly Ascanio, had reported scurrilous doubts about his willingness to go to the beleaguered walls in Rome's defense.

The gravest charge against Pompeo, one that Ascanio at least
seems to have believed fervently, smacked of opera buffa. Puccini's
comic *Gianni Schicchi,* first performed in 1918, retells the very ancient story of a rogue, relegated by Dante to hell's eighth circle,
who climbs into the still-warm bed of a recent corpse to dictate a
convenient false will.[41] Pompeo, Ascanio charged, had perpetrated
just such a fraud at the death of their aunt Lucretia, slipping an impostor behind the curtains of her bed to lay down cozy terms.[42]
Here, either life or fraternal slander may have imitated the art of a
famous story.

At first glance, Ascanio's charge seems ludicrous. Lucretia,
Geronimo's widowed sister, had been deeply involved with the
family. Remember, she had been one of the three executors the patriarch assigned to warrant his eldest sons' worthiness to inherit.
Geronimo, who clearly trusted her, had also left her as the sole and
busy guardian of his five minor offspring.[43] After almost six years
as her brother's active agent, Lucretia took sick and, on her
deathbed, on 24 January 1554, dictated or handed over a will not
easily counterfeited. The document, five crowded pages long,
teems with minute bequests to retired maids lodged downstairs
and to daughters of favorite serving women and lists assorted
medals, gems, and silver salt cellars, bowls, ewers, and candelabra
secreted in strongboxes in monasteries and houses around the
city.[44] No impostor behind a curtain could have kept such privy

details straight. Furthermore, the notary by her bedside, the usual Bernardino del Conte, had for years been a Giustini confidant. He too had served on the triumvirate who vetted the accession of the eldest sons. Also among the witnesses at her bedside was Antonio Cagnetto of Parma, long the tailor of the Giustini and, in his career, witness to at least eleven Giustini acts.[45] Clearly, not even a false Martine Guerre could have faked such a will in such a company. Furthermore, Lucretia's Giustini niece Cecilia claimed three years later to possess a draft in her aunt's own hand.[46] So Pompeo is easily cleared of Ascanio's scurrilous slander.

Or is he? In her will, Lucretia left her house to Enrico de Tucchi, a kinsman of her late Tucchi husband.[47] Less than four months later, in April 1554, Pompeo appeared before the faithful notary, del Conte, as "legatarius, tam vigore testamenti quam codicilorum *ut ipse asseruit* [italics mine] per eandem Lucretiam conditorum." That is, "legatee by virtue of the testament and of the codicils, *as he asserted,* established by the same Lucretia." So armed, he claimed, Pompeo took possession of Lucretia's very substantial house, opening and closing its doors in the usual token of ownership. As often, the tailor, Cagnetto, witnessed. Two questions: what were these codicils, if they in fact existed, and why indeed did Bernardino del Conte neither have nor know them? And what ever happened to the evanescent Tucchi claim to Lucretia's fine house? Was Ascanio on the trail of real subterfuge: either a spurious claim to a fictitious paper or, even stranger, a canny *beffa* (hoax) from behind bed curtains?[48] Was Pompeo a furtive cheat little better than his shady brother?

The younger Giustini sons seem much more after their father's own heart. At Geronimo's death, the eldest of the three, Pietro Paolo, was twelve. The father, in his will, stipulated that the boy could be universal heir if, by twenty-five, he had won his doctorate in law.[49] Should Pietro Paolo fail in his father's academic ambitions for him, the next brother in line would inherit in his place. The three younger brothers all duly took paternal wishes to heart. By the fall of 1552, Pietro Paolo, at seventeen, was already a doctor and out from under his aunt's tutelage.[50] By the summer of 1557, the young man was well established. Now a Roman citizen, he had become, like Geronimo before him, an advocate of the Consistory.[51] Since 1552, he had owned his father's old house, received from his brothers in a series of property swaps.[52] By the summer of 1557, he dwelt there with a young wife.[53] Although he sometimes gambled with his rambunctious bigger brothers, he seems to have gone on to be a pillar of both family and community.[54] He four times held offices with the commune, in 1570 acceding to the high honor of *conservatore,* one of the three chief executives of Rome.[55] His notarized acts show him as a consolidator of his properties and a sponsor for his younger brothers, with whom, unlike Pompeo, he had much business.

Like Pietro Paolo, the next son, Cosmo, and the youngest, Fabritio, also studied law. Cosmo was at Padua by 1551, Fabritio by 1554; by the summer of 1557, the two were well along.[56] These two juniors, however, unlike Pompeo or Pietro Paolo, failed to set up patriarchal houses of their own; they just lived together, probably in rented quarters, not in Rione Parione but a few blocks farther north, by the church of Sant'Agostino. Neither ever fathered Giustini sons; Cosmo entered the church sometime before October 1561.[57] Fabritio picked a fight, was banished for the killing, and died in Gubbio.[58] As he lacked heirs, his brothers carved up his assets.

Like their brothers, the Giustini daughters had varied familial roles. In our story, the three sisters played kin politics differently, for they diverged markedly in character, age, and experience. As with the sons, the goals and actions of each woman reflected her position and her history.

The eldest, Silvia, as befitted the firstborn of all eight Giustini children, had some seniority and clout.[59] Her husband enhanced her political momentum, for Bruto della Valle, an only son, belonged to an exalted Roman family in a palace just three blocks away. Her parents had by 1543 secured the match with 4,000 scudi, a solid dowry to which her father's last will later added 500 more.[60] By 1557, Silvia had borne children; her loyal wet nurse, Clementia, figures importantly in the play below.[61] The round block letters of Silvia's signature, inelegant but self-assured, attest to her character and literacy.[62] So do fourteen letters to her husband, whose estates she ran when he was out of town. To judge by what she wrote, Silvia was forceful, competent, self-assured, and passionate about her children: come back, she told Bruto, for they grow better when you are here. Silvia was also deep in the uneasy family politics of her natal clan. She had a superstitious streak; a pretty toddler's bad fall and bruise made her fear the evil eye. But she was also worldly enough to keep her absent husband abreast of the rumored fates of cardinals.[63]

The second sister, Cecilia, or Cilla, as her family often called her, was far younger than Silvia; at her aunt Lucretia's death in 1554, still unmarried, she received a special legacy for her hope chest.[64] Indeed, grilled three years later about Pompeo's alleged fraud at the aunt's deathbed, she was quick to protest, perhaps disingenuously: "I do not know anything about it because I was a child [*putta*] and went up and down playing."[65] Cecilia had a dowry 500 scudi bigger than Silvia's and as prestigious a marriage—to Tiberio Alberini, second surviving son of an old noble house and brother of Califurnia, Pompeo's wife.[66] In the events of July, while Silvia stormed and raged, Cecilia strove for compromise. Her more pliant tactics perhaps reflected not only personality and conflicted loyalties but also youth and inexperience.

Vittoria, the youngest, was unlike her sisters, for by the time she was five, Geronimo, like many a wellborn parent with a glut of daughters, had singled her out for the nunnery.[67] As his testament put it, she was "not very healthy and not suited to matrimony."[68] "And so," the father's will went on, "in the meantime he desires that she be placed with some nuns while still a child." For the purpose, he decreed, Vittoria should have a more modest monastic dowry of 500 scudi, plus 50 ducats yearly for pocket money. But Geronimo left an escape hatch. "In the event that the aforesaid Madonna Vittoria does not want to enter a nunnery and is marriageable, then he left to her just as much as he left to the aforesaid Cecilia for her marriage."[69] Geronimo stipulated that in that case, upon her betrothal, the moneys for Vittoria's marital dowry would be bled from his sons' assets.

The Giustini brothers proved they knew full well how lucrative their baby sister's religious vocation would be, and how costly its demise. Over Ascanio's opposition, Pompeo and Pietro Paolo lodged Vittoria as a pensioner, not at the nearby Castellane convent, where she had studied as a child, but at a nunnery at the other end of town, San Lorenzo in Panisperna.[70] But Vittoria balked hard against her fate. When the assistant prosecutor and his notary examined Silvia at home on 26 July, one week after Vittoria's

death, she told them (Latin summary in italic type, Italian transcription in roman type):

> *She was asked if she knew that the aforesaid Vittoria wished to marry, or did she*
> *wish to lead the monastic life.*
>
> *She answered:* She had little wish to be a nun and said that she
> did not wish to be a nun.
>
> *She was asked: Is it not true that the aforesaid Messer Pompeo made the*
> *aforesaid Vittoria enter a monastery by force, and she refused, saying she did not*
> *wish to go in, and Pompeo whipped her for many days before she entered, to keep*
> *her from marrying, for she had a dowry of 5,000 scudi assigned to her, and he*
> *could make money from her?*
>
> *She answered:* I do not know if Messer Pompeo struck her on
> this account, but in my opinion, I could imagine that they wanted
> her made a nun, Messer Pompeo, and the others, instigated by
> him, in order to win this dowry for themselves.
>
> *She was asked why the said Messer Pompeo made the said Madonna Vittoria*
> *leave the house of the said Pietro Paolo one month before she died, at a time when*
> *she was healthy.*
>
> *She answered:* I do not know that he did it for any other reason
> than that she left the house of Messer Pietro Paolo because the
> sister-in-law was young, and at times she [probably Pietro Paolo's
> wife rather than Vittoria] left the house, and to Pompeo this did
> not seem correct behavior. I know no other reason.[71]

By the summer of 1557, Vittoria had resolved that the nunnery
was not for her. At her brothers' great expense, she was determined to marry. For her, then, the dowry promised by her father's
will was a precious lifeline. As death closed in on her, she clung to
it with shipwrecked desperation. Sadly for her, gold scudi bought
no safety against the ravages of hectic infection. As her life slipped
away, she must have felt that her brothers schemed to pry her from
her inheritance while she still breathed. And, indeed, two rooms
away, four of them, all but Ascanio, gathered in the sala (public
room) to agree to force a will. Their real goal was not actual sei-
zure but control postmortem. Of these fraternal plotters, the
three who had studied law must have known well that a proper testament might be needed to forestall equal division among siblings
of both sexes. What went to sisters, in effect, would only enrich

their husbands. Regarding an unmarried sister's death intestate, the Roman statutes were perplexing, but the rules of *ius commune* held that, without a will, the 5,000 scudi would go seven ways, benefiting, therefore, the married sisters and execrable Ascanio.[72] With a will that forced Ascanio and the sisters out, each remaining brother would receive a quarter. As often happens in families, money, an end in itself, also served as an expressive instrument for settling emotional accounts.

We have now set the scene well enough to let the characters speak for themselves. Nevertheless, the historian does not retire from the scene. Rather, from here, most scholarly remarks retreat into the notes and stage directions. Still, between the acts, the script will pause for commentary.

In the dialogues that follow, quotations of direct discourse (dialogue) from the manuscripts appear without extra punctuation. Where my sources have only indirect discourse, as in "He said that . . . ," I use parentheses to show that I have taken small liberties to re-create direct speech. I place a few surmised words in square brackets. Nothing else below is of my invention.

ACT I: THE EVENING OF 17 JULY 1557

We are upstairs in the substantial house of the second Giustini brother, Pompeo, midway up Via di Parione. The dwelling is big enough to let servants wander out of earshot from our scene of action. The house has three shops on street level, rented out, perhaps with small apartments above them for the shopkeepers. On an upper floor is a large public room, or sala, off which sit first an antechamber and then the bedroom where Vittoria lies. Behind the bedroom is a retrocamera.[73] From the northern windows one can see the nearby façade of Santa Maria della Pace, the Giustini burial church.

SCENE I: PROBABLY IN THE SALA

Present are Pompeo; his younger brother Doctor Pietro Paolo, a lawyer about twenty-two years old, who dwells in what once had been his father's house, one block to the south; and his minor brothers, Cosmo and Fabritio, still law students, who live in yet a third house, by Sant'Agostino, not very far away.

We cannot hear the words, but we know that the brothers discuss the news that the physician has said that their fifteen-year-old sister, Vittoria, must surely die. She has made her confession to the priest. Should they now broach with her the issue of a will? If the girl dies intestate, the brothers fear, the two surviving sisters and, through them, their husbands, Tiberio Alberini and Bruto della Valle, nobles of prominent Roman houses, could receive equal shares of her sizable inheritance, 5,000 scudi. "It is more proper that the men get it than the women,"[74] they agree; by "men" they mean themselves only, not their in-laws. A ticklish question then arises: what should we do about Ascanio, the black sheep, the one who disgraced our house by marrying that whore, that ex-courtesan, Laodomia? Should we say anything to Vittoria about leaving Ascanio out?

Fabritio: No, let's not say anything about Ascanio. Let's just leave it to her.[75]

But who is going to raise the matter of the will? Nobody has much stomach for it.[76] In the end, the unpleasant task falls to Pompeo, the soldier, the second eldest, the master of the house, and the leader of all the brothers, except Ascanio.[77]

SCENE 2: VITTORIA'S BEDROOM

This is the room, and probably the very bed, in which Aunt Lucretia died three years earlier.[78] Some hours may have passed since the fraternal parley. It is now about one hour after sundown. Vittoria lies very sick. She has an acute fever and a pain in the gut. Clementia, a widow of twenty-seven and wet nurse for the children of Silvia, the eldest sister, tends Vittoria.[79]

Vittoria: Something is gnawing at my insides, in my stomach.[80]

Pompeo enters and approaches the bed. He leans over the girl, probably settling himself near her head on the wide shelf that runs around three sides of a lettiera, the usual bed of state of the well-to-do.[81]

Pompeo: Vittoria, now that you have confessed, don't you want to take communion too?
Vittoria: (Yes.)
Pompeo: Now that you have arranged things with God, it would be a good thing if you also arranged things with the world as well. You should make a will. Don't be alarmed by this. You

know that those who are well do it too, the way our parents did, and others too.[82]

Vittoria (*bursting into tears*): Why are you saying this, Messer Pompeo? That means I'm going to die. That's why you're saying this to me.[83]

Pompeo: That's not it at all. Rather, I just want you to know that you can dispose of some things.[84]

Vittoria (*perhaps mindful of her beatings at Pompeo's hand when he tried to force her to become a nun and forsake her dowry*): [But what will happen to my dowry?]

Clementia: Madonna Vittoria, try to content your brothers. If you do this thing, they won't take it from you if you make it through.[85]

Pompeo: I don't want you to leave anything to Ascanio, because he is a good-for-nothing, dissolute character. He is here in Rome and he has never come to see you.[86]

Clementia: That cannot be!

Pompeo: Upon my faith as a gentleman, he's in Rome![87]

> At this point, the crunch of carriage wheels resounds on the street below. Nurse Clementia exits to greet her mistress, Madonna Silvia, the eldest of the Giustini siblings. We hear salutations down below as Clementia helps her mistress off with her street clothes[88] and then the sound of footsteps on the stairs as Silvia comes up, crosses the sala and then the antechamber, and enters the bedroom with Clementia and with two other servants of hers, Francesca and Lucretia.[89] Pompeo still leans over the bed. Vittoria is still sobbing. She can barely speak.

Vittoria (*reaching out her arms*[90] *to Silvia and crying, in a gasping voice*): Madonna Silvia! Madonna Silvia! Madonna Silvia! Help me! Help me! Pompeo wants to assassinate me. He wants to make me make . . . I don't know what . . . I don't know what . . . Pompeo wants me to have them make a will. Some sort of will. I'm not going to die![91]

Silvia (*to Pompeo, speaking sharply and perhaps shrilly*): Oyme! There will be time to make a will! She's not so sick as that! Don't assassinate her this way! (Let her rest!)[92]

Pompeo (*rising*):[93] What do you mean, assassinate. So, me, I'm as-

sassinating my sister for her property! I'm not a man to assassinate anyone.[94]

Silvia: That's not what I mean at all. I am saying it because she is
sick.[95]

Pompeo: (Stop your screaming; you are bothering the girl.) You
came here to wreck my plans.[96]

Silvia: If I'd thought any such thing, I would not have come here.[97]

*At this point, Cecilia, the younger married sister, and Fabritio, the youngest of
the brothers, come rushing in, alarmed at the sound of shouting.[98] Offstage, a
serving woman of Silvia's, probably Lucretia, rushes off to the houses of Pietro
Paolo, just down the street, and of Cosmo, who lives with Fabritio near Sant'
Agostino, some blocks away, and fetches them to calm this family fight.[99]*

Pompeo: Get out of here! Get out of here!

Silvia: *Oyme!* Good Lord! Why this? I . . . For one single word! I
meant no harm![100]

Pompeo *(angrily puts his hand on his dagger, though he does not unsheathe it,
and lunges toward Silvia):*[101] Get out of my house. Otherwise you
will make me do something big, something crazy.[102]

*Silvia ducks behind the bed to avoid injury. Fabritio and Cecilia lay restrain-
ing hands on Pompeo.[103]*

Silvia: I'm going! I'm going!

Pompeo: Out! Out![104]

*Pompeo grabs Silvia by the sleeve, still shouting, "Out of here!" and drags her
roughly by the arm[105] down the stairs, as she cries bitterly all the way. He re-
leases her in the street, without her head shawl.[106] She is thus in a state of extraordinary undress for a proper Roman matron, who, when in public, should
always cover her hair. Silvia sends one of her serving women to her house, the
della Valle palace, a few blocks away, to fetch the coach[107] to carry her back
home. Silvia then heads down the street toward Pietro Paolo's house, just fifty
paces[108] to the south. But Pompeo, having second thoughts, runs after her,
catching up with her halfway to their brother's dwelling. He then leads her back
to his house. He tells the magistrates later that, had it been daylight, he would
never have gone after her.[109]*

SCENE 3: DOWNSTAIRS IN POMPEO'S HOUSE

Silvia and Pompeo go back inside to await her coach.[110] The argument breaks out again, just out of our earshot, rehearsing the same claims, reproaches, and protestations. In the midst of the wrangle Pietro Paolo and Cosmo arrive. As they enter, Pompeo is urging Silvia to be gone. Silvia is telling Pompeo, yes, go she will. The youngsters Cosmo and Fabritio take Pompeo's side, but Pompeo does most of the talking.[111] Pietro Paolo, the eldest lawyer, is perhaps more reticent. Cecilia too has come down the stairs. We hear again the sound of wheels. The coach has come back to fetch Silvia home. It is now about two hours after nightfall.[112]

Cecilia: (Silvia, don't go! It's the wrong thing to do!) [113]

Silvia makes as if to leave, then, afraid that Pompeo will force Vittoria against her wishes to make a will, stops.

Silvia: I want to see my sister die.

Silvia then heads back up the stairs. The others follow.[114]

SCENE 4: THE SALA, ON THE SAME FLOOR
AS VITTORIA'S BEDROOM

The brothers and sisters pace up and down the sala, arguing still. Present are, in order of declining age and prestige, Pompeo, Pietro Paolo, Cosmo, and Fabritio, on the one side, and Silvia and her young sister Cecilia, on the other.[115] Silvia is still berating Pompeo. Eventually, Pompeo sits in a chair.

Pompeo: (Silvia, pipe down. Don't keep breaking my head like this.) [116]

Clementia, Silvia's wet nurse, slips back into the bedroom; from there she can still hear the loud wrangling in the sala.[117] Pompeo puts his hands together.[118]

Pompeo: I beg you, Silvia, for the love of God, get out of here before you drive me to do something crazy. You came here to block this will. You think you are going to inherit something.

You will have nothing from it. I will make this will come about and I will do so to spite you!

Silvia: (That's not what I came for at all. I don't want property.)

At this point, Tiberio Alberini, Cecilia's husband, comes into the sala, but, a mere in-law and also the brother of Pompeo's wife, he keeps his discreet counsel and says nothing. He may sense that any intervention on his part, given his divided loyalties and contradictory material interests, could only backfire.

Cecilia: (That's not it at all!) Don't bother yourself about that at all. Send for a notary, and we will renounce anything that might be coming to us. (We just want the girl left in peace.)

Silvia: (Go ahead! Send for him!)

Much of the reading of this entire drama hinges on the meaning of this gesture by the two sisters. If, as is likely, they in fact really put love and nurture ahead of money for themselves, these words are serious, if only as an impulsive sacrificial gesture. If, rather, their solicitude for Vittoria covers for covetousness, then the offer is a sham. A cynic would be quick to note that, indeed, nobody sends for the notary.[119]

SCENE 5: IN VITTORIA'S BEDROOM

This whole scene is only at the word of Fabritio. It may therefore be a fiction, for here Vittoria seems suspiciously compliant. The dialogue does not jibe with Pompeo's and Cecilia's stories of later struggles to persuade the girl. Fabritio, the youngest brother, enters, salutes Vittoria, and sidles up to the bed.[120]

Vittoria: I see that Pompeo wants me to make a will. (I know that I am going to die. I still feel all right [about it].)

Fabritio: Don't worry. It's all to avoid quarrels with the in-laws. If you don't make a will, the sisters will come into it too. It's much better that the property stay with us brothers, and besides you know which of us is bad and which is good, and who loves you. You know what Ascanio has gone and done.

Vittoria: (Tomorrow morning I can do it. Just leave me in peace this evening.)

SCENE 6: BACK IN THE SALA,
WHERE THE WRANGLE CONTINUES

Pompeo: (Shut up, both of you!)

Silvia *(after a brief silence)*: Just you please let me say two words and then I promise I'll hold my peace.

Pompeo: (Go ahead. Go do so!)

Silvia: All you brothers are assassins and traitors. Now I've a load off my mind!

Pompeo, who has been sitting on a chair, rises in fury and reflexively puts his right hand on his dagger hilt but does not draw the weapon. In a rage, he goes up to Silvia and gives her a solid slap to the face.[121]

Pompeo *(as he slaps her)*: (Now I've a load off my mind too!)

A slap to the face, in sixteenth-century Italy, is both a formal social sign and a powerful blow to self-esteem. The other brothers and also the brother-in-law all dash across the room, lay restraining hands on Pompeo, and check him. Cecilia rushes protectively into the space between her struggling brothers and her sister.[122] *Things calm down a bit.*

Silvia *(addressing Pompeo)*: I said it about everybody! It doesn't fall to *you* to hit me![123]

Pompeo: It most certainly does fall to *me*, because I am the first of all of us.[124]

As things settle down, Tiberio Alberini goes back home.[125] *Pompeo's wife, Califurnia, enters. Silvia retreats to a corner, very quiet, but anxiously watchful. Pompeo goes in and out of the bedroom. Pietro Paolo and Fabritio drift off, heading for their houses and for bed.*[126] *Cecilia too heads home to get some sleep, having had a long hard session keeping watch the night before in Vittoria's room.*[127]

SCENE 7: THE BEDROOM

Silvia is just out of sight, having stationed herself in the back room, behind Vittoria's bedroom, where, though she cannot see, she can hear everything, at least imperfectly. She will stay there all night, keeping vigil, afraid to come closer lest

Pompeo and his wife accuse her of interfering with Vittoria, but watching lest her sister die or Pompeo molest her further. Cosmo hovers briefly over Vittoria. We cannot hear his phrasing but we know the subject.

Vittoria: Leave me alone. Leave me alone. *Orsù,* I want to sleep.[128]

She turns away from him. Pompeo comes and leans over Vittoria. We cannot make out his words, but we later hear from Silvia that he long hectored the poor girl to make her will and to cut Ascanio out. Finally, he too gives up. Silvia keeps her vigil till dawn and beyond.[129] At some point in the evening, Pietro Paolo sends a servant of his out to the nearby dwelling of Bernardino del Conte, the family's trusted notary, with word that, come morning, he might be needed.[130]

First Intermezzo

This first act reveals the alignments in play. On the one side is a tight male coalition, probably long tacit but certainly sealed aloud by the hurried fraternal parley in the sala. There, the four Giustini men place their material interests and the solidarity and honor of the lineage, narrowly defined as male, ahead of both their sister's heart and Ascanio's purse. Sensing urgency, they delegate to the eldest among them, Pompeo, the distasteful task of broaching the subject of a will. Ranged against their design is a looser, less explicit coalition of the three sisters and their female servants. We know that Silvia, the eldest sibling, has opposed Pompeo's earlier campaign to deprive Vittoria of her dowry by whipping her into a nunnery. This evening, her legacy once more under fraternal pressure, Vittoria reverts for help to her old ally. The elder sister arrives in the very nick of time, ruining, as Pompeo says, his designs, for Pompeo clearly needs female intercession to convert Vittoria; his yoked appeals to peace with God and brothers are making no headway. Groping for a go-between, he finds one in Silvia's servant, Clementia, only to be interrupted by her mistress's tumultuous burst into the bedchamber. Silvia's outcry illustrates one side of female power; her passion trumps her brother's cloyed reasoning. Her anguished reproaches, invoking the principle of mercy, both shore up Vittoria's will and stall male plans. Pompeo's rage against Silvia, whether calculated or not, seems at first to serve his end; he simply removes the obstructress, throwing his sister in disarray into the nocturnal street. But, as Gandhi knew, victimhood, when it shames, wields power. Pompeo, having overreached himself in familial and Roman eyes, must fetch Silvia back.

Silvia's purposes are multiple. She and Cecilia may hope, by stalling, to thwart a testament and so share in the bequest. Nevertheless, probably more urgent in their eyes is to protect Vittoria, from bullying and from the twin specters of a lost inheritance and death. Together with Cecilia, against Pompeo's fixation on contracts, divine and human, Silvia advocates and flaunts a stance of sacrifice.[131] Thus, to set an example for their greedy brother and to seize the moral high ground, the two sisters offer to surrender all material interest. At the same time, Silvia labels her opponents as tenants of the low ground. She ladles out reproach, bandying terms like *traditore* and *assassino,* words redolent not of religion but of honor. Pompeo's riposte, the slap, a shaming blow, also belongs to honor's realm. With it, he checks Silvia, forcing her into a different discourse and a new stratagem. She reverts to sacrifice, retreating into the back room to take up a vigil—a ritual stance, sanctified by familial and Christian piety—from which her brothers dare not dislodge her. That is, she appeals to her rights to exercise compassion: she "wants to see her sister die." Her act of witnessing, a deterrent to Pompeo, is thus girt morally. Silvia's pious desire overrules her brother's anger, checked also by the presence of the other siblings. Thus, the evening sees Pompeo's tactical defeat. Yet the next morning will turn the tables to bring him strategic victory.

ACT II: THE MORNING OF 18 JULY 1557

All action (in one scene only) is upstairs in the Giustini house. Pompeo still hovers over Vittoria, urging her to make the will.

Pompeo: I want you to make me, Pietro Paolo, Cosmo, and Fabritio heirs. As for Ascanio, I don't want you to leave him anything, for he has a horrid reputation. He is a bad character, and the disgrace of our house. Furthermore, he has known you were sick for days and he hasn't ever come to see you.[132]

Pompeo again appeals to Clementia, Silvia's wet nurse, who compliantly addresses Vittoria, but to no avail. The apothecary bustles in with futile medicines and then departs.[133] Pompeo then collars Cecilia.

Pompeo: (Ask her to make the will to leave the brothers quiet, so that they can be in peace and not have to litigate with these Della Valle and Alberini.) [134]

Cecilia: No! You must really think me out of my mind, to do something so much against my own interest![135]

But Cecilia at last surrenders her qualms, her own interests, and her husband's. Though the account here is from her testimony, she never tells us what thoughts and feelings finally rally her to Pompeo's design. Cecilia goes to Vittoria and speaks to her gently.

Vittoria: Pompeo tormented me all night long to make a will and to do what the brothers want.[136]

Cecilia: [Vittoria, you really should make the will.] (Keep your mind on God and on the good of your soul. And leave your brothers in peace, so that they won't have quarrels with the others. That is all it's for.) [137]

Vittoria: Well, I am content. I am willing to do it to content you. But last night I didn't want to. You can send for the notary.[138]

The other brothers gather in the sala, keeping out of the way of the priest, Father Ambrosio, from the church of San Tommaso, just across the street, as he gives Vittoria communion and last rites. As soon as the priest has finished, into the bedroom comes Bernardino del Conte, the family's middle-aged, red-bearded, trusted notary. With him, at his summons, enter Pompeo, all three younger brothers, and Cecilia. In too comes Giuliano Blandino, used-clothing merchant from down the street and old family friend, a frequent signer of Giustini contracts.[139] Silvia is still in the back room, listening. Bernardino moves to the head of the bed.

Pompeo: [Vittoria, do you want to give any of your property to anyone in particular?] [140]

Vittoria: (What will happen to my dowry if I do?)
Bernardino: (Don't worry. If God gives you his grace and lets
you live, nothing will happen. You could make fifty wills and it
would not put you at any disadvantage at all.) [141]

*Vittoria is at last content with this answer. Bernardino, unlike the brothers
who have bullied her, she can trust.*

Vittoria *(turning to her brothers)*: I would like a grace from you. I
would like to leave three hundred, four hundred scudi for the
sake of my soul.
Pompeo: Not only three hundred or four hundred, but a thousand!
Do with your property whatever you like.

*As Bernardino begins to write, Vittoria makes the customary bequests of
25 and 50 scudi for the dowries of the daughters of various women of the household, to a total of 400 scudi in all.*[142] *Then Bernardino asks that witnesses
be summoned. Cosmo and Fabritio scurry off around the house and out into
the neighborhood, rounding up a sizable company of witnesses. As Bernardino takes down the will, some of them wander in. They are not needed to
hear Vittoria's dictation of the will but only to swear to her assent to its proper
transcription when the notary reads it back to her. Some are house servants,
others neighbors. From outside, there are a merchant from Gubbio, caught
on his way to Mass at Santa Maria della Pace, who lives down by Ponte Sisto,
in another part of town, and who has property dealings with the Giustini; a
grain merchant;*[143] *a druggist; and a Frenchman named Etienne de Montréal.
From the household, there is one of Pompeo's servants and one of Fabritio's.
Cosmo later turns up with a painter from the street down below and a brace
of notaries, but by now there are already so many witnesses that these are
sent away.*

Bernardino *(to Vittoria)*: (And who are your principal heirs?)
Pompeo: [Vittoria,] look. We don't want you to leave anything to
Ascanio, because you have been ill and he has been in Rome and
he has never come to see you.[144]
Vittoria: (I want Pompeo, Pietro Paolo, Cosmo, and Fabritio.)
Bernardino: (Are you sure you want it that way?)

As Bernardino has the witnesses hear the stipulation of the will, Etienne de Montréal, the Frenchman, who has arrived after Vittoria began to speak, notices that Ascanio's name is missing.[145]

Etienne: But Messer Ascanio won't get anything![146]

Cecilia *(having acquiesced to the making of the will, had clearly not intended this effect)*: Why are you doing this? That's a very wrong thing to do, leaving nothing to Ascanio! Isn't he your brother, like the others?

Pompeo: Leave her alone to make the will freely and do what she wants, and don't get yourselves mixed up in it.[147]

Vittoria: No, I don't want to. No! No! I don't want Ascanio to have anything of mine, because he has brought little honor to our house. I don't want Laodomia to have my property.[148] No, I'm not leaving Ascanio anything! Don't talk to me of Ascanio. He never came to see me.[149]

Somebody of the family: [That's the way it is. She is not leaving him anything.][150]

Bernardino *(turning to the collected witnesses)*: Take notice! Note that not only does she name him, but she also expressly says that she does not want to make him an heir.[151] *(Turning back to Vittoria)* Name your heirs one more time.

Vittoria: I leave Messer Pompeo, Messer Pietro Paolo, Messer Cosmo, and Messer Fabritio as my heirs.[152]

In his draft, however, Bernardino does not record Ascanio's exclusion. Once the witnesses are assembled, Pietro Paolo does not stay to hear the entire dictation of the will. He withdraws, heading off to his house in the company of a physician named Stefano, who had paid a call on the patient. His absence matters to what will happen in the evening.

Vittoria: Messer Bernardino, this document that you have made: in whose hands will it remain?

Bernardino: (It will remain in my hands.)

Vittoria: You won't give it to anybody?

Bernardino: No.

Vittoria: Now I am content.[153] Praise God, I've done it. I'm as happy as if I were well and getting out of this bed.[154]

At this point, there arrives a physician with a clyster for one last enema.[155]
Bernardino and the witnesses withdraw to the antechamber, where Ber-
nardino writes out the names of the witnesses.[156] *They sign and drift off. Three*
hours later, about the eighteenth or nineteenth hour of the Roman day (noon
or 1 P.M.), young Vittoria dies.[157] *When she dies, Vittoria's face, which had*
been fever red, turns spotted and then, as she cools, blackens all over.[158] *We can-*
not see this scene sharply.

Second Intermezzo

Now we know precisely how Vittoria dictated her final testament.
This is precious information, for seldom can historians of any
epoch see a will in the actual making. Our near ignorance is trou-
bling because wills are altogether crucial to the social history of
the Renaissance Italian family. Many astute historians use them
intensively for several purposes: to trace fluctuations in piety and
charity, to explore material culture, to uncover attitudes to the afterlife, to unravel inheritance strategies, to ferret out the subtle
changes in the power and position of men and women.[159] A large
scholarly literature thus tends to assume that a testament ex-
presses the intentions of its maker. Yet one lesson of Vittoria
Giustini's story is that some wills are the product of several minds.
Indeed, that Vittoria, so young, made one at all is due first to her
wealth and then to fraternal pressure. Nevertheless, despite her
capitulation, it would be wrong to see Vittoria's will as a mere dik-
tat. Rather, its contents reflect an uneasy collaboration, in which
Vittoria, Pompeo, Cecilia, the notary, and even the witnesses par-
ticipated. This collaborative process cannot have been unique; on
those who tally wills it urges caution.

Pompeo's victory probably owes less to his lumpish eloquence
than to crucial allies. As morning begins, he still appeals to Vittoria's solidarity with the Giustini house, vituperated by Ascanio's
infamy, and plays upon her sense of hurt that her eldest brother
has not come to her sickbed. As yesterday, he turns to the nurse
Clementia, whose interventions still fail. Then, somehow, Pompeo brings Cecilia around and she converts Vittoria. Unlike Silvia,
Cecilia seems unaware of the plot for Ascanio's exclusion; her ad-

dress to Vittoria makes better sense if she does not know, for her words turn on the theme of peace. Let there be peace between Vittoria and God and between the brothers and their in-laws. Possession is not the rhetorical issue; rather, the point, Cecilia says, is familial concord. Had she suspected the long and violent family quarrel the will would kindle, she might have eschewed this irenic theme. This speech of Cecilia's does the trick; Vittoria takes up the testament as a pious act. Nevertheless, she remains fearful that, by the bequest, she will jettison her dowry. It takes a second ally of Pompeo's, the notary Bernardino, who as a family friend enjoys her trust, to reassure her. At the end, wary as ever of her brothers, she wants assurance that Bernardino, not Pompeo, will hold the will in hand.

The elder sisters' desire to include Ascanio illustrates a difference between male and female conceptions of family interest. Although married, Silvia and Cecilia retain a strong attachment to the paternal house; Silvia's letters prove this well.[160] For them, harmony is a central concern. Even when quarrelsome, they take up cudgels in the name of peace. Fearing rancorous conflicts, they work to mollify fear and grief and anger. Silvia strives to spare Vittoria; Cilla interposes her body between Pompeo's fury and Silvia; both sisters work to spare Ascanio Pompeo's contumely. In this pursuit of tranquility, the women compromise their own comfort, safety, and wealth and risk Pompeo's dudgeon. They are also content, on Ascanio's behalf, to compromise the family's collective honor. Pompeo's priorities are radically different. For him, the wealth and collective honor of the male lineage are paramount. Ascanio, having disgraced himself, must be cut out, humbled, shunned. In Rome, women, though themselves quite capable of pursuing honor with violent words and acts, nevertheless often work to mitigate the damage wrought by the proud male yen for vengeance.[161] As the next act will show, in this female ambition, the two surviving sisters fail utterly. Vittoria's bend to Pompeo's push will have dire results.

ACT III: LATE AFTERNOON OF 18 JULY 1557

It is six hours later, the late afternoon of the same July day. The sun will go down in two hours, and already midsummer heat is beginning to abate.[162] *To*

*our left, we see a Roman street. A wall, with a door, blocks it off from an en-
closed courtyard that fills most of our stage. To the right stands a garden, a few
steps up, and beyond it rises the residence of the youngest Giustini brothers,
Cosmo and Fabritio, from which drifts the buzz of six male voices*[163] *and the
light sounds of a small dinner party. Among the guests is Pompeo and red-
headed Marcantonio di Cantalmaggio, a young merchant from Gubbio, who,
in concert with a fellow townsman who was witness to the will, does business
with the family.*[164] *The swallows, almost surely, are beginning their usual
wheeling, raucous celebration of the end of day, skimming over rooftops and
dodging among spires and chimneys. In the street appears Ascanio. At his side
walks Giuliano, a young servant, perhaps African, with a belted sword. Ascanio knocks. A lackey, François the stable boy, crosses the garden, opens the
door, scrutinizes the visitor, at last recognizes him, lets him and his man in, and
relocks the door behind them.*[165]

Ascanio (*calling upward toward the sound of the party*): [Cosmo, come on
down!] I have to have a word with you.

*Cosmo, who has just about finished eating, quits the dinner party and descends
from the garden to the courtyard.*[166] *What passes next is in earshot of the din-
ers, who listen rather carefully. Probably, it is suddenly too quiet.*

Ascanio: Cosmo, are you content to think the way our brother
Pietro Paolo does? (He just ceded me his share of my share.) [167]
Cosmo: (Look, Ascanio, I didn't know what's in the will because I
wasn't there when they made it. Were I to see the will, I would
not want to depart from the opinion of my sister. I am willing
stand by this in court.) [168]
Ascanio: [Fabritio, come on down here. How about you? Are you
willing to do what Pietro Paolo just did and give me your share
of my share from the will?]

Fabritio detaches himself from the dinner party and descends to the courtyard.

Fabritio: (Ascanio, I was there only at the end of the will-making.
I'd been there earlier, many times, but you couldn't hear a thing,
she was in so much pain. I found out more clearly from the others that she didn't leave you anything. Be that as it may, I want
to stick with what the will says, whatever it says.) [169]

Cosmo stays for a bit, listening, and then returns to the garden. He converses with Pompeo. He then comes back to the top of the stairway and calls down.

Cosmo: Ascanio, get it into your head that I want to observe the intentions of the testatrix.[170]

Ascanio (*waxing angry, begins to raise his voice; to goad Pompeo, he fetches up the story of Lucretia's false will*): (Cosmo, you have been talking to Pompeo. He won't get away with this false will the way he did with our aunt's.) Pompeo, you just watch it, or I will tell the world that you are a scoundrel and a traitor. (I'll tell about this false will and that one of our aunt's that you had them forge.) [171]

Pompeo comes down the stairs, dressed for dinner in his doublet. He is unarmed; perhaps he left on the dinner table the dagger he had carried the day before.[172]

Pompeo: Ascanio, what is this? What is this you are saying? What is all this shouting about? (Your sister's will was well made. There's no need to get you dragged into this! You know that already.) [173]

Ascanio: What do you think I am?[174]

Pompeo: You know well enough what I think of you. You mean nothing to me. Go on, get a move on! Get out of here! You have no business being here.[175] I think you are . . . I think you are a mortal enemy.

Ascanio: It's on other things than this that I should spend my time with you!

Ascanio bites his finger at Pompeo, a classic obscene gesture of scorn and defiance.[176] Pompeo at once spins around and thrusts his bottom in Ascanio's direction, roaring.

Pompeo: [Ascanio], I want you to stick all the nose you've got up my ass.[177]

Ascanio reaches for the dagger at his hip and lunges toward Pompeo.[178]

Ascanio: You have assassinated me.[179]

*Marcantonio di Cantalmaggio, the dinner guest from Gubbio, leaps at As-
canio, clasping him to prevent an attack on Pompeo.*[180] *Pompeo rushes at Giuliano, Ascanio's servant, who is standing by the courtyard wellhead, grabs the
youngster's sword, draws it, and dashes toward Ascanio.*[181] *Several bystanders
converge to seize Pompeo. In their hands, he trips and falls; Giuliano's sword
goes flying. At once, one of the servants picks it up and hustles it out of range.
The air rings with profanities. Pompeo recovers his balance, breaks away,
sprints up the steps into the garden, and returns brandishing his own sword.*[182]

Pompeo: Out of here Ascanio! Get out!
Ascanio: I intend to stay right here.[183]

*Hurling oaths, the two brothers go at one another. François, the French stable
boy who had first let Ascanio in, comes rushing from the house hauling a cor-
sescone, a kind of halberd, either to support Pompeo or to break up the fight.*[184]
*Two or three other servants, similarly armed, gallop in his train. While the oth-
ers swarm defensively around their master, François closes with Ascanio.*[185]
Under the press of numbers, Ascanio backs toward the closed door to the street.

Ascanio: Come on out, Pompeo! Come on out! I'll prove you are a
traitor and a fraud and a forger.[186]

Ascanio's cape falls from his shoulders.[187] *Servants rush to open the door,*[188]
*and Ascanio, still shouting, backs into the street. Pompeo plunges after him, As-
canio draws, and the two brothers duel ferociously with sword and dagger. Two
servants with their halberds join the fray on Pompeo's side.*[189] *At this point,
neighbors begin to gather. Among them are Lorenzo Quarra and Jacobo dello
Stincho, both domiciled near the Minerva church, a few blocks away, and
Agostino Bonamore, a druggist whose own sanguinary marital troubles of 1558
have already appeared in print.*[190] *Not intimates, these men nevertheless know
the Giustini family, or at least their house and name. They have come running
at the racket of the fight. Jacobo now swoops in to separate Ascanio from the
servants.*[191] *Three or four of the many soldiers who fill the wartime city appear
in the street. Seeing Ascanio outnumbered, they draw their swords, drop capes
to elbows for nimbler fighting, and scramble to his aid, shouting.*

Soldiers: Don't be afraid, gentleman sir! Nobody's going to get
away with bullying you. What's going on here? Back off! So
many men against one![192]

Fabritio has grabbed at François to restrain him, telling him to back off, for Ascanio and Pompeo are brothers. Still, the soldiers turn on François and easily disarm him.

Fabritio: Let go of him. He's my servant![193]

A soldier aims a blow at Fabritio, who is encumbered by long clothes unsuited to fighting, but does no harm.[194] At this point, various bystanders, including house guest Cantalmaggio, break up the fight.[195] Ascanio, still defiant, lingers at the gateway, refusing to leave until he has his cape back.[196]

Cantalmaggio *(to the Giustini crowd):* Leave it to me. I'll give it to him.

He fetches the cape, brings it out to the street, and protectively fastens it around Ascanio's shoulders. The three townsmen offer to escort Ascanio but, when he refuses, go their way.[197] Pompeo retreats into the house, bleeding from a minor finger wound. Miraculously, no one else is hurt. Ascanio and his servant, Giuliano, head off. With them is a servant of Cencio Capizucchi, a well-known soldier, an in-law of the Giustini, and Ascanio's partisan and patron. Cantalmaggio escorts them as far as the nearby church of Sant'Agostino, scolding Ascanio about how it is no good thing when brothers fall out.[198] The soldiers come up.

Soldiers: Gentleman sir, we are soldiers. We were afraid you would be murdered. We joined with good intent.[199]

Cantalmaggio now returns to the Giustini house. Ascanio sends his servant ahead to organize supper. He himself then heads to the palace of the governor of Rome, intent on lodging a complaint. There ends what we can reconstruct well. The busy story of Vittoria's will, however, goes on for at least six more weeks. And then its epilogues, in family politics, will run on for years.

EPILOGUE TO THE DRAMA
This final scene is altogether male. The very tensions the three sisters have hoped in vain to smother explode in an almost fratricidal fight. Ascanio, on the scent of his purloined legacy, contests at once his own exclusion and Pompeo's ascendancy over the younger

siblings. He has, he claims falsely, already winkled a quarter share out of Pietro Paolo, probably the brother least dependent on Pompeo, and now hopes to use that false report to pry two quarters out of the younger brothers. The wrench in the works is Pompeo's unexpected presence at their house for dinner, stiffening Cosmo's and Fabritio's backbones. Ascanio begins with a simple appeal to match Pietro Paolo's generosity. His rhetoric flaunts no higher principles of fraternal or pious love. The brothers, fortified by Pompeo at their shoulders, demur in the conveniently impersonal language of the law. To cow Pompeo, Ascanio falls back on blame and threats, calling the new will false and paragoning it to Aunt Lucretia's shady testament. But here Ascanio's courtyard campaign for money stumbles, for, true or not, his charges do not cow Pompeo; they goad him to scornful obloquy. Ascanio ripostes with a mocking hand gesture too offensive to ignore and Pompeo at once replies with worse. Pompeo's obscene derision boxes in Ascanio, who is left no choices but flight or fight. The ensuing melée spills so little blood that one suspects a tinge of pantomime. The neighbors and soldiers who come running, in the customary way, to break up the fight may, in fact, to wary combatants, have been welcome.[200] Ascanio, breaking off with obligatory swagger, even before supper resorts to law, grasping at the criminal court for domestic leverage.[201] His campaign, however, as we shall see, will bring him, not familial satisfaction, but legal travail.

At the governor's, Ascanio launches a florid denunciation. For all he knows, Pompeo has poisoned Vittoria. Certainly, he has been beastly toward her; he has whipped her to make her take the veil and shed the dowry. Furthermore, these past two days, he has hounded her to force an unfair will. To top things off, three years back, when Aunt Lucretia died in that very room, Pompeo played his outrageous trick with the talking corpse.[202]

The governor bans Vittoria's burial. Learning of the decree, Pompeo goes to see the governor but is not allowed to speak to him; that morning, the magistrate took a purgative to clear the gut. Soon, all over Rome, Pompeo hears rumors, as Ascanio spreads the word that his brother forced the will. The tale has reached their kinsman Capizucchi and their mother's brother, Giovanni Vicenzo di Fabii, who back Ascanio.[203]

The court is swift. It orders a quick inspection of the corpse.

Then, on 24 July, just six days after the sister's death and the brothers' duel, it hauls in Pompeo's servants to inquire about the nature of Vittoria's illness and the circumstances of her will. Two days later, a prosecutor and notary interrogate Silvia at home, long and closely. Her testimony damns Pompeo's conduct. Yet when the court raises Aunt Lucretia's suspect will, Silvia, swearing that she would never destroy her brother, refuses to comment. "Oh, I do not know, and if I did, I would not say it, either to the governor or to the pope if he commanded me to, where I know that it might mean my brother's death." [204] That same day, the court grills Clementia, Silvia's wet nurse, who on every point backs her mistress firmly.

For nine days the record goes silent. Then, on 4 August, the prosecutor and his notary appear in the palace of Cecilia's husband.[205] They serve Cecilia with a warrant: she must testify or pay a 5,000-scudi fine, a hefty sum, as big as Vittoria's contested legacy. Preferring silence, Cecilia balks long and hard, but, brandishing their warrant, the men of the law extract from her a reluctant testimony that, when she at last lets loose, backs Silvia's version wholly.

The same day, Pompeo himself testifies in the governor's residence before a heavy legal team: Chief Prosecutor Pallantieri, a judge, and the governor himself.[206] He tells a moralizing tale that highlights his benevolence, Vittoria's gratitude, and Silvia's hysteria. He also tells a sheepish, bowdlerized version of the courtyard fight, omitting his haughty challenges and anal taunt.

The court then pursues accessory witnesses. Four days later, it begins to investigate the fight, questioning first the guest from Gubbio, Cantalmaggio. Over the next few days, it interviews three Giustini servants and Ascanio's page, who all defend their respective masters, and two of the three men who came to break up the fight.[207] It fails to trace the soldiers. Then, on 9 and 10 August, the court interrogates three of Silvia's servants: Lucretia (who had known Vittoria for years), Francesca, and Clementia again. All tell the same story, excoriating Pompeo, pitying poor Silvia. And the magistrates return to Silvia, who, to the court's careful question, reaffirms the formal charge: this will was made "by force." [208]

On 12 and 13 August, the court grills the notary, Bernardino del Conte, who defends the propriety of the will and of his own conduct and parades the very Christian contentment of the dying girl. For the next eight days, the tribunal surveys the witnesses to the will, all of whom, in self-justification, claim to have seen no threats or pressure.[209]

The magistrates then return to the Giustini. On 15 August, the court quizzes Fabritio, who backs Pompeo and berates Silvia for her usual shrilling.[210]

Then, on 19 August, the court questions Tiberio Alberini— Cecilia's husband and Pompeo's wife's brother, strung taut between wife and in-laws. Underlining his impartiality, he announces that he had gone to the sickroom "to do a charitable deed."[211] To keep his distance, he reports as hearsay the pressure on the girl and prudently keeps his thoughts to himself. Tiberio depicts the drama as turning on Vittoria's comfort, not on the sisters' gain. Nevertheless, unlike his wife, he does portray Cecilia as alert to her own monetary interests. The court never quizzes Silvia's husband, absent from the death.

The magistrates then increase their pressure on the two elder Giustini brothers. Between 24 and 28 August, the court questions further witnesses to the courtyard brawl. By now, both brothers are under investigation for breach of their old truce, imposed years back by an earlier governor.[212] The first day of September finds Ascanio a prisoner in Tor di Nona jail, examined by an assistant prosecutor about the recent brawl, about his other armed fights with Pompeo a few years back, and about the peace then imposed, now broken, and its 1,000-scudi guarantee, now risking forfeit. The next day, the same officials quiz Ascanio about his fishy five cards in a four-card hand and about his fraternal quarrels. Ascanio blusters, whines, ducks, and weaves. He is remanded to jail.[213] On 6 September, Pompeo too is confined, in Corte Savelli prison. An assistant prosecutor examines him about the broken fraternal peace and about his subversive remarks in the presence of Isabella de Luna, a famous Spanish courtesan, where he boasted of friends in the Imperial and Spanish army that had just made hash of the pope's forces. The court also probes his failure to rush to the Roman walls when the enemy troops made their recent feint at Porta Maggiore, Rome's backdoor.[214] On 9 September, the court quizzes Ascanio about the brothers' broken peace, but Ascanio tries to keep the discussion to the courtyard brawl.[215] On 12 September, Ascanio, still in jail, blusters that there are dire things against Pompeo and secrets about his marriage that he will tell, but only into the ear of the governor himself.[216]

On 13 September, Pompeo is placed under accusations, released, and given three days to prepare a defense. The formal charges include falsifying the will of his aunt Lucretia, forcing Vittoria's will, and poisoning his sister.[217] As for Ascanio, we have no record of either release or charges. He may well have had no trial, for Roman legal processes could break off at any point. Sixteenth-century criminal proceedings are tips of icebergs of conflict, negotiation, and settlement. So, for Ascanio, as often, no sentence survives. Pompeo's case does go through; he is vindicated on every count. The sentence, dated 7 October, first notes in passing the dismissal and replacement of Prosecutor Pallantieri (but not his jailing) and then lists the major charges, all rejected. For Ascanio's campaign for vindication, revenge, and cash, the sentence is a solid check.

But not checkmate. Ascanio soldiers on and, eventually, half succeeds. For what happens next, there are no trials, but family letters and notarial acts help piece together an epilogue of spite and fervid bluff and barter. It is clear that for Ascanio the bond between brothers that squeezed him out of his rightful share in his sister's goods is a deep wound that chafes and throbs. It is hard to assay his mix of motives; likely, the denial of patrimonial goods, in a world where one is what one owns, strikes at the root his pariah sense of self. Central to the imbroglio, also, is the status of Laodomia, ex-courtesan, semisecret wife. Ascanio strives—with her active help—to cobble Laodomia, willy-nilly, into a true Giustini. The couple will try several ploys: to secure her hold on Ascanio's own property, to forge social ties to family members and their kin and to elite Romans, and to link her, by charity and acts of patronage and piety, to Roman institutions the Giustini themselves have favored.

Ascanio and his family will scrap and skirmish for three more years. Then, in the summer of 1560, death will cut him short. Meanwhile, his siblings' lives are far from dull. Silvia has a baby, Orazio; her letters to Bruto are full of the pregnancy, family news, and her wish to have her husband home with her.[218] Both Cosmo and Fabritio win their doctorates in law.[219] Cosmo takes his holy orders and, in the fall of 1558, rents space with Pietro Paolo in Via di Parione, ensconcing himself, four servants, his mule, and his coach.[220] And Pietro Paolo, to judge by notarial papers, remains the axle around which most family business turns.[221]

Pompeo, two-fisted, rambunctious, cruel, still attracts trouble the way a homebound trawler draws circling gulls. A sentence of February 1558—the trial is lost—lays on a fine and exile for a drubbing he and his servants bestowed on a debtor's procurator at Pompeo's doorstep.[222] Pompeo had grabbed the man by the chest, berated him, hit him, and ordered his servants to club him "in various parts of his body." Just as Pompeo was reaching for his dagger, passersby stopped the fight. Three months later the court suspends the sentence, but the troubles go on. In June, writing Silvia's husband, Pompeo mentions touchy negotiations with the governor about a pending trial and a cardinal's safe-conduct scheme on his behalf. He adds that in her husband's absence he has instructed the coachman that Silvia is not to leave home without one Lavinia, who should keep watch on her—fraternal solicitude.[223] And in January 1559, we know from Silvia's reproachful comments, Pompeo leads his brothers in some shifty plot. Though the details escape us, Silvia's feelings do not:

> You should know that my fine brothers have betrayed Cristofano. They made Ascanio be the spy, and they had him arrested in his house. This is the good deed they did him! . . . Pompeo was the ringleader in the whole affair—so that how far you can trust the lot of them it is not my affair to tell you.[224]

Yet Pompeo has no monopoly on Giustini violence. On 4 September 1558, Fabritio throws an egg. We lack trial papers to explain his motives, but the surviving court sentence suggests why.[225] Romans often threw playful, expressive eggs during Carnival, first loading them with flattering perfume or with spiteful stink. But Carnival was in February, not September. Fabritio is on horseback, armed, and hedged with armed footmen, in a very public space, Piazza Navona, just three blocks from home. Gentlemen did not go shopping, on foot or horsed. Nor are raw eggs easy to cradle with reins in hand. So when Fabritio, in the saddle, clutches his fragile missile, he must be hunting a coveted and chosen target.

Cencio Dolce! He was Ascanio's gaming partner, his denouncer in court, and the recent author of the shrill pamphlet that trumpeted his cowardice and treachery. Is it on Ascanio's account that Fabritio lofts the egg or on Fabritio's own? Without the trial, we cannot say, nor do we know just where on Cencio the egg lands. But when the inevitable fight breaks out, Fabritio's sword finds Cencio's thigh, slicing it so deeply that Cencio soon dies and Fabritio is banished from Rome. He goes to Umbria, Giustini home turf. He never comes back; in June 1559, in Gubbio, he too dies.[226]

Before Fabritio's death in exile, Ascanio too falls gravely ill. We first hear of his sickness from a letter of Silvia's to her husband on 19 February 1559. After reporting on her troubles finding a good coachman—she has hired five already—she adds:

> Ascanio is terribly sick. The physicians have given up on him as done for. Maestro Franceso [a medical man] is angry and won't go there anymore and says that it is tuberculosis. They say that it isn't, that it is an almost plaguelike fever; he's come out in pocks. I don't think you could find a worse illness than what he has. I don't think he is going to die, as they say he will, for it seems to me that his spirits are fairly good. Pietro Paolo and Califurnia have quarreled.

Silvia then goes on about the bonfires to celebrate a tax reduction and about rumors, nearly true, that Carlo Carafa will lose his cardinal's hat.[227]

Though Silvia's letter does not explain Califurnia's falling out with Pietro Paolo, Ascanio seems the likely cause. Just eleven days earlier, Pietro Paolo and Cosmo notarized their donation to Ascanio of their own two-quarters share of what should have been Vittoria's 1,000 scudi left to him.[228] The very next day, Ascanio drew up his will and testament and notarized it in the very house where Pietro Paolo and Cosmo lived. The double transaction, obviously, signaled a single deal. Ascanio's will, like many, wades deep in family politics. It requires careful parsing.

As is usual with Italian testaments, the will begins with funeral arrangements and charitable bequests.[229] Ascanio asks to be buried at Santa Maria della Pace, the church that holds his father's memorial bust and his sister's bones, and leaves the monks a bequest for annual masses for his soul. He sets up masses at several other churches, among them San Marcello, the home of the Confraternity of the Most Holy Crucifix that, should his heirs not observe his will, will inherit in their place. He then turns to Laodomia and stipulates that she should extract what is coming to her as her dowry from a 6,000-scudi bond of his on the Ancona public debt (the Monte). Ascanio instructs his heirs to pay a servant his unpaid wages. He offers a generous 100 scudi to the nunnery at Montecitorio called "Della Castellane." This house, like the Giustini family, has ties to Città di Castello. It is here that Vittoria spent some of her girlhood; her own will rewards an old teacher among the nuns.[230] Ascanio singles out two other nuns for special gifts. Then, with Vittoria still in mind, Ascanio, with pious malice, bequeaths to the Confraternity of the Most Holy Crucifix "for the salvation of his soul and the remission of his sins" "the half of the share of the legacy of the late Vittoria, his sister, due the testator, which half portion were and are held by Pompeo and Fabritio, his brothers," and, for gravitas and punch, notes the names of two lawyers fully informed about the matter. After one more gift to a Castellana nun, Ascanio turns to secular debts and credits: some money in Laodomia's hands to be paid some wards of the noble Paola Cenci, some money owed him by his kinsman ally, Cencio Capizucchi, and a sum of 155 scudi due him from Pompeo. And Pietro Paolo owes him a substantial 1,200 scudi; this money should go to Laodomia, and with it she should pay off assorted debts to noble Romans. Pietro Paolo himself should cover a lesser debt remnant of 32 scudi.

The will then takes careful steps to protect Laodomia from Ascanio's brothers' grasp.

> He said and declared that all the linen cloth and the woolens and the utensils and domestic goods and the dresses belonged and belong to Laodomia, his wife, and that he left and granted them and anything not enumerated here to the said Laodomia, under her own authority, so that she need not take them from the hand of the heir and that she could have and hold them.[231]

Ascanio, here, may have in mind, inter alia, the goods Laodomia had brought with her to the marriage, perhaps many of them the

THE LAST WILL OF VITTORIA GIUSTINI · 111

fruits of her career as courtesan. Likewise are Laodomia's, the will adds, all the papers made out in her name and all the goods and moneys they enumerate. To separate them from his estate, he leaves them to her. He then spells out that, as implied above, for her dowry she can have 1,500 scudi out of the 6,000 he holds in the Ancona fund.

After disposing of a mail shirt to a kinsman of his mother, and some sleeves of mail, the will then ladles bile onto the Giustini siblings.

> He left, by the law of inheritance and to provide for what they
> can ask for on any cause and occasion, to Messers Pietro Paolo,
> Pompeo, and Fabritio, his aforesaid brothers, and to Cecilia, his
> sister, one scudo for each of them, and in this, he made them his
> heirs with the desire that they be able to seek nothing else from
> his goods, whatever the cause and occasion.[232]

But what of Silvia, his sometime advocate? To her Ascanio leaves 500 scudi, half of them from the Ancona Monte and half, pointedly, to be taken from the quarter of the Vittoria inheritance passed him the very day before by Pietro Paolo. Ascanio, here, is sowing dragon's teeth of family discord, setting Silvia against the others, probably to Pietro Paolo's embarrassment. Then, to complicate things yet further, Ascanio's will pivots neatly and gives right back to Cosmo the Vittoria money Cosmo had given him the day before.

Finally, as is normal, the will names the universal heirs, the ones who enjoy the goods but pay the debts and probate the estate. The value: as usual, not specified, and hard to estimate. The heirs: Valerio, Pietro Paolo's little son, and Laodomia, half and half. Laodomia, though, as husbands often specified, would forfeit upon remarriage. Her choices: on the one hand, a chaste widowhood or the nunnery or, on the other, the dowry and nothing else. In the latter case, Valerio, Cosmo, and the Confraternity of the Most Holy Crucifix would split the inheritance three ways.

There are big losers by this will: Pompeo, Fabritio, Cecilia, stripped and smacked across the face. Pietro Paolo wins big, through his son. Cosmo and Silvia come out in the middle. And Laodomia also wins, both goods and status.

But with Ascanio nothing is ever simple. A few weeks later, on 16 March, Silvia writes Bruto:

> This evening Laodomia sent me word that Ascanio is angry with her, and that tomorrow he intends to make another will and that he does not intend to leave her anything, neither to her nor to Pietro Paolo. I swear to you that he has it on his mind and that he could do it. For he is discontent with everybody. He sent for me, but I don't want to go there, for they already say that I am putting him up to it. And Cosmo and Pietro Paolo give me dark looks, and God knows that I never said anything, or had anyone say anything, to him.
>
> Ascanio is somewhat better now that Maestro Francesco [the angry physician, again] goes there. But it is a sickness that lasts long and never heals. Here, the word is that that person [i.e., Francesco] cannot comfort him and that at any moment he could die.[233]

Ascanio is as good as his grumblings. Just under two weeks later, his notary, Curtio Saccoccio, writes out a little protocol to the effect that Ascanio has delivered over a will, signed by his own hand, to be unsealed upon his death, and adding that he thereby annuls his prior testament.[234] Saccoccio, not having drawn this new will up, does not write it out; we can only imagine what havoc it intends. Word of the new will leaks slowly; Silvia will not report it to her husband until three months later.[235]

A few days later comes Fabritio's death in exile and, shortly after that, Pompeo's delivery to Ascanio of a quarter of Fabritio's legacy. The document cites "the fraternal love Pompeo has always felt toward Ascanio" and "his illness and consequent need." Nevertheless, Pompeo cannot bring himself to deal face-to-face with his ailing, reprobate elder brother but sends envoys to deliver the word and the legal paper. Later that day, in a separate document, Bernardino del Conte, author of so many Giustini protocols, registers Ascanio's solitary gratitude.[236]

Ascanio lives another year, with Laodomia, in their house in Rione Monti, across town. He sets his hand to Laodomia's legal papers when she buys a coach and horses and lays in hay and grain to feed them.[237] Then, as the end nears, once more he calls his notary,

Saccoccio, and makes yet one more will, the actual last one. Again, it is worth reviewing, as each detail speaks to family tensions. At the very center, still, is the issue of Laodomia's place in the Giustini firmament. The will begins, again, with burial at the Pace church and then enumerates five pious confraternities, the Most Holy Crucifix among them, to escort the corpse. The will then sets up an annual mass at a Geronimite church and, more importantly and at higher cost, weekly masses sung by the Pace monks. It then gives the Castellane nuns 50 scudi for his soul and another 50 on the condition that, upon his death, they accept his wife for free as lodger. Moreover, it stipulates, the nuns and tertiaries can keep all his silks. Thus, the will installs Laodomia in a house the Giustini patronize. The will then instructs Laodomia and the Most Holy Crucifix, together, to pick four girls to receive dowry gifts of 25 scudi each. Then comes a surprise: 800 scudi owed by Pietro Paolo should go to Pompeo's young son, Guglielmo, as should the whole thousand from Vittoria. (By this time, thanks to two brothers' grants and Fabritio's death, three-quarters of her legacy to Ascanio, still distinct in his reckonings from other assets, should have come his way. Has something mollified Ascanio on this point?) The will remembers Silvia but this time gives her only 100 scudi, not 500 as earlier. Pietro Paolo, Cosmo, and Cecilia receive nothing whatsoever. Rather, everything, everything, goes to Laodomia, but under a condition close to Ascanio's heart.

> In all his other property, mobile and stable, he makes and nominates as universal heir Madonna Laodomia, his wife . . . with this condition, however, that she never make an agreement concerning this legacy, neither with his brothers nor with his kinfolk, nor with any person.[238]

Clearly, he still fears his brothers' interference and, from the grave, wishes to protect his wife and to exorcise the lure of compromise. Laodomia should live chastely, the will goes on, or forfeit to the Confraternity of the Most Holy Crucifix or, if it defaults, to the syphilitic hospital, the Incurabili. Nevertheless, this time Ascanio is much more generous to Laodomia: should his wife choose to marry, besides what she is owed and what is plainly hers—"like the coach, the horses, and the monies spent on hay, the mules, the house in Tivoli, her money in the banks" and other sums she knows about—she can have 1,000 scudi if the husband is a gentleman in the judgment of the executors and of the three religious companies beneficiary to the will. But if in their judgment the husband is not Ascanio's equal, the 1,000 will shrink to 50 scudi, and that much only if he is *"honorato."*[239]

Nice try! Does it work? As children say, "No way!" The real and symbolic capital at stake is just too great, and Laodomia, as widow, is too weak to fend off the Giustini and their friends. She tries hard. With Ascanio gone, in late September she makes legal moves, probably with the support of Cardinal Crispi, to have an inventory of his goods.[240] But the Giustini soon shift to block her. Pompeo, with typical uncouth directness, supplements law with fists and blades. At Christmas, a diplomat writes the duke of Mantua:

> A strange affair took place, some twenty days ago or thereabout, but word has not gone around the court. It seems that, some while back, one Ascanio da Castello, a Roman gentleman, married a woman of ill repute and then he died, leaving Pompeo da Castello, his brother, and this woman. And between them arose a legal quarrel, and it seems that this woman had the favor of Cardinal Crispi. This Pompeo went to her house, and under pretext that he wished to talk with her, it seems that he grabbed her by the waist and uttered an infinity of curses and threats. And aside from the ruckus he made, this Pompeo also had a swarm of bullies [*bravi*] down below, and they say that they had unsheathed their swords. And, since there were no other witnesses, it has not been made more public nor denounced to the courts or to the pope. They will just let it go, according to what I am told.[241]

Meanwhile, the Giustini seize their brother's goods and haul their case against the will to a papal court, the Sacred Rota, where, in summer, it still hangs. Laodomia and her partisans, presumably Cardinals Crispi and Capizucchi, parry with an appeal to the court of the senator of Rome, who rules for Laodomia and retakes the property.[242] In June 1561, the prospect of a long fight and endless legal fees spawns a compromise. Because we cannot estimate Ascanio's debts and assets, it is hard to say how much Laodomia loses in giving up her husband's very final will. But we can see how much she gains in her long campaign to become a Roman lady.

The compromise itself is fascinating. The parties sign in the house of Laodomia's champion, Cardinal Capizucchi, who looks on. Laodomia, through a newly appointed "curator," makes a formal renunciation of everything left her by Ascanio, even of her dowry and all her own old properties: the house in Tivoli, the furnishings, the investments, her credits owed by assorted Romans. She gives up the coach, the horses, the three mules, the oats, the wheat, the hay; the *concordia* (agreement) enumerates all these goods. In exchange for these concessions, Pietro Paolo and Pompeo, present in the room, pay out on the spot 1,400 scudi, cash, and surrender a draft on the Morelli bank for another 1,200, payable five months hence. Laodomia in exchange surrenders further claims on goods and dowry. The brothers promise to cover without exception Ascanio's and Laodomia's outstanding debts to "apothecaries, servants, merchants, tailors, and silk dealers." Furthermore, in accordance with Roman statutes, on the estate's behalf they will reimburse Laodomia's outlay for mourning garb. As heirs, the Giustini swear that Laodomia will feel neither the benefits of nor the burdens on Ascanio's estate; no creditors can pursue her, not even the Celletti family's heirs in Tivoli. By mutual consent, Tiberio Alberini's brother—Cecilia's brother-in-law, Rutilio Alberini—agrees to represent Laodomia's interests in these matters.[243]

Now that her fortune is rock-solid, Laodomia sets out to organize her widowhood. She plays her elite network to settle her endowment in safe hands; one week after the compromise, she invests 3,500 scudi in a mortgage (*censo*) yielding 8.5 percent, secured on one of the estates of Cardinal Farnese. One of the Capizucchi and a noble Mattei act as her guarantors.[244] Two days later, she contributes to the mortgage 800 scudi, furnished by Ascanio's old soldier-friend Cencio Capizucchi. The notarial record shows that she is living, as Ascanio had wished, in the Castellane nunnery. Laodomia's signature proclaims her deliciously now-secured social identity: "The very magnificent Madonna Laodomia Rasa, wife-who-was of the good memory of Messer Ascanio Giustini." But prayers and bells are not the life for her. One month later, Laodomia buys a house in Rione Monti and arranges for the present tenants' departure. Cencio Capizucchi is her witness.[245] One month later, though in good health, Laodomia draws up her will.[246] It is a fascinating document, for it shows in many ways how the ex-courtesan is remaking herself, finally, as the widow of a gentleman. Ascanio, however dubious in life, is now shrouded by the respectable pall that cloaks the dead. From the afterlife, he is a useful ally in her campaign to cast off her origins.

The will illustrates this campaign. Most of it is in Italian, not the usual Latin, perhaps because the testatrix can read the spoken language; we know she signs her name. It begins, as usual, with funerals. Laodomia asks for burial—where else, after all!—in Santa Maria della Pace or at the Trinità if her heir prefers. Right by her husband and his kin! She may have smiled at how the Giustini would cringe to hear the news. Having married off two maidens, the will next leaves 30 scudi to the Giustinis' pet nunnery, the Castellane. She then promises to pay off her serving girls and lays 20 scudi for masses on San Pietro in Montorio, not a Giustini church, so far as I know. She spreads the income of her first post-mortem year across five confraternities, including Ascanio's favorites—the Incurabili and the Most Holy Crucifix. She leaves mattresses, sheets, blankets, bed hangings, embroidered shirts, and a table with its ornamental carpet to a young female friend, plus an ample dowry of 300 scudi for her wedding. Then, the faithful wife, she distributes all her remaining furniture to the poor, "for her soul and for that of her husband." The will returns to the nuns at the Castellane house: another 150 scudi, divided among the nunnery itself and five lay sisters, three of whom also appear in Ascanio's will, all to have as well 2 more scudi annually for life. In addition, the nunnery should pick two girls for dowries at 25 scudi each. Next: more masses at her burial church, one a week for her and another "for the soul of the aforesaid late Messer Ascanio, her husband." The will then returns to Tivoli, where she and Ascanio had lived, to settle money on the more virtuous of the sons of the Celletti family. Though the *concordia* had handed all old Celletti claims over to the Giustini, here Laodomia, for some reason, is reaching back across the agreement to make a settlement of her own. The will then sets up as executors the Confraternity of the Most Holy Crucifix, Ascanio's own designated agents in testamentary affairs. The will scatters remnants of a reserve fund on the poor, again for her soul and her husband's.

The will then takes a very odd turn, addressing Curzio Saccoccio, the notary, a man otherwise, in the way of notaries, professionally invisible:

> Item: she wishes that her heir, inscribed below, should, for remuneration of the labors of me the notary, inscribed below, undertaken in the *concordia* between herself and her husband's brothers, make a dress of velvet for Delia, my daughter, when she gets married, of a color that my daughter chooses, and, if she desires to become a nun, the equivalent in money.

So Laodomia probably rather liked her settlement with Ascanio's brothers! Our only proof.

Finally, as is normal with wills, Laodomia names her universal heir. It will be "Antimo, firstborn son of the noble Messer Cencio Capizucchi, cousin [*fratello consobrino*] of her late husband." Cencio has run through this story, playing cards with the Giustini brothers, supporting Ascanio after the duel, funding and advising Laodomia's widowhood. Here, she rewards his loyalty handsomely. But she lays on interesting conditions: her fortune of 4,000 scudi—which she spells out (3,500 with Cardinal Farnese, 300 in a mortgage on her house, and 200 to be laid into a new mortgage)—will be under strict entail.

> Should it happen that the aforesaid most reverend cardinal buy back the aforesaid mortgage, the said four thousand scudi should be invested at once in so many mortgages or perpetual *monti* [bonds] with the stipulation that such monies are the legacy of this testatrix and that there be an eternal memory of the fact, and they can never be put in hock or alienated in any way, nor from the principal can there be taken a single penny [*quattrino*] . . . and she wishes that the inheritor be always the firstborn male, the natural descendant of the house and family of the said Messer Cencio, ad infinitum. And in the absence of males, let the firstborn female, likewise legitimate and natural, succeed, ad infinitum.[247]

Fascinating! But why this? Is Laodomia, childless herself, trying to create an enduring legacy in the form of an adopted lineage in an allied family? Or is she merely taking further steps to keep importunate Giustini from tugging at the corners of her fortune? Or is she just conforming the terms of her gift to a Capizucchi taste for entailing their own property? This last is less likely; they, after all, could do it later. Whatever Laodomia's reasons, there is more here than meets the eye.

Note how her story ends. We can trace Laodomia a little further, as she makes improvements to her house and as she hires a young teenaged girl to be her servant.[248] And then her notarial footprints fade. But in 1575, when fierce Cencio Capizucchi dies after years in service as commander of papal troops, on his deathbed he tells the world that Laodomia has been his secret wife.[249] Since when? Why and how? It would be nice to know! For her, a victory to savor, but the secrecy points out its flaws.

We know some other fates as well. Cosmo, the churchman, would live into the 1570s and, says his tombstone in Santa Maria della Pace, leave all his goods to charity. Pietro Paolo would remain a successful lawyer. Pompeo would lead a roiling soldier's life. In 1563, he would have a civic moment, elected *caporione* of his district.[250] All other news of him is missiles, swords, and trumpets. In 1564, Pius IV would make him artillery captain.[251] Somewhat later, he would sign on as lieutenant to a colonel, Count Annibale Altemps, but then would cross his master, who, in April 1567, would try to have him killed. Pompeo would survive his bullet wounds, whereas Cardinal Altemps and his minions went to jail.[252] By November, Pompeo would be well enough to brawl in council on the Campidoglio; the pope would jail him for it.[253] Two years later, in the street of the Banchi he would violate an expensive peace pact with an agent of the Colonna, come to blows, and flee town to duck the fine.[254] At some point, Pompeo entered the Venetian service: in April 1571, he would be under arrest for raising troops, against the rules, inside the Papal State.[255] In May, he would be freed with Venetian help to carry on his command. By December he would be dead, of wounds suffered in the great Lepanto naval campaign against the Turks, but inflicted not at sea but on Corfu.[256]

As for the women, Silvia lives long, dying in 1591 after forty-eight years of marriage and widowhood. She survives her husband by more than twenty years and all her siblings too.[257] Genealogies show seven children, the Orazio of her 1558 letters being sixth in line. I suspect that the tables err and that Orazio is child five, born one year after his sister Vittoria, who marries in 1571. If born in the fall of 1557, this new Vittoria would have been fourteen at her wedding, young but not abnormally so in her social class. Silvia must have commemorated her poor sister in the Italian way, by quickly "remaking her" in christening a daughter. Silvia, in her last child, erects one more living Giustini memorial; she calls him Pompeo. When the soldier brother expires in Corfu in 1571, Silvia, after twenty-eight years of marriage, is forty-three or so, probably at the end of childbearing even had her husband not died that very year. This new Pompeo would marry an Alberini—circles were small among Rome's elite—and would name his daughter Silvia.

Silvia's great misfortune is to see 1582 and all the calamities that rained down on her nephews, Cecilia's sons. Cecilia herself and Tiberio have left the scene, and luckily. For it is a Greek tragedy fit for the house of Atreus. One son, a knight of Malta, would die on the scaffold for an absurdly botched shooting—for honor's sake, masked, at night, in Carnival. A few months later, another son, quarreling over possession of a footstool, would stab and kill his brother. The whole lineage would gradually go under.[258]

We can step back from our story to see what it tells us about the politics of family life. The drama around Vittoria's deathbed offers a minor study in social control. Note the many faces of control, which came from every side. The units, both controlled and controlling, varied in scale. The events around Vittoria's bed and in the brothers' courtyard were instances, in the small, of large social processes proper to the Giustinis' class and their time and place: the transmission of property, its concentration in the lineage, the familial restraint of errant kinsmen, the policing of destructive behavior, the maintenance of male power in the face of female resistance.

What machinery wrought these effects? As always, one side of social control is the work of extrasocietal forces—states, churches, and systems of ideas—to discipline society. In the story of Vittoria's will, however, there was little such activity. The state—the governor's criminal tribunal, the Roman statutes, and the civil law of inheritance—did help shape events, but its force, largely negative, merely fenced in the possible, perhaps restraining the brothers from violence or a peremptory grab of Vittoria's inheritance. Nevertheless, as so often in premodern Rome, the state was conspicuous largely in its absence. This was a self-help world, where control, often, was far less institutional than social. The strongest forces brought to bear on Vittoria, Pompeo, Ascanio, and the others came not from courts and palaces but from forces far closer at hand. Social control had social roots.

Self-help thus pervaded the family conflict around Vittoria's bed and legacy. For instance, Pompeo used, not legal processes, but force of will and hand to direct the outcome: leaning on Vittoria, haranguing, dragging, and slapping Silvia, cajoling Cecilia, and dueling with Ascanio. His main resources were personal and familial; as "the first of all," he could concert his brothers' campaigns against Ascanio and the sisters, and as head of house he could pressure Clementia and male servants to back him. Pompeo succeeded least with the sibling next in line, Pietro Paolo, a married householder and lawyer with a doctorate, who more readily broke ranks, perhaps offering compromise to Ascanio. Ascanio likewise preferred self-help, turning to the state—going to court—only when his own eloquence and arms fell short. In this light, how should we gloss Ascanio's move from words, first to a taunt, and then to steel? Have we loss of self-control here or subtle control, by violent means, of others? Did Ascanio's insult try to define a boundary his brother should not cross? Did the sequel, two years later, when Pompeo volunteered a share of Fabritio's estate, in some way reward Ascanio's pugnacity? When Ascanio did turn to the state with his denunciation, it was to enlist it as an ally in his campaign for revenge and gain. As often in Rome, ostensibly public justice served private ends.

At first glance, the women might seem paragons of weakness. Bullied by her brothers, Vittoria in extremis buckled, yielding all. Cecilia melted, mediated, and mollified. In the back room, Silvia quivered, impotent and silent. This view echoes the pessimism of some historians of gender.[259] Yet, in fact, female agency was everywhere. Vittoria, even in the clutch of death, could still thwart her brothers, as she did when well. Cecilia, and even the servant

Clementia, possessed skills at mediation useful to Pompeo. They did not bargain with these skills, but Cecilia at least withheld them for a while. Silvia, though in the end she failed to deter Pompeo, could discomfit and obstruct. There is strength in anger and, as often for underdogs, even more in martyrdom. In the nocturnal street without her shawl, smarting under Pompeo's slap, or hovering in the back room, Silvia mobilized opposition. When Pompeo struck, everybody rushed to quell his wrath. Just as the males had their phalanx, so had the females. Silvia, Cecilia, and their serving women locked elbows to protect Vittoria and afterward, as witnesses, remained as unanimous in their condemnation of Pompeo as the male brothers, servants, associates, and friends remained in his defense. This female solidarity surely reflects lines of clientage that fostered loyalties among the women, just as on the male side of the political divide that split the larger family.[260]

Here, as often, males and females differed in strategy and tactics. As we have seen, male politics protected the property and honor of the lineage. Ascanio, having forfeited respect through his perfidy at gaming and disgraceful marriage, was better out than in. In accordance with honor's ethic, his offenses demanded retribution: the loss of legacy and, when he bit his derisive finger, a cascade of demeaning insults. Blows, of course, merited blows. In family politics, the men could avail themselves of brute force and of public institutions. Female politics was more housebound in means and ends and far less tied to honor. As we have seen, the sisters' goals were ambiguous. At times, they seemed to forestall Vittoria's will to protect their stake. More often, however, they seemed less keen to amass scudi than to assuage pain and forestall anger. Thus, again and again, Silvia and Cecilia buffered the assaults sanctioned or excused by the vengeful, grasping honor ethic. They preferred compassion and tranquility to pride, to righteous retribution, and to their lineage's repute or wealth. They protected underdogs: Vittoria and even Ascanio. Cecilia shielded Silvia. In bargaining, they proffered sacrifices, abandoning their shares to secure domestic peace and to buy a little calm for poor Vittoria. Thus, the drama of Vittoria's death illustrates at once male hegemony and female accommodation, mediation, and subversion. As in other Renaissance Italian families, female resistance to honor's claims, by tempering male impulse, in subtle ways helped to pro-

mote the survival of the social unit, so easily sundered or lacerated by honor's harsh imperatives.

History as dramaturgy, although it invites such hypotheses, cannot itself give rise to theory. The scope is too narrow for classic induction. Yet a play, by its very richness of detail, does test the tensile strength of hypotheses wrought elsewhere in the forge of wide research. The great virtue of history as drama is in its capacity to expose what the Americanist Rhys Isaac calls the "lacework" of the past, the knotted, complex, patterned skein of relationships that determined choice.[261] The play's the thing, wherein to catch the conscience, the consciousness, and the calculations of all the players. On the written stage, agency rules. Freedom bumps up against restraint, feeling hustles thought, and reflex kicks out, not at random, but along lines patterned by culture.

The Giustini story is polyphonic. Many voices, many themes, and many conflicts shape it. It has all the bustling noise and sweep of an aristocratic house, an open place, full of news and traffic with the city and distant zones of Italy. The family itself, despite its raucous, fractious ways, is, for its time and place, reasonably normal. The drama, then, is most instructive if we let it show the rhythm and complexity of the interplay of age, gender, kinship, service, clientage, rank, and neighborhood, and the clash of styles and values, on two densely busy patrician days.

Chapter 4, by contrast, is claustrophobic. It pits a single household, a lute maker and his cloistered female family, against an overweening, predatory neighbor. I choose to tell it, protagonist by protagonist, from inside the artisan family. Three young women and their two bastard infants define its parts. Meanwhile, through all five stories runs a common adversary, exploiter, and sometime benefactor, Alessandro Pallantieri, Rome's chief prosecutor. Pallantieri, a perverse, vicious man, like many such, repeated his obsessive acts of cruelty. And his acts of kindness. Nevertheless, we do not loop in static circles, quite, but slowly twirl forward, for the tale takes years. Protagonists have time to mature, age, and sometimes die.

The story is ugly, painful, and deeply sad but, I sometimes feel, redeemed to austere beauty by the women's nobility in the face of so much suffering and abasement. It is fascinating too for its sexual politics and politics of sex. For, here, though we have a triple inequality—of official power, of class, of gender—again and again the women speak out, make bargains, help fashion rules, and, in myriad ways, resist the higher powers that oppress them. Their armory contains only the weapons of the weak: resistance, not outright rebellion. They subvert and evade oppression and, at rare moments, lash back with irony and reproach. We could thus read the whole story as a domestic epic of oppression and gritty resistance across a gulf of class and gender. But shades were in fact far grayer; as often, when exploitation grinds down its heel, queer accommodations and unwholesome collaboration sprout from the trodden ground. Read, then, for ambiguity and shadow.

In stories, villains work better when their villainy is alloyed, nuanced, and contradictory. Alessandro Pallantieri, by such a measure, is a delicious malefactor, a mawkish predator. Utterly appalling as he is, I hope you still enjoy him.

Chapter 4

"THIS IS MY DOWRY"

The Vile Loves of Prosecutor Pallantieri

THE CRIMINAL COURTS IN SIXTEENTH-century Rome quite often jailed not only suspects but witnesses. Their motives might be one of several—a shady reputation, crucial knowledge, a propensity to flight. Against absconding, courts often held goods and capital hostage, in pledge against failure to appear and testify. But when witnesses were poor in goods and in wealthy friends, it was hard to extort sureties to pin them to their forensic duties. Any of these reasons, alone or in combination, may have put Lucretia, a young married woman, mother of several young children, in jail. Whatever cause imprisoned her also jailed her sisters Faustina and Livia and her father, the German lute maker Cristoforo Gramar. All four, none of them suspects, had been locked up for about three months, since October 1557, in Tor di Nona jail.[1] Indeed, of the whole family, only Lucretia's brother, Stefano, and Lucretia's new baby and young children remained at liberty.

The legal drama that distressed and trammeled Lucretia's entire family was a long, snarled affair. Their collective story of private griefs and sins, by accident of law and politics, had tangled with a much wider contest pitting great men of state. It was a vindictive struggle quite political at heart but robed, as so often in Rome, in the solemn mummery of law.

Lucretia, her sisters, and her father bore witness, alongside many, many others of assorted sex, age, office, station, faith, and birthplace, at the ten-month trial of a fallen high official of the Papal State, Alessandro Pallantieri. Pallantieri's tumble had been swift and painful. On 6 October 1557, he had been the *procuratore fiscale* of the Papal State, its mighty chief prosecutor. On 9 October, he slept the first of some six hundred nights in prison. On the surface, his trial probed corruption and the abuse of office; like many functionaries of the Papal State, Pallantieri had waxed fat off the shady avails of office.[2] Nevertheless, peculation and graft were only a false front for less seemly motives for his dismissal, arrest, and prosecution. We must step back a bit and unravel them, for indignities suffered in 1557 would shape Pallantieri's subsequent career and spell a prince's and a cardinal's doom and, at last, his own.

On 13 July 1555, after twenty-five years of public service to five popes, Pallantieri became *procuratore fiscale*.[3] It was a consummation long devoutly wished and keenly sought; back in 1549 the death of Paul III had snatched the dangled job from his eager grasp.[4] In the early 1550s, he had written Julius III a needling memorandum parading his suitability.[5] Now, at last, just two months into the stormy papacy of Paul IV, his wish came true. Pallantieri himself, on trial, recounted how the news came through.

> When they had before the pope the congregation, with many cardinals and his most-illustrious lord-nephews, about appointing officials, I had heard that Ottavio Ferro had been made *fiscale* and that he was coming to Rome. I took it easily and continued in my office, neither thinking nor hoping more. And then it happened one day in the pope's antechamber that His Excellency the lord duke of Paliano [a papal nephew] called me, without my thinking anything of it—it was all for the goodness and the kindness of His Holiness—and took me by the hand, saying, "Be of good cheer!" And when I asked him what the matter was, he told me, "I don't want to tell you. Enough! Be of good cheer!" Another time, in the same place, His Excellency called me, and grasping me by the hand and after many words, before he left, he said [in

biblical Latin], "'Ye of little faith, why did you doubt!' You are the *fiscale,* made by His Holiness. Get your *motu proprio* [commission] made, and I will have it signed for you."[6]

Although a prosecutor, and not a minister of state, a Roman *fiscale* waded knee-deep in high politics, for alongside assorted common frauds and homicides were cases that ramified, whenever the great had broken laws or laws bent to break the great. Nothing better illustrates the mix of law and policy than Pallantieri's prosecution of the greatest of them all, Emperor Charles V and his son Philip, new king of Spain. Serving the pope's goals and his nephews' dynastic grasping, in late July 1556 the *fiscale* lay a legal brief against the monarchs, in the Consistory.[7] A trial of sorts ensued; the legal case was one of several casus belli. When, in September, war itself broke out, for the papal armies things went fast from bad to worse. Carlo Carafa, the cardinal nephew (acting chief minister), rushed to France to beg support and soldiers. In his absence, he left a council to conduct the war. Among its members was his private secretary, the learned Florentine exile Silvestro Aldobrandini, a stubborn republican who hated Spain for installing the Medici autocracy. Aldobrandini, bitter and loyal to his cardinal, remained a trenchant hawk. Against him on committee sat a coalition, a dove flock of war skeptics fluttering around the cardinal's brother, the duke of Paliano. Before the cardinal returned from France, the peace party in March 1557 drove Aldobrandini from office, a broken man. Leading their cabal was Alessandro Pallantieri.

Cardinal Carafa was livid. At his trial three years later, fellow cardinals would report, "they said that Cardinal Carafa threatened to hang Messer Alessandro Pallantieri, for he had been the cause of driving off Messer Silvestro."[8] Though he never hanged him, the cardinal did drag him from office into prison. It took Carafa a full six months to plot this coup. Despite his potent enemy, Pallantieri, it seems, felt safe. Pallantieri later testified that just four or five days before his arrest, at the weekly Inquisition, the pope himself had turned to him, saying, "[You are *fiscale*] to maintain us here."[9] Lulled by blandishments and his survival, he was taken aback by serried shocks. Three hours after sundown on 6 October, he learned from a letter from his son in Bologna that Sebastian

Atracino, chief judge there, had been called to Rome, by Carafa, to be *fiscale*. Urgent news! Pallantieri's spare tale of what happened next cannot mask his dismay and shock:

> I climbed into my coach and went to the palace to find Cardinal Carafa and the duke. I found that they were not there, that they had gone to supper in the house of the chamberlain. So I went back home without talking to the one or to the other.
>
> Early next morning I went to the palace. First I found the cardinal's room locked. I went to the duke and asked him about the news I had in this letter.
>
> His Excellency told me that he knew nothing about it.
>
> Then I went to the room of the Most Illustrious Cardinal, where in the antechamber I found [the judicial official] Giulio Spiriti.
>
> It was opened, and the two of us went in together, and I found the cardinal and, if I remember well, Signor Bartolomeo [Camerario] di Benevento [head of the Grain Office, *commissario* of the army, and ally of Pallantieri's], Signor Cesare Brancaccio [as recent governor, ex-boss of Pallantieri and still Carafa's protégé], Signor Don Antonio Marchese, and the signore *fiscale* here [Atracino], whom I greeted.
>
> And then the lord duke came, and after him monsignor the governor of Rome, to whom the cardinal spoke at the window, and having talked and left the window, in the middle of the room, he said, "Pallantieri, go with the governor here and do what he tells you."
>
> I told him, "As you please, Governor!" I followed him and en route he told me that the cardinal had commissioned him to come to my house to fetch my papers. "Let's go take some breakfast there, at the house."
>
> They took all my papers, without exception, and then monsignor the governor told me that I had to come to jail.
>
> I told him, "Please!" So we boarded my coach and they brought me to Tor di Nona [prison]." [10]

Like Cardinal Carafa, Alessandro Pallantieri had a vengeful streak. He never forgot, never forgave, this day.

Before this rough tumble, Alessandro Pallantieri had enjoyed

A remnant of the Pallantieri palace in Castel Bolognese. Photo by the author.

a splendid public career. Though not noble, he came of a solid family from a Romagna town, Castel Bolognese. The fifteenth-century palace of the Pallantieri clan still faces the Via Emilia, the ancient great road that links the southern cities of the northern plain. Born in 1505, Alessandro took his doctorate in canon and civil law at Bologna.[11] His wife, Gentile, was a wellborn Bolognese, as was his mother.[12] The marriage was unhappy; after a daughter and three sons were born, the couple separated. By his arrest, Alessandro and Gentile had dwelt apart for thirteen years at least; in all that time she had never lived in Rome.[13]

Much of Pallantieri's long career in public office entailed legal work in assorted corners of the Papal State. His first job, in 1532, was as prosecutor near home, in the Romagna.[14] A bit later, he worked in the Marches.[15] Then, briefly, he served as governor of Cesena and later substituted for his future rival, Silvestro Aldobrandini, ruling Fano.[16] The next year, 1534 or 1535, Pallantieri governed Perugia. Abusing judicial powers by fetching a female prisoner to his room at night, he landed in prison; his patron, the future Cardinal Gambaro, bailed him out.[17] Undented by his seamy slip, he flourished. "I never liked to run after offices; offices ran after me."[18] Disingenuous; the first claim was false! Sought or seeker, Pallantieri went on to serve as judge (*auditore*) under Cardinal Grimani, his and his father's patron.[19] After a Viterbo stint, Pallantieri took his first Roman job, as criminal magistrate for the Camera Apostolica.[20] For the rest of Paul III's reign (to 1549), Pallantieri ran assorted missions, mostly based in Rome. The year 1540 found him in Pavia, prosecuting the bishop for assorted crimes.[21] Contented with his work—as he told the court—the pope and Cardinal Farnese then dispatched him to Ferrara, Spoleto, and Rochetta and then, from 1541 to 1542, installed him as *luogotenente* (judge) and then governor of Ascoli.[22] There, his tenure was tumultuous; he led a force of 400 soldiers to seize the castle; he sparred with the city council, who threatened appeal to Rome; and, at the end, he suffered judicial review (*sindicazione*) in Ascoli and then Rome for his political and sexual conduct.[23] Yet his career still bloomed. Pallantieri remained a criminal judge and, late in Paul III's reign, made diplomatic missions to the Imperial court at Ulm (1547) and to the Netherlands, for eight or ten months (1547–48), to negotiate sales of papal alum.[24]

Despite the long, high climb, Pallantieri became restless. Married, he could not take ordination.[25] Pallantieri, in court, quoted the jovial Julius III, always a tease:

> He praised me more than I deserved and put his hands on my shoulders, "Be of good cheer, for in any case I want to make you a fine prelate with this wife of yours."[26]

Since most high offices in the Papal State went to clergy, Pallantieri eyed greener grass in Genoa, Milan, Siena, and Naples.[27] Meanwhile, still criminal magistrate for Rome's governor,[28] he lobbied Julius for a more potent job: *procuratore fiscale.*[29] The pope's brother Baldovino del Monte, he claimed, championed his career and his promotion.[30] Julius, however, heaped on missions elsewhere—to Camerino, Ravenna, Spoleto, and Todi—and then, in 1554, made him head of the Grain Office (Annona). Pallantieri then scoured the Patrimony of Peter, a fertile district northwest of Rome.[31] As Annona *commissario,* he was at once merchant, administrator, judge, and high constable. He could investigate growers

and sellers, jail them, try them, and confiscate their beasts and produce. He could mandate reports on stocks and force sales at cheap,
decreed prices to help the state feed Rome. It was a perfect job for
graft and double-dealing; Pallantieri cashed in fast. His biggest
coup was offloading confiscated grain to a complaisant Toscania
merchant, Paolo Vittorio, cozy cheap. Vittorio sold his haul not in
regulated Rome but on the open market; on the sly, he slipped Pallantieri half his profits. Other merchants quickly smelled the rat,
for Pallantieri and his town council allies blocked their bids to buy.
"Pallantieri does not buy a *rubbio* (measure) of grain in Civitavec-
chia that he does not gain a scudo on," they sneered (an exaggera-
tion, because the going price at Rome ran at four scudi the *rubbio*,
but proof of gossip's bite and drift). Two years later, to wreck Pallantieri's career, Cardinal Carafa unearthed these patent scams.[32]

The arms of casa Pallantieri bear three avian legs with ample
claws, clutching orbs (*palle,* "balls," punning "Pallantieri"). Eagles?
Falcons? Vultures? Whatever the raptor, the shield is apt; Alessandro Pallantieri was rapacious and cruel. He could be grasping, overweening, and harsh, and, in lechery, high-handed and
slovenly. And yet he prospered, rising high in public service; vir-
tues and talents must have outshone his vices. Certainly, the great
often esteemed and championed him. Under Julius III, at the
Vatican he was a welcome guest, a ready partner at the pope's own
gaming table, as at other tables in other palaces. When on trial and
laboring to explain his suspect wealth, seemingly the fruit of graft,
he blamed instead his skill and luck at gambling. Pallantieri's story
was a lapwing tale, peeping drollery and drooping wings of anecdote to coax prosecutor from quarry. Yet, even if embellished, his
account paints a handsome picture of Vatican life under Julius:

> And since, at the time of Pope Julius, both His Holiness and the
> cardinals and the bishops and all the court gambled, I was caught
> up in the dance too, gambling with the others, and His Holiness
> sent for me almost every day to have me come and play. And
> among the other times, when I went to the villa of His Holiness
> to bring complaint of certain things that Signor Ascanio Colonna
> was doing to keep provisions from coming to Rome, His Holiness
> said nothing to me about this except, "Make yourself welcome!
> Just now, we were missing a fourth player!" And when I told him

that His Holiness had laid on my shoulders the burden of the Grain Office and that there was need to attend to other things than playing, His Holiness replied, "I am amazed at you! Is there lack of grain in Campo di Fiori [a market]? Stay here to eat. And eat with Michelangelo, and order something good!"

And another time, when he had me called to the palace to gamble, I told him, "Holy Father, I have things to do. I have won some scudi. I wouldn't like to lose them." His Holiness said, "You have to play. If you lose, it does not matter. I will show you how! Find something to steal for you and for me!" So I played many times both with His Holiness and, in his presence, with his brother, Signor Baldovino. After the midday meal, it was the only thing they did, and I was almost always among the invited.

And when I went to a banquet, when I played with His Excellency [Del Monte] and with cardinals and other prelates, it was my good luck that in the house of Monsignor Pavia, who was governor, I won several thousand scudi, as all Rome knows.[33]

This Monsignor Pavia, once the bishop of Pavia, was the very man whom Pallantieri had prosecuted back in 1540. As governor, he had become Pallantieri's boss; that the two could later work together hints at qualities that, despite his flaws and vices, buoyed Alessandro's career: a nose for politics, good timing, a sense of just how much to dare ask for. His popularity at the gaming table suggests good company. Certainly, his testimony reveals sharp intellect and pithy, forceful speech, formidable in court and entertaining at table: To know a man, "you have to keep his company for years and years and eat a bushel of salt with him."[34] Rebutting an alleged lapse in giving a receipt: "In Rome I plant no seeds in bacchanalia's woods" (i.e., "I don't sow the wind").[35] About a family of alleged reprobates: "People like that are repulsed by laws and canons."[36] And note this tremendous oath right in the face of his old grain-scam accomplice, Paolo Vittorio, who, a contrite and hostile witness, contradicted him in court:

But God can show a miracle, right now, on my person if I do not speak the truth, as I pray with all my heart that if he ever did mir-

acles, he should do so now. May the fire of Saint Anthony burn
me visibly, right now, and may God send down on me and on my
house, my sons and daughters, the final ruin and all the maledic-
tions that can possibly be sent if ever Messer Paolo [Vittorio]
here ever asked me for a receipt.[37]

Such, then, was Lucretia's adversary in court. Odd, though, to
call him "adversary," for, after all, Pallantieri stood accused and
Lucretia testified against him. By *inquisitio*'s normal procedures,
where judges conducted the investigation, Pallantieri, like other
suspects, would have enjoyed little freedom to parry testimony.
Normally, in the preliminary hearings (the *processus informativus*) of
a sixteenth-century trial, suspects could not counter damning evidence. Usually, they were absent. Witnesses spoke in camera, before judge, prosecutor, and court notary only. No defense counsel
looked on. When suspects themselves appeared before the judge,
they could only guess what their adversaries knew. Only later,
when the court issued transcripts of the interrogations, with
names removed, could suspects and counsel frame their defense.
The only exception to this habit of keeping defendants ignorant
and off balance was the rite of *confrontatio*, where the magistrates
brought a witness and the suspect face-to-face. But even then the
questions, normally, were the magistrate's alone. Pallantieri was
more fortunate because early in the trial he won the right to conduct his own defense. To his aid, he brought his wits, his prosecutorial guile, and his well-honed sense of evidential doctrine. There
ensued a courtroom drama much closer in symmetry and spirit to
modern Anglo-Saxon practice than to *inquisitio*'s usual uneven
battle. Lucretia, for instance, first testified three times alone: on
12 October just after her arrest, on 21 October, and on 22 November.[38] But then, on 28 November, she retold her tale under the
ex-prosecutor's ferocious cross-examination.[39]

Three days later, at last, came torture. Did the magistrates finally torture the shady ex-prosecutor? Not at all! Rather, they
strung up innocent Lucretia. Thanks to the notary's typically patient, zealous record, we can listen in.

Lucretia was brought to the torture chamber, stripped, and
asked to reaffirm her testimony. She did so. To quote the record:

And while, at the lord's command, she was stripped, she said of her own accord, "I cannot speak falsely, and I have spoken the truth. Why don't you give the rope first to him?"

And his lordship asked her to speak truly: was what she said in her examinations true and said as truth? And he said she should avoid lies and imputing any falsehoods.

She replied, in tears and grieving as she was bound, "I have spoken the truth. I use falsehood with no one. Oh God! Oh my God! I would never have believed that he would have had the will and the nerve [*la faccia*] to deny wrong, and if one speaks the truth, it is worse, and if one does not say it . . . You could kill me! I have told the truth."

And she was crying, saying, "Oh God, I have spoken the truth."

And then, by the orders of his lordship, she was raised up.

She began to say, "Oh God, I have spoken the truth! I cannot say anything different! Woe is me! What have I been brought to? He has done wrong and I suffer this! This is the profit that comes of it! This is the dowry that he gives me!" And, suspended, she began to cry out, "Oh woe! Oh woe!"

She was asked to tell the truth.

She answered, "Yes! Yes! I have told the truth. Oh woe! Oh woe!" And since she persisted like that in what she said for the space of a Miserere prayer [perhaps three minutes], his lordship ordered her to be let down gently and to be put back in solitary with the intention of continuing.[40]

Modern observers are often shocked and scandalized when they encounter judicial torture of crime's victims. Citizens of the United States, though often complaisant with their own system's savage punishments, so recoil at the cruelties of the old jurisprudential inquiry that they misprize their logic. A like confusion holds for Europeans, as *Artémisia,* a deeply muddled French film about the celebrated woman painter's rape trial, makes patent. In the movie, blood gushes from the hands of the unhappy artist, tortured to renounce her love for the painter Tassi, who had raped her. Cinematic melodrama overstates torture's mayhem and miscasts judicial goals. In the real trial, the court tortured Artemisia to do her a favor, to help her right her wrong.[41]

By the logic of early modern Italian law, jeopardy to pain, like any other jeopardy—to goods, to reputation, to station—held a speaker hostage. A stake, any stake, fostered telling the truth. Those with social, political, or moral assets thus usually escaped torture. Torture fell on those who, in judges' eyes, had little to lose but bodily integrity and comfort. Lucretia had three strikes against her: her modest social station, her gender, and her sexual history. To further their case and help her prove her point, the judges did her a favor: they strung her up. The session was the shortest possible; the pain, largely, pro forma. The court's purpose: to corroborate a story it already believed.[42]

Now, *in dolore*, as *in vino*, often *veritas*. Or so the doctrine went. Lucretia's painful courtroom drama can be read as visceral and raw, and her words as true. At the same time, it still was drama, and real as were the pain and angst, Lucretia may have known she had a role to play. The torture, for her, offered an opportunity, the chance to speak with the privileged force of pain. When better than on the rope to declare the irony of her dowry of anguish! Whatever did she mean? Let us go see.

PART I: LUCRETIA'S STORY

In 1532 or early 1533, twenty-five years before the Pallantieri trial and eight years after coming to Rome, Cristoforo Gramar, a German lute maker, took a wife. He married Adriana, daughter to a wholesaler near the Pantheon.[43] The bride was only fourteen or fifteen; at her death twenty-three years later, she was still pretty; Lucretia said of her, "When my mother died she was 37 or 38, for she was young and she had been respectably good looking."[44] Between her father's contribution and a subsidy from the Annunziata fund, the young bride had brought a modest but respectable dowry—seventy scudi.[45] At the time, Cristoforo was a mere tenant, lodged in a baker's house.[46] But shortly after marriage, probably with the dowry money's help, he moved his new wife to their own house. During Pallantieri's trial, the family still had rights to it. Fittingly, the dwelling stood on Via dei Leutari, Lute Makers' Street.[47] The house lay on the street's west side, near a notorious landmark, the battered antique statue called Pasquino, Rome's nocturnal posting site of anonymous lampoons.[48] There Cristoforo made and repaired lutes, sold lute strings, and, with his wife, produced four daughters and a son. If further offspring died in infancy or childhood, we never hear of them. Lucretia, the eldest, was born in 1535 or so.[49] We lack the birth year of the second daughter, Martia. Faustina, the third, was born around 1541.[50] Livia, the youngest, came into the world in 1543 or 1544.[51] Adriana may have joined in picking her daughters' names, for, like hers, all come from ancient Rome. Not only was Adriana Roman in birth, taste, and classic nomenclature, but she was literate as well, teaching school for both girls and boys.[52] Doubtless that is why Livia, and perhaps her sisters, could read.[53] The son's name, Stefano, Christian like his father's, was in flavor not Livy or Suetonius but New Testament; we do not know his age.[54]

Pallantieri, as cross-examiner of the Gramar daughters, strove to pry from them hints of scandalous living. His needling questions and cavils availed him only the young women's indignant and generally convincing denials. If they spoke truly, as girls they had lived an almost cloistered life, seldom venturing out except to go on local pilgrimage to the classic Seven Churches.[55] As youngsters, they had played downstairs in a sheltered courtyard with the children, mostly girls, of a saddler's family in the building.[56] They had seldom ventured into the lute shop. Still, they could look down in on it; we know this because, when Bonaiuto, an elderly Jew, purchased lutes, they would stand atop the stairs hurling anti-Jewish insults: "cur-slaughtered-by-Jewish-ritual-butchery" (*cagnaccio sciattato*). The anecdote is revealing in many ways; not only does it show what the girls could see from upstairs, but it illustrates as well the pervasiveness of the harassment Roman Jews suffered and, intriguingly, also demonstrates the penetration of Christian Roman speech, even in the mouths of cloistered little girls, by the Italo-Jewish term for ritual butchering, a word of Hebrew origin.[57] Few outsiders ever came upstairs from shop or street into the family's quarters. Cristoforo's customers and clients stayed below, among the lutes.[58] And rare indeed were outsider males in the intimate upstairs. A few times Stefano invited in a lute teacher; Lucretia, to avoid him, chastely locked herself in the kitchen and never spoke to him.[59] Stefano took brief instruction from three more teachers for one month each, always downstairs in the shop, and then, eventually, taught Lucretia how to play.[60]

Other male traffic was slight. Twice a Franciscan friar, a cousin of Adriana's, spent the night; a young priest came once, nine years back, to hear confessions.[61] The steadiest male traffic involved the textile trade, for Adriana and her daughters rounded out household income by sewing and tailoring on commission. About once a month a merchant's agent, Ambrosio, visited the kitchen with orders, fresh stuffs, and pay for work completed.

> When he brought us his piecework, sometimes we stayed at the window, and he talked with our mother in the sala, and we told him if we were short of thread or silk or asked, "What work do you want us to do?"[62]

Women also came by with clothes to work on; one sometimes brought along her little boy.[63] For the girls, home was sheltered; they peeked at the world through the slatted wooden blinds or eavesdropped from upstairs.[64] Neither daughters nor mother had been much calloused by traffic with Rome's rough-and-tumble habits. The family's very modesty and caution, in the hands of a man so perverse as Alessandro Pallantieri, would set a crowbar to its door.

Pallantieri was their neighbor, just across the street. He had moved there in 1546, after two years lodging up by San Salvatore in Lauro.[65] He used the house at first on loan, rent free, from a god-kinsman of his named Angelo di Todi, a notable for whom Pallantieri did legal work and who lodged there when back in Rome.[66] Then, on his Flanders expedition of 1547–48, Pallantieri lost control of the house. Upon returning, he had to lobby to pry out two nobles, Antimo and Onorio Savelli, the latter a two-fisted feudal magnate whom Pallantieri was to prosecute in 1566 for countless thuggish crimes.[67] Early in the rein of Julius III, Angelo and two of his sons were murdered; Pallantieri went to Todi as the papal investigator.[68] Amid the Todi denouement, Alessandro bought the dwelling outright, and then the house next door, pouring into embellishment a cascade of coin. In court, his loyal notary-amanuensis, Agostino Merulo, put the outlay at 4,000 scudi, a sum fat enough to dilate judicial nostrils.[69] Pallantieri himself admitted coyly in court to "a few hundred."[70] Doubtless, he laid out more, and fast, for before Paul III died in 1549, the jurist fêted pope and court at home.[71]

In the summer of 1548, just back from his Flanders mission, Pallantieri noticed Lucretia.[72] The youngster was barely past childhood: "I was thirteen, going on fourteen, years old."[73] It was June, before the great solstice festival of Saint John the Baptist (24 June). As Lucretia remembered it:

> Living at my father's house, I sometimes went up to the roof to water some herbs, and Messer Alessandro Pallantieri, who then lived across the way from our house, as he still does now, from his windows began to watch me and to talk to me, saying, "Do you want me to come help?" and things like that. I paid him no heed, for I did not want to consent or to attend to his affairs.[74]

A light beginning, but the judge's attentions fast gained weight.

> This Messer Alessandro began to do crazy things, for in the evening, after dark, from his house he threw stones through our window and made a racket that the neighborhood could hear. And from the very beginning, he wanted to flirt with me.[75]

Pallantieri soon began to lean on Adriana, to awe and menace her with his clout in Rome. Back then he still was just a lieutenant— a judge—at the criminal courts. But, he intimated, he could rise. Lucretia again:

> He held off a bit and then began to speak to my mother. He was at the window of his house, and my mother was in her room across the way. According to what she told me, Messer Alessandro spoke to her, pressing her to let him come to our house to talk to me. She did not wish to consent. He grew angry and berated her. Among other things, I heard that one time, when Messer Alessandro was talking to my mother about this matter and chiding her, my mother asked him, "Will you ever be governor of Rome?" He answered her, "I may not be governor of Rome, but I have the power to make things happen." And so, the two of them departed angry from the conversation, and these things went on for about a year, my mother told me.[76]

The pressure on Adriana grew and grew. Pallantieri threw stones into her bedroom, uttered threats, and came knocking on the door. "Sometimes my mother would sit spinning by the door to keep my father from hearing the noise."[77] Lucretia remembered how, in the evenings, she would hear Pallantieri's door open before he came to knock.[78] All this while, Cristoforo knew nothing. Finally, toward fall, Adriana gave way to the threats and pleadings. She let Pallantieri in.

> He asked her just to let him come inside the house, for all he wanted from me was to talk to me, and he swore and promised that all he would do is speak to me, . . . and finally he wore my mother down to let him enter in the evening.[79]

It must have been late, for Cristoforo, if we can believe him, had already gone to sleep.[80] As soon as Pallantieri entered, he came up the stairs. Frightened, Lucretia ducked into the kitchen, "where there was no light, or anything."[81] "But he came up and went into the kitchen, where I was. It seemed to me he knew the layout of the house."[82] Pallantieri lavished no blandishments or foreplay: "He put his arms around me and did everything he could to know me carnally. I did all I could to help myself, with my mother's help. She got in between us, so that evening he did not do anything."[83]

Naturalists have marveled at the eerie calm of the Sumatran monkey as it lies, unresisting, in the jaws of the Komodo dragon. Narcotized by hopelessness, it just lets the hulking reptile ponderously shift its grip, the better to swallow it alive. The monkey seems shocked immobile, dazed by doom, by immensity and power.

Weeks passed. Adriana seemed paralyzed. She sought no help, from her husband, from anyone. What could she do? Where could she turn? After all, that looming man across the street, with his sword, his long purple robe, his bulk, his long beard verging on white, was the law itself.[84] Then Pallantieri returned to his attack, first with saccharine apologies and promises—"swearing we should fear nothing because he would not do that rude thing he did the other evening"—and then once more with a blunt stab at rape.[85] Even after the second attack, the mother opened the street door yet once more. It was by then late October or early November 1548, three weeks after the first visit. As Lucretia told the court:

> Another evening, he came the same way. I retreated to my bed-
> room, to a chest near the bed. My mother was there too. He could
> not pull my mother away from me, and he grabbed her and, if I
> remember well, he threw her to the floor, and he put out the light
> and said that in no way would he leave until he had done every-
> thing he desired. So, with my mother crying and trying to pull
> him off me, Messer Alessandro, on that chest, had sex with me,
> and he made me hurt and made me bleed. And he was the first
> man who ever had carnal dealings with me. I told him to leave
> me alone, but he held me in such a way that I could not move and
> he did what he wanted. And he stayed awhile, until around mid-
> night, and that night he only did it to me once.[86]

Adriana, however complicit and however much she had seen this coming, was torn to shreds. "She grew ill," Lucretia said. "For three days, she neither ate nor drank."[87] "All she did was cry. And think of it! My father didn't know what was the matter. And she wouldn't tell him. He asked her, 'What's the matter with you?' She pretended she was sick."[88]

Pallantieri, meanwhile, began troweling the ground for his new back garden of earthly delight. As if in court shaking down a sus-pect, he planted here and there the seducer's standard threats and promises. Keep your mouth shut, he told the girl, and "he would be the family's source of good."[89] The same mix of threats and prom-ises pinioned Adriana; a week later she opened the door again.[90] There ensued a few weeks of frequent sex, and by Christmas, little Lucretia was pregnant.

That did it! Adriana was caught. "I am afraid my husband will find out. If he finds out, I am ruined."[91] To understand her an-guish, we must unravel not only her own dilemma but her daugh-ter's and her husband's. Her errors could cost her husband dearly, in both honor and money. Careless historians sometimes write that in the Renaissance a girl had a stark double choice: fierce vir-ginity till marriage or whoredom. Reality was far, far grayer. In the marriage market, except among the highest classes, a hymen was in fact just one commodity among many at play. It was a great asset, just as its absence was a costly liability. But other things, wealth especially, could retilt marriage-market scales. A nonvirgin was shamed but hardly damned if her family could proffer assets with which to endow a marriage or, at higher price, a nunnery berth. Thus, Adriana, like any wife, owed her husband good custody of his daughters, for a slip on her part or theirs would cost the father grievously not only in repute but also in extra dowry outlay. So what Adriana now needed, with Cristoforo's help, was a device to hoist their daughter back up, to replace her hymen with cash.

And who had the money? That lizard, Alessandro.

In Renaissance Rome, women, even when victims, enjoyed far more initiative and power than we often think. Not Cristoforo but Adriana bearded the bully: he would have to set things right. As Lucretia remembered the story, her mother had always been her protector:

> My mother decided that my father would have to find out. And she told Messer Alessandro, "Now that you have done the wrong, it falls to you to make it known and to arrange things as much as necessary."[92]

Or, in another version:

> She told Messer Alessandro, "Now that you have done me wrong, it falls to you to make reparation, and that you tell my husband, so that I not take the blame."[93]

Do not take this to mean that Adriana was so afraid to tell her husband that she wanted Alessandro to bear bad tidings. Her design was subtler; he must formally declare his liaison, man-to-man with Cristoforo, to guarantee Lucretia's future. Adriana, to lay the ceremony's groundwork, advised poor Cristoforo well ahead. "To win him over, she told him, 'We could get some profit from it.'"[94] From then on, his ignorance was just pro forma, like so much else on that extraordinary night when the judge paid an awkward social call on lute maker and family.

It was Christmas Eve, three hours after sundown, when our contumelious Scrooge visited his humbler neighbors.[95] Watch how Lucretia told the court it happened:

Messer Alessandro came to our house and knocked on the door.
My father went to the door and asked what he wanted.

Messer Alessandro said, "Open up! I want to say a word
to you."

And so he opened for him, and he [Pallantieri] went on up.

And he told my father, "I want you to give me Lucretia, to
come to my house this evening."

So my mother called me, for I was in the kitchen. And I went
there.[96]

In her testimony, in the face of Pallantieri's forensic scoffing, Lucretia threw in a homey detail to give the ring of truth:

And you said, "I have burnt my finger."
It began with that.
"I have heard that that varnish that you use is good for burns."
And so my mother went and put a little on his finger.[97]
And then he sat awhile there, in the kitchen by the fire. And
then he said, "I want Lucretia to come to my house."

And so my father did not answer, neither yes nor no; he remained utterly astonished. And my mother was caught off her
guard. They said, one to the other, "It is better that we let her go,
so that it come out in the open."

And Messer Alessandro led me into his house. Here is a memory mark: he went first! I don't know if he went to take away the
lights along the stairs or to make the servants go to bed. And then
he came for me and I went with him to his house.[98]

Livia, the youngest, though only five back then, still remembered
how, as Pallantieri led her off, her big sister picked up her cape.[99]

This whole incident badly needs decoding. Decoding indeed,
for every action, from proffering a burnt finger, to sitting by the
fire, to setting the stairs in darkness, to crossing the street and entering the judge's house, dripped meaning, patent to the protagonists but veiled to us. What happened here had a template, a
model, in Renaissance marriage custom. Usage left it to a husband
to feed, house, clothe, and protect his wife, to support her children, to guard her chastity and reputation. A man who took a wife,
or his senior sponsors, first negotiated carefully with her parents

or guardians and then, before witnesses, made promises, signed papers, gave a ring. And finally, amid festivity, music, and joyful racket, the groom led his bride, under neighbors' eyes, by torch or daylight, in procession to his house. The precise details varied from town to town, but the essentials—negotiation, exchanges, promises, the woman's ceremonious public transfer—were constants. Now what of Pallantieri's nocturnal visit? In some ways, it inverted a marriage ceremony. In the place of witnesses, notaries, and paperwork is the privacy of Cristoforo's house. In the place of gifts is a dab of lute varnish on the judge's scorched finger. In the place of a noisy, festive procession is a furtive scuttle down dark stairs, across a silent street, into a sleeping house. But the meaning was clear: Lucretia, albeit furtively, would enter Pallantieri's house, bed, and family just long enough to lay symbolic claim to his paternity; the unborn child would be conceived a second time, under its future father's roof. A nine-month deadline urged speed. Pallantieri, a bully, was cunning and false; the very skills and vices that pinned defendants to the mat and gave him the edge in politics bent and bound Lucretia and her family to his foul will and whim. But, still, still, he was a father. Something in him, feeling or principle, made that count. Adriana must have sensed that fact and seized it in a desperate bid to save what could be saved—a future for her daughter.

Cristoforo, in court, was mealy-mouthed—for good reason, as we shall shortly see. He told a fishy version of the whole tale, devoid of rape, where at the Christmas parley Pallantieri spelled out his promises.

> He said, "I want to bring this girl of yours to my house for the holidays."
> I said a bit of a no.
> He answered, "I want her, and I will do all that is necessary to have her married, and everything."
> And this was on Christmas Day. And so I let him take her, and he promised me that he intended to marry her off and to give her her dowry. That is all he said to me.[100]

The falsity of Cristoforo's story of the seduction casts a shadow on his version of the rest. He magnifies his reluctance, puffs up his

success at bargaining, and erases Adriana's role. Still, perhaps Pallantieri, as Cristoforo claimed, did spell out a promised dowry. But
Lucretia, alert to dowry matters, said nothing in court about such
an offer. Whether or not he said so, however, Pallantieri, by taking
Lucretia home, shouldered two burdens—to the mother and to
her child. And everybody understood.

At Pallantieri's house Lucretia lay low. She stayed three days, or
four or five, she said; Cristoforo and Faustina, however, both said
a week.[101] Lucretia remained in Pallantieri's bedroom throughout;
there he lay with her and there she ate the food he brought her
from his study, where servants left it.[102] Much of the time, her sister Faustina, then eight, stayed with her. Faustina told the court:

> At the time that he [Pallantieri] had sex with Lucretia, I stayed
> eight days [i.e., a week] in his room. I remember that, at the time,
> one night Lucretia and I slept in the same bed. He was in the
> middle. He did not have sex with me then, but he had sex with
> Lucretia. And the other nights I stayed in the trundle bed, for I
> did not want to lie in the big bed, even though he wanted me to
> lie with them.[103]

We have plentiful evidence from assorted Roman trials that Renaissance sex fairly often took place in company; neither the lay of
rooms and furniture nor values fostered privacy. Still, this story
also points to Pallantieri's own sexual bent for youth and squeamish spectators; likely not for warmth—even in chill December—
but extra tingle, he urged the child back in between his sheets. The
greatest puzzle here: why would parents who had cloistered their
girls to guard their purity then slip their eight-year-old across the
street? Odd!

At her stay's end, Pallantieri brought Lucretia home, again after
dark.[104] And then, at her house, he carried on his carnal traffic. He
first showed up on the eve of the Feast of Kings (6 January 1549),
and then many times thereafter. When there, he often fondled the
younger sisters.[105] Heading out, he would don his cape and sword
and slip across the street. These visits were nocturnal, stealthy, and
long, up to five hours; across the street, amanuensis Merulo grew
weary waiting upstairs for the master to come home.[106]

At home, Lucretia's pregnancy was no secret. Even little Livia, only five or six, heard about it from Pallantieri himself, from her mother, and from others of the house.[107] Her child's memory pinned the birth—on the Feast of San Bartolomeo (24 August 1549)—to some late-summer figs she ate just before the baby came.[108]

Lucretia bore her son cut off from neighbors; she had no midwife and, of course, no festive childbed guests. Only her parents were there to help.[109] The next evening, at Pallantieri's behest, Cristoforo smuggled the newborn away to the house of a godkinswoman of the judge.[110] The mother would briefly see the little boy again, two or three months old, at Pallantieri's house but would come to know him only three years later.[111] We will tell his story in a moment. First, though, we must help Lucretia shake off Pallantieri.

The court never asked Lucretia how she felt about being raped, about being bound over to her rapist as his concubine, about bearing his child, about losing the infant. Little in early modern Italian law invited such sympathetic questions, for the law's concerns were elsewhere: the violation of fathers' rights and offenses to the canonical rules of marriage and kinship. Unlike modern magistrates, sixteenth-century judges had little interest in or tenderness for a woman's autonomy, security, self-respect, or sanity. Nor did male feelings matter, since the law, like the culture as a whole, dealt in externals: loss to limb, to property, to social reputation. At the same time, sixteenth-century culture also discouraged Lucretia from spilling feelings about herself. Rape and unwilling sex, back then, were primarily social, not psychic, facts. Thus, both law and culture kept Lucretia from grieving before the court. Nonetheless, her long testimonies brimmed with feelings. Above all, there was sorrow and pity for her mother. And as her torture session shows, she took no pains to hide her spite toward Pallantieri. Face-to-face, she told him, "I have had the damage and the shame and it is on your account."[112] About her father, she wore a mask, saying little, pro or con. As for the baby lost at birth, though she voiced no grief, she did stake a maternal claim to him, through pain. We learn of it in a wry exchange. Pallantieri, full of sophistry, wagered to Lucretia's face that she could hardly prove the boy, now eight, was really hers; after all, for years she never saw him. Against his logic, she played her maternal instinct:

> She was asked [goes the Latin summary of Pallantieri's question]
> could it not be that the said Orazio was born of another woman
> than she, and that she is deceived in this?
>
> She answered [in Italian]: In the name of God, I am not
> fooled, for I felt him well enough when I made him.[113]

Notice that the making, as she understood it, was not the conception but the birth; making Orazio, to Lucretia, was of course not
theirs, a shared labor, but hers alone.

We moderns, with all our present beliefs, dogmas, values, fears,
and obsessions surrounding sex, gender, youth, innocence, power,
and trauma, will be inclined to label Pallantieri a foul monster and
to toss him scornfully onto history's ash heap. But we will learn
more if we stay our indignant arm and scrutinize him closely, for
though often vile and monstrous, yet he was a complicated, nuanced man, at once villainous and oddly tender. And he haunted
his times, not ours. Let us watch astutely his treatment of Lucretia—his diminutive surrogate wife—of her whole family, and of his
newborn son.

Fatherhood, back then, had conventions of act and feeling. We
cannot gauge the sentiments, but perhaps more than just good
form brought Pallantieri to Lucretia's childbed in the evening of
the day when she gave birth. "He brought three scudi and said,
'Buy yourself some pigeons.'"[114] Pigeon flesh—light, delicate,
expensive—was thought noble and curative.[115]

As this gesture shows, Pallantieri hoped to keep the liaison
alive. In time, he returned to Lucretia's bed. She, however, sought
desperately to end it fast.

> Our affair did not last much longer, for I was scared I would get
> pregnant a second time. I tried my hardest to get away from him,
> and so, when my father had a match in hand, I did not look to see
> if it was good or bad. To leave the house as fast as possible, I took
> a husband.[116]

As the liaison unraveled, the couple quarreled: "Sometimes we got
angry at one another. Sometimes he came; sometimes he didn't.
And he wanted me to become a nun. I did not want to."[117] For
some three months before Lucretia's marriage, sex ceased.[118]

Early in 1550, Cristoforo found a candidate for husband: Giovanni, a fellow lute maker, surely a professional acquaintance.[119] Though he must have seen it coming, Pallantieri clearly had short warning of the actual match. With his man lined up, Cristoforo, about to negotiate marriage terms, darted across the street to cash in on promises made at Christmas past. Or so he hoped.

> He went to tell it to Messer Alessandro, who then was *luogotenente* of the governor. And my father told him, "I have found a match for Lucretia, and she accepts it. We would like to know what you would like to give."
>
> Messer Alessandro answered, "I don't have a way at the moment, but still I will give something. Make yourself credible in some fashion. Make your arrangements, and I will come this evening and I will bring you something."[120]

When, twenty-one years later, Alessandro Pallantieri made his will, he would leave sixty scudi each to six poor maidens for marriage.[121] That figure serves as yardstick for what he did that evening for Lucretia and explains how she took it. She told the court:

> He came, and he brought me twenty scudi, and he counted them out to me. And I did not say, "Thanks!" I did not say anything at all.
>
> And he said, "What an oaf this girl is! She does not even seem pleased!" And that was the end of our relationship.[122]

Alessandro paid in gold.[123] Faustina would tell the court that he laid out so little because he was peeved at Adriana, who thwarted his yen to bed the younger sisters.[124] Though the Annunziata confraternity, by policy, endowed only virgins, for Lucretia it somehow coughed up more than did Alessandro.[125]

So it was that Lucretia, bride at fifteen, moved out. She achieved motherhood speedily; in the next two years she bore two more children.[126] We can glimpse her, married, when for a week Livia, then six or seven, slept with her in her bed after the birth of her first child, a girl. The visit worked because the husband had not yet rejoined his wife in bed.[127] As the family grew, the couple moved, in 1552 or 1553, to a bigger house; Giovanni may have prospered.[128] Not all income came from trade in lutes, for they took lodgers, in-

cluding a posse of Germans, five or six acquaintances of Cristoforo's, who spoke no Italian.[129] Lucretia stayed in close touch with
her family, alert to their interests; we see her visiting in Easter
week of 1553 and playing host to sisters down to the 1557 trial.[130]
Lucretia's womb was fertile; to the eve of Pallantieri's arrest, babies
kept coming. But, as her words show, hasty marriage had not eased
her heart. In the winter of 1556–57, she fell into love or tenderness
with Alberto, a boarder, a man of higher station. He had been a
tenant earlier and returned for a second, longer stay. The pair first
had sex together a year ago, outside the house, and then, through
much of 1557, husband, pregnant wife, and boarder-lover shared
the family table until, in June of 1557, Giovanni moved to Venice,
abandoning his wife and children. Alberto then moved in to share
Lucretia's bed at home.[131]

Pallantieri, who knew this story well, as he knew the whole Gramar family inside and out, schemed to extract details when face-
to-face in court. His aim, consistent with Italo-Roman evidentiary theory, was to lame his adversary witness in her moral
standing and thereby sap her testimony's probatory force. His success here may have spurred the judge's choice to torture her, to
make good her lapse from chastity and so render her more credible. The exchange, too long to quote in full, was laced with feeling. Pallantieri had plodded on, drawing out a catalogue of boarders. In what follows, the questions—recorded in the usual
Latin—are his.

> He [Pallantieri] asked her whether anyone named Alberto had
> stayed in her home.
>
> She answered, smiling, "I remember now what you are trying
> to accomplish! But I did not remember that. I began for you
> from the beginning, with the first one, who was called Messer
> Marco. But Messer Alberto was the last one. But he is not at my
> house any longer."
>
> And to a question she said, "This Messer Alberto was in the
> house down to the time I had the baby and I came to the gover-
> nor and I was examined and put in jail." And to the same ques-
> tion she added, "Messer Alberto lived in my house twice. The
> first time, he was there for some three months, and now he has
> been there a year."

She was asked how she knows that Alberto left her house, and does she know where he went?

She answered, "I know that he changed lodgings and that he had put his books in order before I came to jail. And Livia also told me so yesterday. But she did not tell me where he went to live. She said he had paid seven scudi for the house rent, for the patron wanted to carry away our furnishings from the house. And no man has had more compassion on me than he."

She was asked if Alberto ever knew her carnally.

And he [Pallantieri] first turned toward her and said that she had to tell the truth. And she answered, "You should talk! You go trying to dig up certain things. I am here on account of you, not on account of him! God knows I have had worse from you than from him!"

And the *fiscale* [Atracino] asked what she meant by those words and told her to answer the question.

She answered: "I mean that I have been shamed and slandered by you and I have never had sex with anyone except with you and you make it seem as if we [sisters] have had sex with everybody. And a fine fix [? one hard word] it would have been if it had not been for Messer Alberto. He has paid my expenses and shod and kept my children, and he has paid the house's rent, and he has had my friendship for the past year. And this is something that every person knows—if he has done well by me or not."[132]

By now, we can fathom Lucretia's declaration, when the judges hoisted her up, that the rope and pain were her missing dowry. As she told the court, since she had come to jail, the old woman who watched her children had died and her new baby had fallen sick. Her husband having walked out on her, the man she loved and counted on had moved away to parts unknown. As we shall learn, that was not the end of the damage, but to see the rest, we will have to read Faustina's story, and Livia's. In the meantime, let us learn the fate of the child of rape, Orazio.

PART 2: ORAZIO'S STORY

The account of Orazio's first eight years of life complicates and nuances our tale yet further. For it adds shading to Pallantieri's own tangled emotions, sometimes cruel, sometimes tender, and it lays bare some of the complex exchanges that fed the growing symbiosis of two households face-to-face across Via dei Leutari.

Pallantieri, in court, maintained that Orazio indeed was his, but by a servant, not by Lucretia.[133] His motives for this imposture will come clear in Faustina's story. Accordingly, he pretended that he and not Lucretia's father had carried the baby off, one day old, to find a wet nurse. Knowing better, the court threw its knowledge back at him, naming names.[134] Pallantieri was more faithful to his Christmas undertaking to protect the child than to his promise to help the mother; he paid the baby's keep as he was shuttled from house to house in search of milk, shelter, and good care. Hoping to mask the mother's identity, Pallantieri smudged the details. There was a wet nurse; he forgets who or where. And then there was a wife—he forgets the name—of a policeman of the governor, and then the family of a Maestro Bartolomeo, by the Customs House.[135]

For the baby's arm's-length management, Pallantieri installed an agent, a Jewish woman named Fiorina, then in her mid-seventies, who for five years past had used his legal services and, sometimes, fought him over property.[136] Fiorina loved the boy. Two years later, in 1551 (the testimony is a thicket of allusion), out of affection for the child, the woman surrendered some rights to an inn in the Jewish quarter that held a license to deal in kosher wine.[137] Some of the money went to support her, some went to her agent at the tavern, and some helped feed Orazio.[138] Feeling cheated, in the 1557 trial Fiorina testified against Pallantieri.

In court, Fiorina was far readier than her employer to recall particulars of Orazio's care.

> He [Pallantieri] had me summoned by Agostino [Merulo, the factotum], who came four times. And I went there and asked, "What do you want?" He told me that a little boy had been born. He wanted me to go now and again to the house of the wet nurse to keep an eye on how she was treating him. She was the wife of Cesare the butcher. So I went, once a week or twice, as I could. Then I took him to my house and kept him for some days, and then I found another wet nurse.[139]

When the boy was weaned, Pallantieri brought him home. Or almost home. Fiorina told the court, "Then I fetched him and put him in the house of that lute seller."[140] It was 1552 or 1553; Orazio was three, going on four.[141] Pallantieri only told the court he had hoped that Adriana, a teacher, would instruct him and bring him up.[142] So it was that Lucretia remade her firstborn's acquaintance—as he became her parents' ward, subsidized monthly by his doting father. Pallantieri was the model of paternal solicitude.

> I listened to him learning how to read and sing. And sometimes I went because the child felt sick, when they told me, or because he had worms [real worms or, more likely, diarrhea] and for other reasons, and when Madonna Adriana was ill.[143]

Pallantieri, it is clear, adored the child. He even extolled the youngster's cleverness to Pope Julius.[144]

In 1556, Adriana's health gave way. She sickened and then, on 24 November, Saint Catherine's Eve, she died.[145] Just before Adriana expired, Pallantieri fetched the child across the street to live at his house as a nearly full-fledged son.[146] Orazio became the servants' darling. We glimpse him dancing after supper for their amusement.[147]

As Pallantieri bonded with his little bastard son, other Gramar denizens also slipped, as clients, into ever-tighter orbits around his patronage. Stefano, the Gramar son, moved across the street and began to study with the younger Pallantieri boys.[148] He stayed six months, sleeping in Orazio's room in a trundle bed below the *fiscale*'s bastard's.[149] Then, to further Stefano's career, Pallantieri shipped him to France in the household of his pious colleague, political ally, successor at the Grain Office, and fellow exploiter of pubescent women, Bartolomeo Camerario di Benevento.[150] Finally, in July 1557, Pallantieri, having lost his majordomo, hired Cristoforo himself.[151]

We have explained how money could make good a virgin's lost hymen, repairing honor, hers and her father's, even if it could not patch her body. Pallantieri, with his monthly stipends, his visits, and his favors to the Gramar household, had somehow made the damage to Lucretia good, at least good enough to let the parents

swallow pride and brave the neighbors' muttering. And gossip
there was in plenty: that Pallantieri had fathered babes and slept
with Adriana too, that a Borgia prelate had had the girls. Fiorina,
among others, had burbled in the neighborhood.[152] A sign of tar-
nished reputation was the visit of an emissary from Cardinal Min-
ganelli's household hoping to rent young flesh.[153] In Lucretia's case,
the Pallantieri-Gramar symbiosis was strained, perhaps, but still
tolerable, despite the social rules of their time and place. But the
parents' compromise was stranger still. To see why, we must read
Faustina's story.

PART 3: FAUSTINA'S STORY

When Orazio moved back to the house where he was born,
Faustina was only twelve, at most thirteen. Ever since Lucretia's
marriage, two years earlier, she later said, Pallantieri had tried
"every day" to have her.[154] Orazio's return two years later gave him
the opening wedge.

> At the time he put Orazio, that little boy, in our house, he kept
> coming to our house. My mother did not want him to have sex
> with me or to come. He said that he wished to come and berated
> her. And he sent Stefano, my brother, to announce that he in-
> tended to come. So we had to let him come, and my mother, to
> avoid his obloquy and to avoid its being known, arranged to have
> him come and told him to leave me alone.[155]

Pallantieri hardly heeded Adriana's warnings. He would sit around
the house at night caressing and kissing Faustina or her older sister Martia or both at once.[156]

Morbid compulsions like Pallantieri's have their habits and
their rituals. With Faustina, he reenacted Lucretia's rape, to the
letter. Toward the end of Lent, just before Easter 1553, as Faustina
told the court:

> Messer Alessandro came to our house. He was in a room with my
> mother and with Martia, my sister who is dead, and me. And
> Messer Alessandro went into the room where my mother, my sis-
> ter who is dead, and I were, and he sat at the foot of the bed and

pulled me toward him and without saying a word began to try to
have carnal knowledge of me. And my mother and my sister tried
to pull me from his grasp, but they could not. Finally, there, in
that house, he had sex with me.[157]

Lucretia, thoroughly replaced!

On Palm Sunday, 26 March, Pallantieri returned. He was to
leave town the next day on a mission. Adriana, furious, would not
speak to him. He told Cristoforo to offer his respects to Orazio,
forced sex on Faustina, and slapped her for resisting.[158]

On a Lenten Friday, between rapes one and two, Lucretia paid
a call on her family. She remembered in court:

> I went one day to my mother's house, for she wanted to go to
> Saint Peter's. It was a Friday in March. I found my mother in
> painful grief, very unhappy, for she was crying. I asked her what
> the matter was. She answered, "I am in such pain that I cannot
> say." When I asked what the matter was, she told me, "That trai-
> tor came to our house and he managed to have sex with Faustina."
> She meant Messer Alessandro Pallantieri. And Faustina was
> there, and all she said was that she could not escape his hand, and
> that there was nothing she could have done. So I tried to take her
> to Saint Peter's. I took her, to give her a bit of pleasure.[159]

Lucretia told the court that this was the blow that killed her
mother. "From then on, she was always sick, so that she died from
the unhappiness and melancholy that she had from it."[160]

As with Lucretia, Pallantieri settled into a liaison with his victim. Back from a six-week trip, on the very evening of his return he
came over, overpowered Adriana's vain resistance by strength of
arm, and had her daughter again.[161] Then came the routine, always
in her house, except one night at his.[162] And, as with Lucretia, before long came pregnancy. In April 1553, Faustina conceived a boy.

In some ways, however, this second time was different. For one
thing, it confirmed the family's helplessness. For another, they
knew by now that Pallantieri could default on promises. Early on,
Lucretia warned her sister, "Now you will experience just what I
experienced."[163] And third, they understood the strictures of
canon law and moral practice: sexual relations with a partner's sib-

ling constituted incest. Cristoforo insisted in court that, "half-desperate," he had reproached Pallantieri, that the man had promised to marry the girl off, that he was angry with his daughter. "But my wife said, 'What do you expect? Just let it go!'"[164] Or so he claimed. This picture belies the daughters' descriptions of family dynamic and of Adriana's character. In their versions the father is largely passive or absent, while it is always the mother who struggles and grieves on their behalf. Certainly, Faustina recalled that it was her mother who objected to the breach of moral laws:

> My mother grieved and complained to him that he had had sex with two sisters and that he wanted to do it with the others. He answered, "Leave me alone" and told me to just let her talk.[165]

Pallantieri also told Faustina, "God is merciful. These are sins of the flesh, and Messer Lord God is merciful and would forgive him."[166] Lucretia also protested to Pallantieri about his breach of the incest rules. She averred, "He answered that he did it because he loved Faustina too much. At my house my mother answered him, 'This is a great lie and a great shame upon me.'"[167]

In summer, early in the pregnancy, Faustina's parents discussed abortion. "I told the mother, 'If you don't make her abort, I will kill her,'" said Cristoforo. "I bought certain things to give her to drink to make her miscarry. I don't know if the mother gave them to her. So she made me buy them."[168] Faustina told the court, however, that she took no abortifacients.[169] In early 1554, about fifteen days after Christmas, she bore a full-term male baby.[170] Her labor, long, slow, and painful, produced a stillborn. As with Lucretia, the family called no midwife; only Adriana and Martia were there to help.[171] At daybreak, Cristoforo smuggled the little corpse to Sant'Agostino.[172]

Out of propriety or solicitude, Pallantieri visited Faustina in childbed. Only when she recovered did sex resume. It went on a full year, until, around Christmas 1555, again the girl conceived.[173] As Faustina's belly filled, Adriana faltered and slid toward death. Faustina, in court, linked her mother's death to grief over her family's disgrace:

> My mother grieved a lot over Messer Alessandro, for what he did, for he tried to have sex with all our sisters and she could do noth-

ing about it. And she was never happy when I was pregnant but
desired to die because of it.[174]

Lucretia agreed. In late summer or early fall, shortly before
Faustina again gave birth, she laid her feelings before Pallantieri.

> When my mother was about to die, a little before her death, I
> went to the house, where my mother was sick, to see her. And
> Messer Alessandro came in the evening; it was four hours after
> nightfall. He was talking with my mother, who had passed out
> with a fainting fit. When she came to her senses, my mother told
> Messer Alessandro, "I commend Faustina to you, for I die un-
> happy, leaving her in this condition." For Faustina was then preg-
> nant by Messer Alessandro and about to give birth. He answered
> not to worry, that he would take care of Faustina and of every-
> body. At that point I said to Messer Alessandro, "God forgive
> you, Messer Alessandro, that is the least you can do! You have
> been the cause of her death, for she is dying because of this."
> Messer Alessandro turned to me, saying, "Shut up. You are a
> scamp. A lot you know about this!"[175]

Adriana lived long enough to see the new baby born, but little
longer. In September, Faustina had her baby, a girl. Pallantieri—
was it duty or solicitude?—did visit her before she bore the
child.[176] As Adriana was too sick to help, Lucretia did midwife duties.[177] Pallantieri himself came over the evening after to visit the
new mother; he proffered two gold scudi and marzipan and announced it was a girl.[178] It seems Faustina had not seen the child.
Nor, likely, would she ever.

The *fiscale*—by then he had won his job—left Faustina in post-
partum peace for a month and a half or so and then returned to
sex.[179] Within days of this reunion, Adriana died; it was Saint
Catherine's Eve, 24 November 1556.[180] The evening of her burial,
Pallantieri tried to pay a call, for sex or sympathy. "But we had gone
to bed; he did not enter."[181]

> The next night he came in and told us he had been here. He
> found my sister Livia and me; we were by the fire. He began to
> comfort us and to settle in with us. He took me into the sala and

had sex with me. And Livia stayed in the kitchen. He caressed
Livia too and kissed her and then he left.[182]

With the mother's death, the household went to pieces; in her
last days, Orazio and Stefano had already gone across the street.
Livia soon moved in with Lucretia's family.[183] That left only Martia, Faustina, and the father. Then, sometime in the winter, Martia died, having suffered Pallantieri's gropes but never lain with
him.[184] For seven years, an agent who brought the women cloth-
work, a velvet maker, had aired designs to marry her, but nothing
had come of it.[185] At death, she was perhaps twenty.

On 2 February 1557, Pallantieri temporarily broke off his affair
with Faustina. We do not know why. Likely it was not because he
was tired of her convenient bed but rather because in Adriana's absence the whole Gramar ménage unraveled. On that date, he
wrote a note on Cristoforo's behalf to a noble nun, Laura della
Corgna, asking her to lobby to have Faustina lodged at the Montecitorio convent, home of the Giustinis' Castellane nuns. The
letter worked.[186]

For Pallantieri, Faustina's nunnery was no spiritual retreat but a
handy roof, bed, and board. In his eyes, Faustina was still his to
borrow—coitus only semi-interruptus. In early April, the girl
came out for Easter to visit the Seven Churches with Lucretia;
with Livia, she was to share Lucretia's bed.[187] But Pallantieri sent
Cristoforo, now his pander, to the daughter's abode to fetch
Faustina back to her old house.[188] The place was altogether empty;
Faustina lodged alone, except for Pallantieri, who spent three days
there with her.[189] On four nights in June, when Livia wed, the
same thing happened; this time, Lucretia's husband joined Cristoforo as escort.[190] The final sortie was just days before Pallantieri's
fall from grace: late September 1557. Cristoforo, Livia (conscripted
on paternal orders), and a daughter of Lucretia's arrived at the
convent in Pallantieri's coach to fetch Faustina out to fête Lucretia's most recent childbed.[191] Faustina slept one night at Lucretia's
and the rest in her old house.

Livia, already married, painted the court a lively picture of the
scene. By now, we know the details well enough, the cajolery and
promiscuous fumbling; no need to quote the whole. But note
some details. The two young women were locked in. When Pal-

lantieri came, "Faustina went to the window and said, 'Go to my father, for he has the key.' And he went off and came back with my father, who opened the door and then went back to Messer Alessandro's house."[192] Cristoforo, now Pallantieri's majordomo and melded with the *fiscale*'s ménage, had been reduced by pay from his girls' father to their jailer and their seducer's salaried procurer. Livia remained defiant to the end. She says that the *fiscale* snapped at her, "I am amazed you deigned to stay."[193]

> He took my sister with one hand and me with the other and said, "Let's go the three of us together to the bedroom."
> And he sat us down there, one on one side, the other on the other, and began to flirt. I got up and left them there, the two of them. And before I left he grabbed me by my braids and kissed me on the mouth. And Faustina told him to leave me alone, but he would not listen. I left the room, and he told me to be off. I left him there, and after a while my father came back, so I went back to the bedroom. I had been alone in the kitchen, reading a book.[194]

This is a rare vignette of female literacy, put to use.

On Friday, 1 October, just five days before the arrest, by private coach the fiscale slipped Faustina back into her nunnery.[195] This, though no one knew it, was the end of the affair.

Pallantieri's arrest suspended Faustina's fate. The *fiscale* had often told her that he would marry her off or endow her as a nun.[196] He had as yet done neither; at Montecitorio nunnery, she was just a pensioner, kept on in exchange for Pallantieri's twenty-eight giulii (just under three scudi), paid monthly.[197] At some thirty scudi a year, this arrangement was not cheap: two monastic years would equal a modest dowry; one year cost more than Lucretia's paltry wedding subsidy. When, in early December 1557, after two months' imprisonment, Faustina left Tor di Nona jail, where did she go? Who fed and kept her? We have no idea.

In jail, Faustina, like Lucretia, alone among the witnesses suffered torture. She too was compromised and needed legal bolstering through pain. At the rope, she railed against Pallantieri: "I have suffered other things on his account, and now I suffer this."[198] Hoisted, she began to faint from pain. As quickly as they could, after the standard "Miserere interval," the court released her. "His lordship ordered her put down gently and had vinegar brought and instructed that she be comforted."[199] At that, we lose sight of her.

PART 4: HELENA'S FIRST YEAR

Faustina's new baby, Helena, came at a ticklish moment in high politics. In September 1556, Alba's Imperial and Spanish army was at the gates of Rome. Remembering the sack of 1527, the city feared invasion and ruin. In panic's shadow, Pallantieri, to settle the new child, turned to Francesco Bonello, alias Socio, *commissario* of foodstuffs at Campo di Fiori market.[200] In 1554, Socio had been Pallantieri's traveling notary, buying grain in the Campagna. He was an older man, diminutive, a bit addled. "He drinks his wine unwatered and gets drunk," Pallantieri wrote his accomplice, Paolo Vittorio, advising how to scupper Socio's damning testimony about their grain fraud.[201] When Pallantieri summoned Socio's aid to place Faustina's newborn, the older man's wife had already fled war to Bracciano, miles northwest. The *fiscale* told his crony to find a Corsican or a hills woman from Amatrice or Norcia.[202] Socio shouldered the task. In court he told a bewitching tale of his adventures as the go-between who helped hide philandering's fresh fruit:

> I went to an old woman named Polisena, who was a midwife and who went around collecting the babies that were born. And she also made contacts between midwives and [the foundling hospital] Santo Spirito. I told her, "Madonna Polisena, I want you to find a wet nurse for a gentleman, a friend of mine." She said yes. So I went to find Pallantieri and told him that a midwife would be found, but that Madonna Polisena wanted to know if he wanted her to keep her [the baby] in her house of if he wanted to send the little girl to the house of the wet nurse. He answered me that he wanted the wet nurse to keep the infant in her own house. So I went and made the pact with the midwife, who was the wife of a Hieronimo Acoltatore, who lives on Via Lungara, in Trastevere.
>
> Then I went back to Pallantieri. He told me to stay on alert

because early the next morning, before dawn, he would bring
me the infant or have it sent to me. So, to do my friend a favor,
I stayed two days at home—I never got undressed, for I was
on tenterhooks, expecting him to come. The second night—I
thought that it would be he who came—there came, in the morning before daybreak, a certain Maestro Cristoforo, across the
street from Messer Alessandro, who had an infant under his
cape.[203]

Faustina remembered her father's departure, carrying the newborn swaddled in red woolen bands.[204] Socio, in court, continued
his story:

> So I brought her to that Polisena, the midwife, and I knocked
> on the door. So she got dressed and came down. And the infant
> never cried. I said to Madonna Polisena, "This is that infant of
> that friend of mine. Bring this worthy man [Cristoforo, still pres-
> ent] to the wet nurse and do what needs doing."
> And then I went to Campo di Fiori to write on loose pages the
> grain and wheat that were there. And when I had finished writ-
> ing, I went to Pallantieri's house [just two or three blocks away]
> and I found him home. For it was just a little after daybreak, and
> he was still asleep.
> So I went home and got a bite to eat. And then I went to find
> that Polisena—she has since died. "Well, that baby—is it a boy or
> a girl?" She said, "It's a girl, and I think it was born this past
> night, because I fixed the umbilical cord."[205]

In a later testimony, the old man added: "We unwrapped her and
we saw that the umbilical cord had not been tied; it had not been
fixed. And I told her: 'I'll wager this little girl has not been baptized.'"[206] His story continues:

> Then I said to Polisena, "If this is the baby, it has not been
> baptized." So, then, fearing that the infant might die without bap-
> tism, I went back to Pallantieri's house and told his butler that
> they should let me talk to him about an important matter.
> The fellow told me that he was sleeping, for all night long he
> had been studying. I answered, "Wake him up, for it is a matter

that is quite important to him. And if you are not willing to rouse him, I will start kicking at the door."

So they woke him and I went in. He was there, in bed, undressed or dressed—I could not see to tell—and I told him what had been done and asked him if the infant had had baptism. He said no. I replied: did he wish to have her baptized, and what name did he want us to give her? He answered, "Have her baptized and give her whatever name you like."

So I went home to my house and knocked. My serving woman opened the door for me. I went upstairs and fetched a holy candle and attached a giulio [coin] to it with thread and took it to Madonna Polisena. I told her, "Go to the wet nurse of that infant. Take her this candle and wait here at San Giovanni della Malva, my parish church, for we will have her baptized."

So, not knowing what other name to give her, I had her given the name of my late mother, of happy memory, who is called Helena. And that is what I know of this.[207]

Socio's piety was scandalized by Pallantieri's offhand indifference to the fate of the infant's soul. "It seemed to me very strange that he had taken so little care, for the little girl could have died a Saracen if I had not spoken out."[208] As with Orazio, Pallantieri was careful to keep the bastard at long arm's length. He interposed between the wet nurse and himself a web of go-betweens: Polisena, Cristoforo, Socio. The house of the wet nurse, Giacomina, lay across the river. It was Cristoforo who brought her Pallantieri's money for the baby's upkeep.[209] It was Socio who kept alert to material needs. "Because the little girl had no shirts, I went to Pallantieri's house and made them give me two shirts, old ones. And my wife made me two shirts for the little girl."[210] Pallantieri forbade Socio, who knew Orazio's origins and the new baby's incestuous conception, ever to mention Helena.[211] Still, despite precautions, the *fiscale*'s fatherly impulses gave his paternity away. Offhand as he had been about her name and baptism, Pallantieri still cared enough about Helena's welfare to prowl the street where the wet nurse lived. He owned a garden near San Pietro in Montorio, high on the Janiculum Hill. When the *fiscale* rode there, he would often detour; rather than climb to his vineyard, he would turn hard right just two blocks after crossing the Tiber on Ponte Sisto, pass under the Settimiana Gate, and follow Via Lungara upriver. Giacomina the wet nurse and her neighbors soon fingered him as the secret father of the smuggled infant.[212] Giacomina herself described him to the court; with his white horse, long beard going white, brusque demeanor, black velvet hat or priest's cap, and professional's long robes, he stood out.[213]

Helena, despite her shaky start, survived. Down to his arrest, Pallantieri kept up his payments, twenty-four giulii a month, using Cristoforo as courier and bearer-back of tidings about her welfare.[214] On 4 October, two days before Pallantieri's arrest, Cristoforo paid his call at the wet nurse's house and found the baby in good health.[215] With Pallantieri now jailed, her future, like her father's and her mother's, remained dubious.

PART 5: LIVIA'S STORY

Livia was the lucky one, who alone escaped both death and Pallantieri's talons. It was not that he did not try to snatch her, but first her youth and then, perhaps, her determination and Lucretia's vigilance preserved her virginity, down to her hasty wedding. Born in 1543 or 1544, she was only five when Lucretia, as she still remembered, crossed the street to Pallantieri's house, and only five or six at Orazio's birth. In court, in December 1557, she was fourteen or at most fifteen. Even when small, she had known from family talk about her sisters' liaisons—a deeply painful subject. In court, Pallantieri asked her if she had ever told anyone about the family bastards.

> She answered: "Signore, no, for if I had said it, I would have spoken my shame and my sisters.'" And to the same question, she added: "And, about this, I have never spoken with my husband nor with any other person."[216]

Despite many affronts to dignity and integrity, Livia seems to have kept her equipoise and sanity. "She is always joking," said Lucretia.[217]

About one year back, Livia had had a flirtation of her own with

a neighbor named, by chance, Alessandro. As sometimes happened, a family's attempts to quarantine their daughters proved
vain, even against ordinary suitors and love-bent youngsters far
more anodyne than Pallantieri. In court, to undercut Livia's forensic reputation, the *fiscale* strove to worm out details. Under his
questioning, she told the following tale. Just like Pallantieri with
Lucretia, years before, this young Alessandro had tossed love gifts
onto the Gramar roof.

> Once he threw me a pair of red silk gloves and a missal and a
> ring—that is, a gold band [*una fede*], which he tossed to me up
> on the roof. And I kept them several days. And then my father
> saw it.[218]

The young man must have known the girl well enough to know she
liked books. Before Cristoforo caught on, Livia had showed these
trophies to Faustina.[219] Then, finding a door unlocked, to sneak
closer to the girl the lad twice slipped into the Gramars' cellar.
Livia, under Pallantieri's questioning, recounted:

> One day there came in an old woman who lived in our house—
> her name was Caterina and she has died just recently—and she
> said, "There are people down below." She wanted to go down to
> kindle a light. I was upstairs. And he left. And another time, a
> Sunday morning, when my mother was sick, he came into the
> house and went into the cellar. I went for water and found him
> sitting on a barrel. He told me that he would do me no violence,
> and he embraced me and kissed me. That is all he did; I did not
> stay long, for I had gone for water. He stayed a little while and
> then went outdoors.[220]

Cristoforo, seeing him leave, roared at Livia.[221] Pallantieri knew
about the incident and told Faustina.[222] And after Livia had transferred to Lucretia's house, young Alessandro saw her there and
asked her why she had moved out.[223] And that is all; if more happened, Pallantieri, in court, could never winkle it out of Livia and
her sisters.

Pallantieri had long tried for Livia; originally, Faustina had protected her.[224] But in February 1557, after the big sister had moved to the nunnery, the *fiscale* redoubled his efforts to fill his empty bed.

> After he had Faustina put in the monastery, he wanted me to stay at home alone, and he did all he could to have me too. I had to work hard to defend myself. He grabbed my body, and I threw myself to the ground and hid under the bed so well that I escaped. And he tried by threatening me—he would have me put in jail at Tor di Nona, and he hit me too, when he could not do his will with me.[225]

Swiftly, Lucretia stepped in to rescue her youngest sister, removing her to join her own convoluted ménage. So it was that, in March 1557, Livia came to share a table with her sister and her sister's two rival men.[226]

But not for long. When she married in June, she had a hundred-scudi dowry arranged by Pallantieri's crony Bartolomeo Camerario di Benevento. Although the fellow, as seen already, had his sometimes-lubricious pious female charities, in this case he fronted for his ally to do some good. Amanuensis Merulo testified that Pallantieri wrote out a payment order, contingent on the wedding; Benevento then countersigned it and passed it to the Scarlatti bank. The pious wartime goal: "That she pray God for the conservation of the state of His Holiness."[227] A puzzle here: why would Pallantieri heap five times as much on Livia, who spurned him, as on Lucretia, who bore his son? Was it because Lucretia, once his, had broken free? In any case, Livia settled in, at fifteen, with Maestro Antonio, a shoemaker by San Marcello.[228] When her jailers set her free, she, at least, had a new household of her own to go back to; the husband fetched her home.[229] As we have seen in the tale of Faustina's final visit to her deserted house, Livia's married state did not deter Pallantieri's wandering hands. Still, it kept her out of easy reach.

Even jailing Pallantieri did not shelter Livia from him. In November 1557, shortly before she testified, she received a visit from the ex-*fiscale*'s brother Giorgio and his son Carlo, who strove in vain to sway her testimony.[230]

PART 6: ALESSANDRO PALLANTIERI, THE SEQUEL

Hollywood, with more greed than imagination, in a bid for box-office returns often hangs the dreary title of "The Sequel" on third-rate revisions of second-rate films. Alessandro Pallantieri's subsequent adventures rate higher. They are the stuff of history, in the public record and the subject of chronicles and histories of affairs of state.[231] Though perhaps it should have, his trial did not finish him. Between the prosecution's zeal and heap of witnesses and Pallantieri's own brilliant defense, it went on almost forever. Its 446 folia are replete with fierce Latin disputations on fine points of law, endless recitations of peculations and connivance, and the defendant's own maudlin protestations about his poor health, long confinement, and general persecution. At one point, another sexual victim, now a notary, appears to retell with splendid notarial precision every organ's misadventures one night in bed when, as a lad of fifteen back home in Ascoli, he suffered Pallantieri's importunate advances.[232] In the end, after ten long months of trial, the court condemned Pallantieri, as it had to.

Oddly, we lack the sentence. But we have the absolution, in several copies. It came swiftly with the new regime. No sooner had Pius IV come to power, at the end of 1559, than he sprang the old *fiscale* from his prison. In January 1560, he pardoned him; in March, he set him back in the saddle, *fiscale* once more.[233] The new pope then set Pallantieri at work to build a case against the Carafa clan. Tit for tat! Keen to avenge his own betrayal and arrest, Pallantieri and his governor zealously, and overzealously, compiled their dossiers. There ensued an immense trial of state, a *cause de scandale* that ended with both Cardinal Carlo and his brother, the duke of Paliano, dead of judicial murder. They, and their accomplices, had had their assorted crimes. Most spectacular had been the duke's own judicial murder, by feudal court, of his pregnant wife and her suspected lover. But in fact, the crimes for which they suffered had been political: their attempt to usurp the vast estate of the Colonna barons, favorites of ascendant Spain, and their links to the detested regime of Paul IV.

Pallantieri, victorious, in 1563 rose to the office of governor.[234] By then he was a widower and priest, for only clergy held such jobs. It was as governor, for instance, that in July that year he wrote out the writ against our uxoricide Giovanni Battista Savelli. Pallantieri rode high, grew powerful, and waxed scandalously rich.

And then fortune's famous wheel turned once more. The next pope, Pius V (1566–72), also a zealot, admired his zealous predecessor Paul IV. As soon as he was enthroned, he started to undo the Carafa condemnation, ordering the whole trial reviewed and its papers confiscated. Therefore, in 1567 he removed Pallantieri from Rome to govern the Marches.[235] For two years, the aging jurist still flourished, courting the Jesuits, cloaking his life and persistent sexual vices in public piety, and dreaming of a cardinal's purple hat. But a trick of fate undid him; a friend of his, a virulent satirist named Niccolò Franco, confessed to the Inquisition that he had gathered anti-Carafa scuttlebutt from official court papers at Pallantieri's house. The Inquisition in August 1569 summoned Pallantieri to Rome, jailed him, and tried him once more.[236] It would be the same story of brilliant, dogged, self-directed defense, but this time, much much longer. The Vatican manuscripts heap up to 6,000 folia. I confess, I have not dared look at them.

In the end, the old man went under, tit once more for tat, victim in the end of a colossal string of low blows and counterblows: Aldobrandi's fall, his fall, the Carafas' fall, his second fall. Poetic justice, perhaps. The indictment and the sentence, after a long list of his crimes—forbidden weapons, forbidden pamphlets, the forbidden transcript of the Carafa trial, all in his house, and purloined goods of all sorts—as an afterthought adds "the deflowering of virgins, incest, and adultery."[237] But it names no names; marginalia on the first page of the 1557–58 trial indicate its consultation in 1571, but we have no way of knowing how much then or, for that matter, back in 1558 the judges ever really cared about the misadventures and miseries of Lucretia, Faustina, and their family. Legal marginalia, a sideshow; the crux lay elsewhere, in papal scruples and the rancor of surviving Carafa notables. In June 1571, the state beheaded Alessandro in the courtyard at Tor di Nona jail, just where, a decade earlier, at his prosecutorial hand, had died the duke of Paliano.[238] He went in an aureole of piety, comforted by saintly Filippo Neri but, justly, mourned by few.

Soon after I published in an electronic journal my account of how I used the Savelli murder case to teach first-year students, I received an intriguing letter from a judicial official in Castel Bolognese, Pallantieri's hometown. It was one of those minor search-engine miracles; the official, Paolo Grandi, by vocation a magistrates' administrator, by avocation a local historian, had found Pallantieri's name deep inside my article, under a button to the transcript of the Savelli trial, for Pallantieri had signed the investigation's warrant. Signor Grandi and I exchanged information about the old magistrate, to whom, I learned, the modern official had devoted his *tesi di laurea,* or master's thesis, twenty-two years ago. He kindly sent me his second copy. It has proven invaluable in illuminating the background of my story. In the summer of 2002, Signor Grandi led my family and me on a walking tour of Castel Bolognese; despite the tremendous bombardments of 1945, the Pallantieri palace, though now cut in twain by an urban street, is still there. A convent has swallowed part of it, and a pretty restaurant has colonized the vaulted ground floor. On one courtyard wall are sixteenth-century frescoes, hidden among laundry and potted plants. Modest apartments have divided the upper storeys. With Signor Grandi's help, a local Web enthusiast has set up a page to commemorate a man who, however flawed, was a local son of note.

AFTERTHOUGHTS: SOCIAL HISTORY

Historians of women, of gender, of childhood, or of the family in premodern Europe have to be good sleuths, for until diaries, memoirs, and private letters flourished, in 1650 and beyond, it is hard indeed to know what life felt like, especially for those not rich or powerful. Often, the papers of criminal courts offer the richest and most interesting clues. As they do here, in our story.

One issue in such studies is power. The premodern world was hierarchic, in both fact and principle. Youth deferred to age, servant to employer, commoner to noble, underling to superior, subject to ruler, laity to clergy, matter to spirit, earth to heaven, and, of course, woman to man. But deference was never tantamount to belly-up surrender. So resistance is a subject, as is subversion, via sabotage, mockery, or sheer evasion. And so is bargaining. Early on in the study of gender history, there arose a lachrymose school: all was lost! "Patriarchy" ruled. Women were powerless. There was of course a countervailing triumphalist school, no less skewed. More recently, subtler scholarship has cannily pursued the many shades and shifts of female agency. And, likewise, other scholars have probed the strategies and powers of underlings other than women.

It is for such studies that the Gramar women's tale is interesting, both as portrait of harsh experience and as probe of modes of coping under hideous pressures—legal, moral, economic, social, and physical. The historian seeks to understand their resourcefulness while regarding their stoic ruggedness with sympathy and awe.

⚜

After the bleak tale of Pallantieri and his victims, we deserve something lighter. But our next chapter offers yet another unhappy family. Here again we find guile and cruelty. But this time, by an odd and happy twist of fate, the victim escapes unscathed and the only ones to suffer, aside from the murderous husband, who dies mysteriously beyond our sight and ken, are three baby pigeons sacrificed to forensic science.

Few dire events, except among the birds! Indeed, very little finally happens. But the telling still has goodly room for play, thanks to the tale's archival quirks. The plot failed, but not before the careless plotters put their plans, in veiled language, in several letters and on one queer page of sinister import. These fell into the hands of the court, who with habitual scrupulosity filed them with the trial, where they sat, ignored, for 430 years until, bewitched, I read and copied them.

The chapter that follows offers first that strange document and then those letters, one by one, with scant commentary, to let the plot unveil itself. Its literary model is the epistolary novel, a famous genre invented almost three centuries back and practiced still. Of course, unlike a novelist, I cannot make my letters behave themselves for you. Mine are full of baffling conspiratorial murk. I do my best to unravel the secrets of the plot and then, late in the chapter, suddenly jump from the courtesan's writing table to the prison doctor's studio to watch him practice forensic science on three baby birds. I veer because my documents do; the physician's re-

port survives, bound with the captured letters. We historians follow our papers' lead. Nevertheless, the chapter makes a pitch for thematic unity: plotters' epistles and physicians' reports, I hold, shared an epistemology of risk and stake. To weigh this curious argument, read carefully and skeptically both it and the odd documents ahead.

Chapter 5

THE LADY LIVES,

THE

PIGEON DIES

IT TOOK FOUR TO MAKE THE DOCUMENT: the knight, the friend, the courtesan, and the boy of twelve. But it took just three hands to sign; the youngster lent his hand and pen on behalf of the courtesan, his older sister. Though she could write—her script was clear if wobbly and oddly spelled—she preferred her young sibling's finer penmanship. The paper the boy drafted, though short and simple, would have dire results.[1] It read as follows:

In Rome, 18 April 1582

When, by the hands of God and the Blessed Mary, it should prove pleasing to raise from this life to a better one Felice, my wife, by the present writing I declare, confess, and content myself with all my heart, as God commands, to take as my legitimate spouse Signora Cintia Antelma, a Roman, and I promise and obligate myself to keep her for always, as is proper, and as a husband ought to keep a wife. And, for clarity, both hers and mine, the two of us promise, and we will give our word and faith in the presence of

173

Signore Lelio Perleoni, who will sign the present document and
will obligate himself to maintain the said matrimony, both for the
said Signora Cintia as well as for me, Giacomo. And in faith of
the truth, we have by common accord made this document that
we will sign by our own hands.

    I, Giacomo Teodoli, freely promise, express my contentment,
and obligate myself to the above.

    I, Cintia Antelma, freely promise, express my contentment,
and obligate myself to the above.

    I, Lelio Perleoni, was present and obligate myself as above.

The contracting parties made three copies, diversely aligned but
identical in wording. Cintia kept one; the court notary would find
it three months later in her bedroom, locked away. Lelio kept another, also later impounded with his papers. Giacomo must have
carried off a third; it, like Giacomo, slipped the grasp of justice.[2]

    The paper's sentiment, and its authors', was far from rare: if
ever death should free one of us from a less-happy match, we two
can wed. Extramural love must often have kindled such fantasies
and words.[3] Solemn promises were far less common, for canon law
barred their tainted matches; it took an appeal to Rome to dodge
the ban.[4] Therefore, a formal paper such as this, witnessed by a
friend, was indeed a rarity. To make sense of its twisted roots and
goal, we shall muster what we know about the four protagonists—
their origins, friendships, love, and dark intrigues.

    The first signatory, Cavaliere Giacomo Teodoli, descended
from a great Forlì clan. His ancestors had been eminent Ghi-
bellines, co-leaders of their faction in fierce urban strife. To quell
them, in 1525 the great historian Francesco Guicciardini, as presi-
dent of the Romagna, had expelled their head, Giovanni Ruffo
Teodoli, archbishop of Cosenza and bishop of Cadiz, and flat-
tened the family's fine new palace.[5] Giovanni Ruffo nonetheless
did well in life; he had a long career as papal tax man and diplomat
in Spain (1506–18).[6] In 1525, retiring from the See of Cadiz, he
passed it to a nephew, Geronimo, a curialist who held it for almost
forty years while waxing fat in Rome.[7] Geronimo amassed property: a handsome vineyard just outside the Porta del Popolo and a
comely palace on the Corso, on the west side, just south of the oblong square of San Lorenzo in Lucina.[8] Like many a high church-

man, Geronimo deftly wedged his provincial family into the Roman elite. In the early 1570s, he bought feudal holdings for a close
kinsman, Teodolo Teodoli, in the limestone mountains behind
Palestrina: the high-perched villages of Pisoniano, San Vito, and
Ceciliano.[9] Their upland district was less than fertile, but the feudal rights and two massive castles clinched a noble title: in 1570,
Teodolo became count of Ceciliano.[10] In 1591, the Teodoli took a
nobler title: marchesi of San Vito. The family would hold its own,
intermarrying well and spawning a seventeenth-century cardinal
and an eighteenth-century marchese-architect.[11] Thanks to an
Ottocento merger with the Forlì branch, the house lives on today;
its members still figure in bubbly gossip columns in the Roman
press, and the marchese still owns a painting of the vanished
sixteenth-century Corso palace.[12]

Likely, it was in this palace, then owned by Bishop Geronimo
Teodoli, that Giacomo spent his youth. He was probably the
bishop's nephew, his brother's son.[13] Domenico Gagliardelli, physician to Bishop Geronimo for fourteen years, knew Giacomo very
well.[14] Another veteran servant, of first the aging bishop and then
his heir the count, confirmed Giacomo's presence in the family or-
bit.[15] Giacomo must have enjoyed the country air and pastimes in
the rural fiefs, for letters of 1582 prove that the Teodoli spent time
in Ceciliano.[16] He must have lodged in the hulking castle, with its
crenellated battlements, four great towers, and sweeping view.

It takes sleuthing to place Giacomo, for on several points the
published family trees clash with one another and with testimony
from his trial. Probably he was the bishop's nephew and the father
of Teodolo, first marchese of San Vito. Whatever the precise connection, in the 1580s he enjoyed a monthly stipend from the late
bishop's estate.[17] Giacomo had brothers who wrote him letters, one
a prelate, one a nobleman.[18] Our judicial documents do help place
him in the family; they label Mario Orsini, a figure in this domestic drama, as the son-in-law of Giacomo's wife.[19] The nineteenth-
century genealogist Pompeo Litta confirms this and shows that
Mario Orsini took a second wife, Cornelia Teodoli, in 1582, the
very year of Giacomo's fateful pact. Fallible Litta calls Cornelia the
daughter of Count Teodolo Teodoli but almost certainly she was
Giacomo's daughter, his third surviving child.[20] Orsini, a courtier
of the Tuscan grand duke, descended from a venerable, sprawling

Roman clan of barons, cardinals, and condottieri. The match signals how successful Bishop Geronimo's assiduous campaign to
sprout Roman roots had been. The Orsini marriage was not to
last; if Litta is correct—he often makes mistakes—Mario died the
very next year. His spouse, Cornelia, was far more durable; she
would marry two more nobles and die in 1660—seventy-eight
years later! If, in 1582, she was a fresh bride of sixteen or so, she
lived to about ninety-four.[21] This is a long stretch—for her, for
early modern medicine, and for historians—but not impossible.
Giacomo also had three sons, of whom the last died young and the
first two, Cornelia's older brothers, would in succession hold title
to the marchesate of San Vito. A letter of Cintia's mentions
them.[22] So, in 1582, Giacomo had three surviving offspring, all in
their midteens or early twenties. Though perhaps infatuated with
his courtesan, Giacomo was no puppy.

Giacomo's own marriage, unlike Cornelia's, tied him not to
Rome but to Forlì. His wife, Felice, was a Maldenti. She stemmed
from a patrician family who, like the Teodoli, stood out in the city's
chronicles of conspiracy and mayhem.[23] Their fifteenth-century
palace, with its severe medieval front, great Gothic door, two big
Gothic windows, and squat crenellated tower, still fills a Forlì
city block. Felice probably kept ties to her hometown; a lady-in-
waiting of hers came from there.[24] We know little else about her
save that in 1582 she had shared quarters with her husband, possibly in the Teodoli palace, for at least the past three years.[25] Although, for the year before the pact, Giacomo's passion and attentions had pointed elsewhere, the couple continued to cohabit.

Cintia Antelma, the second signatory, albeit by proxy, seems to
have been a courtesan of middling station. She does not figure in
published histories of her trade; it is thus unlikely that she haunted
the demimonde's glamorous pinnacle.[26] Still, she must have kept a
handsome establishment, for her customers and associates were
clearly gentlemen; she averred in court that those who first brought
Giacomo to her house in the spring of 1581 were men of standing:

> Cavalier Giacomo was tracking me a fair while, till certain gentle-
> men brought him to my house. Then he began to keep my com-
> pany, there, at home. And then he began to deal with me continu-
> ally, at his pleasure.[27]

That last phrase (*come piaceva a lui*) suggests that Giacomo's attentions may have swept other clients from Cintia's bed; if so, he had
passed from mere customer to main lover and then to sole partner.
One more sign of Cintia's louche respectability was that Giacomo,
she says, took no pains to hide their traffic. "The whole world
knew. When he came to my house, he hid from no one."[28] Giacomo was not Cintia's first regular lover; there had been another
man of rank, a signore named Livio Otterio.[29] We know little
more about Cintia: her father was named Giovanni Antelmo; her
mother, before Cintia's young brother's birth, had paired up with
a second man, named Costa; and her literacy, though competent,
was hardly polished. And, of course, she yearned to marry Cavaliere Giacomo. For her, the stakes were high; a hand well played
might win lands and titles for eventual sons.

Lelio Perleoni, third signatory and guarantor, stemmed from
Rimini. There were fifteenth-century Perleoni condottieri and
Perleoni captains for the Malatesta princes. In the mid–fifteenth
century, learned Rimini Perleoni transferred to Venice, married
well, and wormed their way onto the list of citizens.[30] In the
1440s, an erudite Perleoni delivered the funeral oration for a doge
of Genoa.[31] Of Lelio's own precise origins, accomplishments, at-
tachments, and ambitions we know little save that he had tunneled
deep into Giacomo's household; for at least three years he had
lived there as Felice's servitor, her domestic intimate, and Giacomo's. He also kept Giacomo privy company at Cintia's quarters,
where he read him his mail and filed it.[32] Lelio was a gentleman; he
picked his fights with other gentlemen.[33] His script and spelling
were mediocre, as was his bodily constitution. "He is unhealthy,"
said physician Gagliardelli. "He has three problems needing treatment: one in the back of the head, one in the left arm, and one in
the leg."[34] As for Lelio's moral constitution, it bent.

The fourth party to the pact making, but external to the pact itself, was its scribe, Domenico Costa, Cintia's twelve-year-old half
brother. He had a neat hand, far better than Cintia's or Lelio's, and
the precocious worldly wisdom one might expect of a lad housed
in a bordello. In court, self-possessed and wily, he lied as stub-
bornly and astutely as any adult.[35]

Cintia, Giacomo, and Felice would seem to make a classic tri-
angle. But Lelio complicated the geometry enormously, stretching

it to a rectangle of sorts. No sign of sex, in his regard. "Lelio Per-leoni never did it with me," said Cintia. On this point at least, she had no need to lie.[36] But sex or not, there was lively courtship. It is far from clear who did the courting. Most likely, it was chiefly Cin-tia, who, probably with Giacomo's connivance, worked her charm on Lelio to bind him to her in tight alliance, weaning him from any lingering loyalty to his patroness, Felice. The lovers drew Lelio into Cintia's household. He came at any hour, even in the middle of the night.[37] He had easy access to household goods. As Cintia said, "He put his hands in my papers and my property, whatever he wanted. He kept his laundry there, and his shirts, and took them when he wanted."[38]

The tale of Lelio's courtship is hard to reconstruct. When mat-ters came to court, the magistrates grilled the rectangle's two fe-male corners, Felice and Cintia. But the males eluded interview, and, of the females, the first knew little of the tale and the second adamantly refused to tell it. Our best evidence comes from six let-ters impounded by the magistrates, much cited and queried in the trial and still bound with the archived interrogations:

1. From Cintia to Lelio, in her own hand, 24 June 1581
2. From Cintia to Lelio, in her brother Domenico's hand, 11 September 1581
3. From Lelio to Cintia, undated but probably shortly before
4. From Lelio to Felice, 17 June 1582
5. From Lelio to Giacomo, undated but after letter 4, before letter 6, presumably June 1582
6. From Mario Orsini to the magistrates, 1 September 1582

As letters often are, these missives can be opaque; intended for private eyes, they allude to privy matters hard to parse today. Moreover, all but letter 6 are conspiratorial; they take prudent ref-uge in veiled language. Nonetheless, reading carefully, we can tease out the profile of Lelio's turbulent courtship and its final failure.

For all their protestations of love, these letters almost always use the formal second-person pronoun (usually *lei,* sometimes *voi*) and almost never the affectionate, intimate *tu.* Accordingly, my transla-tion renders the pronoun as "You," not "you." Letter 5, however, at a crucial moment, slips down to a telling *tu.*

Letter 1: Cintia, in Rome, to Lelio, not in Rome, 24 June 1581, in her own hand

My Most Esteemed Magnificent Signore,

I would never have believed that You would have come to feel that the signore cavaliere and I loved You so little as You write we do. It is certainly utterly the contrary to what You think. I don't take it well that Your Lordship tells us to have patience, because it is best to say it to us [face-to-face?]. Your Lordship tells us not to worry about seeing [?] the letters that are coming from Forlì, and I tell You that we have not had an answer to those [letters] my Giacomo has written to those signori, and we are very troubled in mind. And Your Lordship does not have to tell us that Signora Ginevra is in Bologna, for a kinsman of hers says so. Ah, my Giacomo, it is not for this reason that my Signore Lelio gets all angry and says that he really knows how to manage things, for he is guilty of every wrong in the world if he reproaches us, for we want nothing other than that this thing be carried off. Your Lordship says that [keeping quiet? one smudged word in the manuscript] will have been a good thing when this thing has been brought to execution, that we have held fast to what many times we had said. I tell You that this is not a reason to get angry or upset, for I assure You for certain as a Christian that if ever there have been good thoughts on it [i.e., we have felt optimistic about it], it is now. But, my Signor Lelio, I pray You not to desire like this to come to Rome until my Giacomo has sent off the signori—his sons. Then some day You can come to Rome, as is the wish of my Giacomo. You will do me the favor of kissing Signor Giovanni's hand. With all my heart I send my best wishes with all those of the house. In Rome, 24 June 1581.

Your most devoted servant,
Affectionate like a sister,
C.A.T. [i.e., Cintia Antelma Teodoli] [39]

Much here is unclear to us: a Signora Ginevra and her trip to Bologna; a Signore Giovanni whose hand deserves a respectful kiss; the letters from Forlì. None of these fall into place. What does come clear is that Lelio is party to some momentous project with Giacomo about which Cintia is coy on paper, and that he is uneasy about its prospects and mistrustful of the couple's commitment to both it and him. He has written as much; Cintia's letter seems to want to steady him, appease his grumblings, and balk his impulse to come to Rome. Cintia, despite her wobbly spelling, seems to have been the whole project's chancellor; the court found in Lelio's papers no letters from Giacomo. Note that Cintia, in signing as "C.A.T.," has, after a mere three months of liaison, annexed Giacomo's final initial to her own; the court itself accepts this cryptic reading.[40] The initials, as statement, are personal and bold. On the other hand, her final salutation, "affectionate like a sister," is the merest epistolary formality. The salutations of her next letter, less than three months later, will take, in both senses, an intriguing turn.

Letter 2: Cintia, in Rome, to Lelio, in Ceciliano, 11 September 1581, in Domenico's hand

Most Esteemed Very Magnificent Signore Brother,

Forever, Your Lordship has shown himself as affectionate as could be and desirous of my every good and honor. And now the time has come to plot by night what one must do by day, and to do for me a thing that is extremely pleasing to me. And if Your Lordship regards me, as You write You do, as a dear—no, rather, a dearest—sister, now the time has come to show me with deeds, and I trust You will not prove wanting. So I pray You and supplicate You with all my heart, for my Giacomo is resolute—no, rather, most resolute—in this affair. It all falls on You because You have the fifty scudi.[41] And You will find me, as Your most affectionate sister, a creature more of deeds than words. And in this I am as sure as sure. From my heart I offer myself to You. Staying with my brother and Felice.[42] From Rome, 11 September 1581.

Your most devoted servant,
Most affectionate sister,
C.A.T.[43]

Lelio should, the letter says, screw his courage to the sticking place. The time has come for deeds, not words. And Lelio has the necessary cash. What deeds? Not clear, but not such as one should put on paper, especially through a scribe, a lad of twelve. Note how Cintia now calls Lelio "brother." This is no longer the clichéd salutation of letter 1. There has been a pact, a formal oath of brother-and-sisterhood. Witnesses in court confirm it, and young Domenico, he will tell the magistrate, has heard the two address one another as siblings.[44] In court Cintia falsely places their kinship pact in the summer of 1582; this letter pushes the date back almost a whole year earlier.[45]

One of the couple's goals was to latch Lelio to the marriage plot. The letters relay glimpses of the cajolery, imprecations, and veiled threats that bound him to the scheme. They bore fruit, for, seven months after Cintia's second letter, the promise paper and its oaths reaffirmed and anchored his support: "Signor Lelio Perleoni, who will sign the present document and will obligate himself to maintain the said matrimony, both for the said Signora Cintia as well as for me, Giacomo." But what did such maintenance entail, and why would last September's fifty gold scudi help Lelio lend a hand? Why had Giacomo and Cintia expended so much effort to court Lelio? Why the rectangle at all?

Sometime in 1582, in the two months between 18 April (the pact) and 17 June (letter 4), a violent quarrel snapped whatever bonds of real or feigned emotions—affection, gratitude, obligation, need, or fear—that had kept Lelio loyal to the lovers' marriage plot. There was a *costione;* the Italian word for quarrel denotes not just words but blows, and the next letters, all Lelio's, suggest a harrowing fray and a trail of dread. All four fighters were from the Romagna: on the one side was Nicolo Castelli from Faenza and, notably, Georgio Teodoli. On the other was Lelio himself and Ottaviano Maldenti, Felice's brother.[46] Scooting for safety into the palace of Cardinal de' Medici, Lelio then turned his coat, but not both sleeves at once. He dashed off three letters that, in the end, blew the lovers' scheme to bits. First came an appeal to Cintia.

Letter 3: Lelio to Cintia, undated but probably early June 1582

Illustrious Honored Sister,

I believe I have the safe-conduct for certain. It is true I wanted to have the dagger. Now it is not needed; the Lord be praised, there is no call to take up arms, both among friends and for the patron. Talking with Domenico, he told me a world of things, offering me in the name of Your Lordship and of the cavaliere not only goods but life [i.e., offering loyal support] and saying that You love me more than you love any other person. Now, I will see. Your Ladyship knows that often You have told me to be careful, for they want to kill me, and that I should bring his servants with me. But now I will see if You love me and if You will love me as You say. See to it that the signor cavaliere will make me a pledge the way they did. He has told You that he wants to kill me and put it in writing and signed it, and because I don't want to put this in writing unless it becomes necessary. And if he loves me as cordially as he says, I will see, for I don't want to be the one who is just, and I promise him I do not want to put myself in jail— except in some way I cannot say—and if he wants to trouble me, I could show the pledge. If not [i.e., if I have no pledge from him], I will believe as I think fit, and I know that if You wish to have things otherwise, I am forced to look out for myself, in whatever way will be possible. I will see how much You have loved me and love me now. I await a reply and I await the dagger with the pledge of the signor cavaliere.

Your most devoted servant,

Most beloved brother if You want me to be that now. I will see and if You hold my life dear, and Your own, with shared love, and I will be disabused about those things that have been told to me, if I am not forced to believe them.[47]

When Lelio dashed this letter off, the break with Giacomo was not yet final. Still, the defiant bluster suggests faint hope of reconciliation. Nor, given his language with Cintia—note his veiled threat to her life in the final salutation—did he expect much help from her. Although sheltered in Cardinal de' Medici's palace, Lelio seems to have felt his life at risk. He bids for tokens of reassurance. In an age when all men carried knives to carve their meat, the dagger from Giacomo, like the pledge, would have been primarily a sign and only secondarily a tool or weapon. Whether or not the oaths and items in fact arrived, the lovers neither soothed nor appeased Lelio. So, very soon, he swung to slash the last shreds of his alliance. As for the matter of the desired safe-conduct, it will soon come clearer.

Letter 4: Lelio to Felice Maldenti, 17 June 1582

Most Illustrious Signora and my esteemed patroness,

I am sending Your Most Illustrious Ladyship the two documents via Signor Mario [Orsini]. You will do me the favor of carrying my strongbox, which is in my bedroom, into Your Ladyship's little chamber. And make sure that nobody looks inside. The cavaliere had come to me and insisted I give him the documents. I told him that when things are done as they should be done, I will not be found wanting in my duty. He said that he will bring me the whore [*la puttana*] this evening; I think it is for this reason. I kiss Your hand with all reverence. With his Illustrious Lordship, 17 June 1582,

Your most devoted servant,
Most Illustrious Signore [?]
Lelio Perleoni

[On the cover:] To the Most Illustrious Signora, my patroness, the Most Illustrious Signora Felice Maldenti[48]

Here, Lelio seems still to expect a paper, perhaps one of the written marriage promises, from Cintia. Giacomo, meanwhile, wants his back from Lelio. The couple are coming over to parley about who holds the papers. Mistrust is rife, and Lelio, writing *puttana*, has turned his back on Cintia. Felice, meanwhile, has seemingly learned of the promise papers by now. Only with this letter of Lelio's, however, does she learn to mind Lelio's strongbox. She does not yet know why.

Letter 5: Lelio to Giacomo, after letter 4, before letter 6, presumably June 1582

Most Illustrious Cavaliere,

Having heard that Your Lordship is acting against me concerning Rocha's death,[49] and having confided this with none other than Your Lordship and with Signora Cintia, I am quit of the obligation I made to You most recently at the house of the Most Illustrious [Cardinal de'] Medici. I have written a letter to the most illustrious Signor Mario [Orsini] that he should enter my house [i.e., "my quarters"], for he will find a bottle of poison with certain powders, also poison. And I have sent him the [marriage-promise?] documents. For I am going to go against You and against what You are trying to do to me. And, furthermore, I am writing him about who was in on the intrigues about this poison. And I hope that the Most Illustrious Cardinal de' Medici will do the favor, by means of the Most Illustrious Signor Mario, so that I can have a safe-conduct to be able to go to the feet of His Holiness. And I will tell the matter and I will have the sample [*paranghone:* the poison?] fetched out to show how to proceed [in court?]. Since You are trying to assassinate me, I want to assassinate You with all those who have consented, and in particular Cintia, traitress, assassin—I don't know what other name to give her. These are the promises made to me. But enough. All turns [?] on who is the traitor and who has consented that I be betrayed in a matter of faith. You have done to me what I should have done to you [*te*]. I am not dead and the time has come that I pay you [*te*] back in kind.

Lelio Perleoni[50]

THE LADY LIVES, THE PIGEON DIES · 185

By this letter, Lelio declares war on Giacomo. He has already taken devastating steps and here, in writing, lashes out, less in hope of gain than for the pleasure of inflicting pain and terror. Note, at the letter's end, his shift of pronouns from the respectful "You" to the here not fond but sneering "you" *(te)*.

Letter 6: Mario Orsini to the magistrates, 1 September 1582

I, Mario Orsini, attest how, when I was in the house of Cardinal de' Medici, where there was Messer Lelio Perleoni from Rimini, the said Messer Lelio took from his tunic two documents—one of which contained matters about marriage with a whore and another of which had other things—that, were I to see them again, I would recognize. He asked me to give the said documents into the hand of Signora Felice Maldenti Teodoli, as I did. Furthermore, Messer Lelio having written that one should take a strongbox of his from his bedroom and put it in a secret place in her rooms, she began to suspect she would find there something of moment. Wanting to see, she called me and had it opened. And there we found, wrapped in a pouch, a bottle that was almost full of a water that seemed ordinary, and in a packet she found a certain white powder that had a smell. The signora took these things, and this being the truth and having been requested, I have made the present attestation by my own hand this first of September 1582, at home.

Mario Orsini[51]

If this last letter is exact, Lelio's note to Felice was not enough. It took Mario's arrival and further papers to persuade Felice to pry open the mysterious box. Felice's own spoken account of what happened next is more vivid than Orsini's careful legal note:

"He [Lelio] wrote me a letter where he insisted strongly that I have a strongbox of his fetched—it was in his room, here in my house—and that I have it taken to the most secret room I had. And he wrote that I have it done in such a way that no one look

inside his strongbox; it was locked and the key was with him. So I
had that strongbox brought into my little room where I do my
hair. But, reading the letter over, I became suspicious, but for the
moment I did not say a thing. And two days later, more or less,
Signor Mario Orsini, my son-in-law, brought me another paper,
sent me by the said Messer Lelio. In it was the promise of marriage between Cavaliere Giacomo Teodoli, then my husband, and
a woman called Cintia Antelma. And Signor Mario asked me,
'What do You think of the paper I brought You?' I told him that
Lelio had written me another letter, in which he told me to keep
the said strongbox. So both of us grew suspicious, and we decided
to open the strongbox to see what was there. And having opened
it with a knife, we found a little pouch full of spools of sewing
thread, and inside one ball of thread there was a little glass bottle,
longish, and almost full; it was missing only a drop [?], with a
clear fluid, tied and stoppered at the top, and when you sniffed it,
it had no smell at all. And in the strongbox, in another corner, we
found a handkerchief, inside of which there was a certain white
powder in a packet. It had a rather nice smell; that is, the paper
smelled because in the handkerchief there were also two pellets of
musk. We took the powder and the bottle—that is, I did, and
Mario—and we put them in a midsized box. And this powder and
fluid—if I saw them I would recognize them."

[The court showed the witness the exhibits.]

"I see this bottle with the fluid in it that you are showing me,
which is the very same, along with this powder that we took from
the strongbox, but it is true that the fluid was a fair bit more than
now; maybe it has been spilled and thrown away. That powder
and fluid—I don't know what sort they are." Adding on her own:
"I can tell you though that afterward in that strongbox I found
yet another paper with a certain black powder inside. I thought it
was gunpowder. Then, having tested it and found that it was not
gunpowder, I gave some of it to eat to a big cat and a little kitten.
The little one died and the big did not."

I, the notary, accepted from the said strongbox a certain black
powder wrapped in paper and likewise another powder, gray,
wrapped in another paper packet, and I kept all these things
with me.[52]

At this point, we can step back a bit to reflect on the political logic of the fatal rectangle of men and women. Cintia and Giacomo, clearly, had courted Lelio to second their cruel design. But many questions linger. Were the fifty scudi for poison? Surely, effective poisons could be bought for less! Did Lelio's signature on the April marriage pact entangle him in a poison plot? If not, why was his signature desired? Did Cintia's old September epistolary evocation of things best schemed at night refer to murder or to deeds less dire? No clarity here, but much shadowy intimation of the outlines of the plot. Also less than crystalline is Lelio's material stake. Were Cintia's and Giacomo's blandishments and imprecations motive enough, or did he expect a payoff? Most likely the latter, but whatever it was, it could not guarantee his loyalty after his quarrel, rage, and fright. One big mystery: why need Lelio's hand at all? Could Giacomo not bring himself to kill his wife? Was he squeamish, or she mistrustful? Was he simply seldom home?

Between the collapse of the conspiracy in June and the resolution of the trial, much time passed. Only on 27 September did Felice at last testify and hand over to the court the second and third powders, gray and black.[53] Nevertheless, in the three months and more since mid-June, much had transpired. Before June's end, the authorities had arrested Cintia and searched her house, seizing a copy of the marriage promise and other suspect papers.[54] They also carried off assorted little bottles; Cintia, on trial, would profess that these held innocent waters for cleaning teeth and settling her tummy.[55] The court had also sequestered papers in Lelio's possession, among them another copy of the marriage promise.[56] Lelio himself, however, slipped their grasp; the trial lacks any sign of his ever having testified. Had he done so, the judges would have been quick to cite his evidence, just as they cited and expounded all they knew in a vain effort to pry Cintia from her obdurate denials. Giacomo too escaped the law. He died. We know neither how nor when, but surely not at the hands of justice, for he too never testified. Lelio, however, got away with body and soul still well soldered.[57] Most likely, as he had hoped, with the cardinal's help he cashed in a safe-conduct and decamped in prudent haste.

For reasons quite unclear, having arrested Cintia in June, the court then let her go, after proceedings of which we have no paper trace. It rearrested her in September, the sole remaining culprit, and tried her. It interviewed her young brother and, to verify his handwriting, made him copy onto the court scribe's pages both passages from Cintia's letter of 11 September 1581 and his sister's name as she had signed it on the marriage pact. Domenico's neat lettering on the transcript apes well the passages penned for Cintia. The court also heard Felice's maid, who had helped open Lelio's strongbox. It took careful depositions from assorted witnesses to the handwriting of the men: a physician, a veteran Teodoli servant, and a banker's son. And it grilled Cintia, who stonewalled to the end. On 19 September, she knew nothing. On 16 October, confronted with detailed evidence from letters and testimony, she knew even less. On 20 October, she remained obdurate. Nevertheless, at the end of that third hearing, the court, deciding it had a case, released her from solitary confinement and placed her, as usual at an investigation's end, in the common quarters of Tor di Nona jail, with five days for readying her defense. Oddly, although Cintia admitted nothing, the court never tortured her.

Why not? Hardly out of gallantry or mercy; Roman courts tortured women without compunction.[58] Rather, despite the paucity of witnesses, the magistrates must have thought they could forgo the usual confession so beloved of Romanized legal practice. They relied instead on their careful judicial empiricism, especially their use of expert witnesses to verify six of the seven incriminating documents (all but Orsini's letter to the court). But their forensic expertise went further. Note the following extract from the papers of the trial. It is in the hand of Giacobo Schala, the court's notary.

1 October 1582

The Magnificent Messer Vittorio, *luogotenente* [a judge], etc., sent the aforesaid bottle in which there was a certain white, clear fluid, and there were the aforesaid white powder in a certain packet and another powder, like the above, which seemed to be of a gray color and was like ashes, and likewise another powder in another packet, which powders and fluid were given, handed over, inspected, and considered by the Magnificent Messer Physician Messer Gismondo Brumano, the physician of the Tor di Nona prison, to the effect that he learn their danger and better and

more expeditiously, and that he make an experiment
[*experimentum*] to see if the said fluid and powders be poison,
and poisoned, and, in sum, whether any of them were poisonous.
Present: Signor Giorgio Faberio, substitute *fiscale* [a prosecutor],
and myself, the notary, etc. And so the powders and fluid were
handed over and given, in the presence of myself the notary
and the said substitute *fiscale,* into the hands of the said Messer
Gismondo the physician, etc., which the Magnificent Messer
Physician ordained, did, and ordered done as follows:

He took three live baby pigeons, without any imperfection
[*macula*]. First he took part of the said black powder and mixed it
with part of the said fluid and gave it to one of the said baby pigeons. It, having taken the said fluid and powder, was not affected
at all but always stayed in its pristine state and had no harm. Second, he took part of the said fluid and mixed with it part of the
gray powder and at once gave it to another of the said baby pigeons. When it took the said fluid and powder mixed together, at
once it almost died, and then it turned, first to one side, then to
the other. In my presence, this pigeon was opened, and its heart
was found to be swollen [*tumidum*] and almost burnt up [*adustum*],
and its tissues were fragile [*fragiles*] and its color had turned livid
[*lividum*]. Third, he took part of the said fluid and mixed in another part of the white powder, which mixture he gave to the
third said baby pigeon, who, having taken the said fluid and powder, stood for a quarter of an hour and seemed to have no hurt.
Then he began to be anxious [*anxiosum*] and to become more and
more sluggish [*oscitare*] and to foam around the beak and to droop
his wings, and in the end he escaped [*evasit,* as in "recovered"] and
had no harm. Having considered all these things perfectly, he
came to this conclusion [*sententiam*]: that the black powder is not
poison, the white has some poisonous qualities but cannot kill
unless given in a certain quantity that I cannot judge, because I
do not recognize the powder itself. The third powder, however,
which is gray, manifestly appears that it is poison, for it was given
in a small quantity and it killed the baby pigeon to which it was
given.

All of this the aforesaid messer physician reported and deposed, with his oath.[59]

Here we have an actual lab report, one of the earlier in medical history to have survived. What does this document teach us about science and about law? And how does it fit into the history of evolving medical and experimental practices? To make sense of this curious text and the set of procedures it documents, it pays to attend carefully to its precise authorship, form, rhetoric, and purposes, for in significant ways this text, despite echoes of current practice, is quite unlike the lab reports written today. A modern scientist or, not rarely, a fat posse of coauthors writes an account of procedures run using excruciatingly dead-pan prose and countless passive verbs, as if to efface all traces of the experimenters' human presence. The experiment, under present rhetorical conventions, should speak for itself, loud and clear.

Not so in 1582; there, the presence of the authors, and of other persons too, is crucial to a validation at once legal and medical. They must be seen. In the pigeon report there are two voices, both first-person singular, one for the law, one for medicine: the notary's and the physician's. In the text, their boundary blurs. But it is the notary who furnishes the literary and procedural frame. Note how his frame, deeply notarial in its conventions, takes pains to lay out, as notarial papers always should, date, persons present, the issue at stake, and facts at hand. The report thus begins, not with biology at all, but law: Messer Vittorio, the presiding judge, sent over the suspicious contents, duly catalogued and described, transferring them to the physician of the jail, whose name the notary writes down, so that the physician might make an *experimentum* for a purpose carefully recorded. The notary thus notes the presence of the substitute prosecutor, Giorgio Faberio, and of himself, both witnesses not yet to the experiment but merely to the transfer of the suspect materials "into the hands" of the physician, Brumano. The document girds itself here, not against skeptical physicians who might query the results on grounds of science, but against any defense counsel who might query what substances were really ever fed to birds. Then, the prosecutor having stepped aside, the notary, with his "as follows," moves to the test itself.

When it turns to the procedure administered, the document mixes notarial and scientific diction. In the notary's voice, not in the modern passive, but in the active, it begins by describing Brumano's acts: "he took" part of the powder; "he gave it" to a baby pigeon. And then, as the pigeons react, the verbs, still third-person active, move to the birds, one by one: "it always stayed"; "it had no harm"; "it almost died." And then, finally, some passives: "in my presence this pigeon was opened"; "its heart was found. . . ." Having given up the ghost, poor pigeon number two was no longer in any state to sustain active verbs. And in whose presence was the opening? For the record, not Brumano's, but the notary's. Then the document returns to active verbs, some for the physician, some for the final bird, down through the third test and into the diagnosis, which, though the physician's, remains in the notary's voice: "Having considered all these things perfectly, he came to this conclusion." And then, suddenly, Messer Brumano seems to break through: "but cannot kill unless given in a certain quantity that I cannot judge because I do not recognize the powder itself." His expert voice, if his it is, is soon effaced with the notarial conclusion: "All of this the aforesaid physician reported and deposed, with his oath."

The document, thus, had a double voice and game, at once medical and legal.[60] Its purpose was both to establish a fact—poison—and to validate not just the fact itself but a meta-fact (a fact about the fact) as well: the legal-medical procedure used. Accordingly, it offers up a nested set of witnesses, all of whom it cites in its quest for legal weight, to Cintia Antelma's judicial detriment. These witnesses are, first of all, the judge, the prosecutor, and the notary himself, and then the physician, and finally the three poor baby birds. As I have argued elsewhere, early modern Italian proof required stake.[61] In this document, the three court officials had at stake their prestige of office. Brumano, the physician, staked his professional reputation; Italian forensic doctors, unlike their premodern English counterparts, enjoyed prestige and perquisites.[62] Gismondo Brumano was no jailhouse flunky; son of a wellborn Cremona family, he had studied at Padua and since 1567 had practiced in Rome as a member of the physicians' guild. He published three treatises, among them one on theriac, the standard antidote to poison. At the end of Brumano's life, Clement VIII would appoint him *archiater,* chief papal physician; he would be, says a biographer, the pope's doctor, friend, and constant table companion.[63] Like the other functionaries, therefore, Brumano could stake his solid reputation to the truth. The men staked as well the reputa-

tions of their institutions and professions, evoked by the ritual
forms and formulae of legal and medical procedure. The pigeons,
lacking speech and reputation, unwittingly staked their bodies.
Their sacrifices had real weight. It may be no cultural accident that
early modern Italians, who so often linked truth to risk and suffering, built their anatomical science on the corpses of paupers
and criminals and, rarely, on their living bodies[64] and on heca-
tombs of suffering pigs, dogs, apes, and other beasts, some cut
while still alive.[65] But we should not push the parallel too far; the
human victim of judicial torture gained credit because, as theory
went, memory or fear of pain urged truthfulness. Animals, however, bore witness just with bodies, not with minds; their testimony lacked all speech, wit, and motive. Pain therefore was, by
logic if not by habit, only accidental to their veracity.[66]

It is worth noting one absent, and ultimate, authority—the
usual *auctores:* Hippocrates, Galen, Theophrastus, Rhases, Avi-
cenna, Averroës, and all the others, ancient or medieval, whose
doctrines inform, validate, and pad almost any work on poison,
from Ardoino in the fifteenth century across Cardano, Paré, and
Mercuriale in the sixteenth to Zacchia in the seventeenth.[67] Why
are they not needed here? Perhaps because, this time, Brumano's
diagnosis is at once firm and incomplete. A more daring report,
hoping to identify the poison, might nervously have shipped authorities on board for ballast.[68] Authorities, in general, were necessary to establish or instantiate general laws and arcane truths.[69]
But Brumano and the notary were after, not a law of nature or a
mystery, but a simple fact: guilt. Thus, they needed to do low-
order induction, a three-step test, to instantiate a mere particular:
these things are noxious. In such matters, authorities, though
helpful, were less pertinent.

Several forensic traditions of rhetoric and practice, some venerable, others novel, mingled in the report on Brumano's *experimentum.* Forensic medicine itself was already very old; it surfaces
in thirteenth-century Bologna statutes and in reports of early-
fourteenth-century physicians' visits, on a court's behalf, to patients and to corpses.[70] By no great chance, the oldest documented
visit, from Bologna in 1302, is a poison case.[71] Fairly quickly, the
Romanizing Italian law of the later Middle Ages devised theory
and practices for the expert witness, the *peritus,* a subject strikingly

little codified in ancient Roman jurisprudence.[72] As doctrine evolved, so did the genre of forensic testimony. There were several usual modes. Sometimes the report of the medical expert just bore witness. At other times, however, surgeons, physicians, and notaries trooped off together, perhaps in groups of four or five, to visit patients and the suspect dead; by the bedside or the sometimes-opened corpse, the experts testified while the notary recorded.[73] Or physicians and surgeons came before a notary and, often, a judge and spoke or answered questions and then swore to veracity, while the notary took down or summarized their depositions and oaths.[74] The police reports and judicial papers of sixteenth-century Rome are full of such accounts, most often of contusions or gaping wounds and of limbs snapped in brawls. There are some poison cases; in these, in general, experts inspected fresh or exhumed corpses, not dubious substances. See, for instance, the examination of Vittoria Giustini's corpse. Our report, in contrast, in describing a methodical test, has a different structure and rhetoric. What are its models? How much, for instance, do its form and tone owe to the recording habits of the anatomists who, in antiquity, the Middle Ages, and the Renaissance, dismantled animals in the name of science? As for the pigeon test itself, as long as there had been cats and dogs around the house, anxious denizens, when leery of the food, had tested it on them, just as Felice Maldenti tried her powder on her hapless cat and kitten. To slake their curiosity about poisons' workings, scientists had done likewise; learned Sante Ardoino slipped sublimate of mercury to his monkey and recorded its agonized contortions.

> I also gave an ape that I had [some sublimate of mercury] to drink, and it had no other effect except what I have said [of human consequences], for it was tormented and often bit its belly and pulled at it with its hands.[75]

As for Brumano's summary of what he found inside the dissected pigeon, it also echoed the language of human autopsy reports. Thus, our physician's tests and their report may mingle the techniques and expository habits of the dissecting room, folk empiricism, medical experimentation, legal autopsy, and—as mental frame—notarial verification.

What makes Brumano's and Schala's test report seem so modern is its air of method: three powders, three birds, three outcomes, a dissection, and a diagnosis, albeit in the combustion language of the humor theory of the day.[76] It looks almost publishable, though a modern editor would object: no double- or single-blinding and no cautious separation of the fluid from the powders, the latter an elementary precaution against contamination's ambiguities. It was not so much modern scientific practice as several flukes of fact that shaped the experiment. Brumano inspected not the corpse of Felice, luckily forewarned, but a rarity, the suspected poison, still unused. And he had not one substance to deal with but three (plus fluid), requiring three young birds. Nevertheless, he could have run the tests in his privy study and then testified in court; we owe it to the court's characteristic Roman-legal scrupulosity with the powders that, from start to finish, the notary kept them and their appointed custodians company and made his record of procedures and their outcomes.

A few years after the Teodoli affair, a physician, Giovanni Battista Codronchi, wrote a booklet, *Methodus testificandi,* laying out a model for reports to courts.[77] Imitating the French surgeon Ambroise Paré, at the work's end he offers several exemplary diagnoses. In important ways, in their rhetorical and dialectical strategies, these set pieces are strikingly different from the notary's rendition of Brumano's tests on pigeons. For instance:

> May God be my help.
> In the case of a violent and premature emission of the fetus, women are more in danger and have greater inconvenience and trouble than in a right and natural birth, as Hippocrates and experience teach. For which reason, in cases of miscarriage, imprisonment is more likely to be questioned than in cases of birth. Thus, since D.M., whom I visited in the prison fifteen days ago, had, as she told me, brought forth a third-trimester fetus and was therefore purging [her reproductive tract] to ill effect and in too great quantity and was tormented by periodic uterine pains, and certain black marks emerged all over her skin, and then she became delirious and often suffered no light fever, as she told me, it is manifest that if she is kept in custody she will not be able to be cured of these symptoms, and she runs the risk of becoming

worse. These things, truths rendered clear by [medical] art, upon request I have put in writing and signed, and I have desired them to be subjected to the judgment of those more expert than I.

Imola, on the day etc.

I, Battista Codronchi[78]

First of all, note the careful scholastic form. Having invoked God's grace, Codronchi begins with major medical premises. First comes a universal statement about pregnancies, perched on the canonical twin pillars of the ancients and experience. He then adds another premise, based on the first, in the form of a universal rule, this time legal, about letting certain female patients out of jail. Second, he lays out the particulars—his own findings—and distinguishes the patient's hearsay from observation. In third position comes his *sententia:* let this particular woman out lest worse occur. In fourth position comes an invocation of his science, and in fifth, mention of his writing and signing the report. Sixth is a gesture of submission to the judgment of those more expert than he. And then, seventh, he furnishes town, date, and signature. The very form itself, the Aristotelian good deductive order, legitimizes the report. Note, also, the many authorities invoked: God, Hippocrates, "experience," medical art, the potential judgment of greater experts. And observe the gestures of submission that, paradoxically, bolster, not undercut, the claim to trust. Codronchi is in the hands of God and the medical profession. His humility, by the logic of the times, should enhance our confidence. Like the signature, the diagnosis could be contested, and so, one wagers, both should be true; the author has put his identity and his judgment on the line.

The chief difference between Brumano's and Schala's exposition on the one hand and Codronchi's on the other, what marks the pigeon report off, is its stress on the steps taken. The scrupulosity about things done is more legal than medical. Where Codronchi takes his authority from scholastic form, ancient precedents, and guarantors, the court notary, by contrast, takes his from the proprieties of law. Judicial and notarial practice privileged sight, and anchored its truth claims, when possible, in recording that the eyes' act had itself been seen and written down. Notary Schala has seen everything: the transfers of the powders, the medical tests, the diagnosis. His presence strips the narrative bare of scholasticism, for it spares Brumano most of Codronchi's strenuous ploys for credit.

All this discussion on the implicit politics of medico-legal texts brings back to mind the plotters' own letters. Renaissance written texts differed from speech. As always, distance—the absence of sight, sound, and touch—changed communication's rules and needs. Lacking voice and gesture, the letter writer, just like the diagnostic expert, needs help to make a case. Remember Cintia's epistle of 11 September, by Domenico's hand. She needs to convince Lelio of her resolve and zeal.

> And if Your Lordship regards me, as You write You do, as a
> dear—no, rather, a dearest—sister, now the time has come to
> show me with deeds, and I trust You will not prove wanting. So I
> pray You and supplicate You with all my heart, for my Giacomo is
> resolute—no, rather, most resolute—in this affair. It all falls on
> You because You have the fifty scudi. And You will find me, as
> Your most affectionate sister, a creature more of deeds than
> words. And in this I am as sure as sure. From my heart I offer
> myself to You.

Unlike Codronchi, to anchor truth Cintia has no Hippocrates, so she invokes the veracity of her ardent heart. She has no putative committee of experts, so she proffers as authorities her own resolve and trust, plus Giacomo's determination. Like Codronchi, she prays and surrenders the very self, in her case not to God but to Lelio. The parallels are striking. But there are differences; Codronchi's insecurity derives from the imperfections of the medicine of his day; his protestations of dependency are formulaic and mild. Cintia, by contrast, must do battle with the dangers, fragility, and patent evil of the poison plot. The stakes and risks, so much higher, hoist her epistolary voice to a shriller pitch. The uneasier the trust, the more hostages it took. In the long run, neither Cintia nor Giacomo could proffer enough to keep Lelio's trust in line.

If our themes are love and death, why, so far, has love had such short shrift? None of our loves have been happy, unshadowed by fear, grief, guile, or malice. The warmest loves have been female: the lute maker's daughters' for their declining mother, Silvia Giustini's for her dying sister, the village women's for dead Vittoria Savelli. Death and loss coaxed out love's voice, at least among the women. From males, meanwhile, we have heard little except the beadle's whimpering refrain and Pallantieri's nauseating blandishments. In the pigeon story, Giacomo, the plotting husband, is almost mute; the most passion we see is Cintia Antelma's, directed not at her lover but at wobbly Lelio.

To give this book a proper ending, we need something sunnier. Or at least a little less dank and murky. So, here, in the tale of Innocentia, we have a happy ending. Of sorts. But, like an old Italian street, my ways and love's are uneven, strait, and beset with sudden twists inviting ambush. So we cannot have our happy love without a dash of irony and pain and without the ambiguity that gives a story sauce and bite.

For symmetry's sake, I start the book's end where I started the beginning. Back in bed. And once more I first take you there and then cruelly make you wait, far too long, while I rummage in my documents to lay out how we all arrived between the sheets. Forgive me, curse me, but in no case skip ahead and spoil the story.

Once more, my theme is textuality. Art. But this time, not all ruminating on textuality and all attempted art are mine: central to what follows is a lover's poetry. It is bad poetry, all thumbs, clichéd, and badly scanned, fitting company for my own counterfeit high literature. Poetry in this tale is not only expressive but instrumental. To see how a lover wields it and how his beloved, like an adept skirmisher, then disarms him and turns it handily against him, follow their plots, and mine.

Chapter 6

THREE IN A BED

The Seduction of Innocentia

THE BED HAD ROOM FOR THREE.[1] ON ONE
side lay Francesca, a governess no longer young.[2] On the other lay
her charge, Innocentia, a young woman of the house, perhaps a
little innocent but old enough to marry. Summoned by the servant, Innocentia had come last to bed. She still wore her shift.
"Take off your shift! The fleas are eating me!"[3] It was the older
woman who spoke and the girl who with some reluctance let the
servant, naked herself, rise up and strip her to the skin.[4] Both lay
down again. But not alone. In the middle of the bed lay Francesca's
ex-nursling, Vespasiano, no longer babe at breast but an archivist
attached to city hall. Full grown, he had other things in mind than
filing papers at the Campidoglio.

Thus begins a tale. Although a tease, I will finally let you see
its end.

But, first, some questions. What is this story's nature and to
what end the telling? As recounted tale, what follows, in subject
and in plot, echoes the Renaissance *novella*. Though actual history,
its events are the novellista's favorite subjects: love, seduction, sly
plots, and barefaced trickery. As with many *novelle,* we are in the
private sphere, in the family, indoors, and, as often, under a blan-

ket. As always, stories about the minor doings of forgotten folk,
when rich in detail, are precious for what they show about the con-
tours of agency: the liberties and constraints of persons usually invisible. For some three decades, such claims have made microhistory's first-ditch defense.[5] I will dig further trench lines and argue,
once my tale is told, that for stories as wry as what I tell here, some
key themes of Pierre Bourdieu's sociology help make sense of all
the ironies.

In what follows, the irony is not, I maintain, only in the lively
telling but also in the events themselves. Some historians would
object. In his trenchant review of Gene Brucker's *Giovanni and Lusanna,* Thomas Kuehn argued adamantly that we historians can
never retrieve the social story from trial documents, for we are
prisoners of our witnesses, who themselves were deeply enmeshed
in the rhetoric and strategies of judicial proceedings.[6] The narrative line, he argues, is merely modern afterthought, and any irony
or other shade or shape is ours only, not anchored in the past. The
best reply to Kuehn and to other, different critics—postmod-
ernists who insist that text is all we readers ever have—is to exalt
triangulation: give us historians witnesses enough to match and
test and we can penetrate the veil of text to discern some semblance of the facts behind it.[7] But, in what follows, we have only
three witnesses, each with a big ax to grind. So our "true" *novella*
will require some sleuthing and, perhaps, some forking paths that
leave its social history in the zone of "maybe." At times, the reader
will choose the plot.

Now, back to bed. What happened next was morally opaque
and raw . . .

But, first, note the paths and plots that brought six legs between
one pair of sheets. Bedtime was late one Saturday evening in early
November 1569, two flights up in a Roman house near Sant'Ivo,
not yet Borromini's gem but already the university chapel. The
house belonged to Giovanni Battista Bucchi, descendant, probably, of a noble Bolognese family.[8] He was Innocentia's stepfather;
the girl, her younger sister, and a seven-year-old boy, Luisso, were
orphans, for their mother, Isabella, had died last January.[9]
Francesca, the governess, already in the mother's service, had
stayed on to oversee the youngsters.[10]

It had been with Francesca's help that Vespasiano came to find himself between two sheets and two naked women, one his former wet nurse, the other his quarry, his beloved, and, perhaps, his half-witting partner in this love intrigue. Their three convergent trails to bed looped and twisted. Like Francesca, the young man came from Poggio Mirteto, on the fertile lower slopes of the Sabine mountains, above the upstream Tiber. We do not know his family's means or station, but at least the lad knew Latin. Vespasiano had entered Rome almost three years back, in the spring of 1566. He had lodged with assorted officials, among them the city's archivist. Moreover, he had attended university lectures.[11] A chance street meeting brought him to Innocentia's house. One day, he and Francesca crossed paths. He did not recognize her at all, but, knowing at once her *paesano* milk-son, she invited him to visit. It was in midspring 1569, just two months or so after Francesca had taken on full-time care of the youngsters.[12] Once home, the woman pressed a drink on Vespasiano. He then spied a dress lying on a trunk. It was the elder daughter's, Francesca said.[13] This small beginning stuck in memory. Vespasiano kept up his visits, but six months would pass before he first saw the dress's owner. When he found her, notably for their hearts and fates Innocentia was grappling for a book.[14] He later told the court how he first laid ears and eyes on her:

> I saw Innocentia because she was having a row with a boy named Alessandro, all on account of a book. And they were making a ruckus that kept Francesca and me from talking—we were conversing about the village. And when I heard the shouting I said to Innocentia—she had a book in her hand and I didn't know what book it was and Alessandro wanted it—I told Innocentia to give him the book and that if she did give it to him, I would bring her another one. And she said, "If you are willing to bring it to me, I will give it [this one] to him."[15]

The book in question was *Book of Virgins,* probably a work by the austere Denis the Carthusian, an encomium to female chastity.[16]

Vespasiano kept his word. A week later, Francesca returned from a noble house where she did laundry to find the master in a rage; he had come home aghast at finding Innocentia and the young man downstairs, together, unsupervised. The archivist had brought the monkish book, and pears and autumn chestnuts.[17] To Francesca, Giovanni Battista ordained: from now on, no more laundry jaunts; she should stay home and mind the children.[18] And, furthermore, Innocentia must let no one in. But Francesca, who had a subversive streak, thwarted the house's closure. She had forged a key, to slip in her own male friends at night.[19] For Vespasiano's visits, Innocentia would use it at least once, but the door was risky. The hinge creaked, and Alessandra, the snooping neighbor woman—owl-eared, eagle-eyed—was a tattler.[20] The girl therefore obeyed her stepfather's orders, mostly, but in form, not spirit, for Francesca encouraged Vespasiano to employ an upstairs opening, the window "by the well." He and his new friend, Francesca's son Domenico—Menico for short—readily clambered through. Innocentia used this opening too, even after dark, to visit neighbors.[21]

Innocentia's enthusiasm for a book piqued Vespasiano's curiosity. He later testified:

> Some days later I came back to the house and spoke with Francesca. Among other things, I asked her if the girl could read well. She said yes. And I said in jest, "We would make a good couple." And she said, "This could be brought into discussion and the thing could really work."[22]

So began a Renaissance courtship. As often, it had several objects. Vespasiano had to clinch the girl's heart and assent, to enlist a go-between, and to win the stepfather over. The first two tasks were easy, for the elder woman played Cupid, piloting his campaign to woo both Innocentia and Giovanni Battista. Vespasiano later told the court, "I believe that Francesca told the girl about how I wanted to take her as wife, and from that time on the girl began to fall in love with me and I with her."[23] In all this, the servant's motives are unclear; she had no material stake. Probably, she reveled in plans and plots that, making her important to everybody, gave her leverage. Certainly, she relished connivance; even before Vespasiano came on the scene, the serving woman had taught Innocentia secret chants and charms, magic for luck and love.[24] To Francesca, as to other women servants in *novelle* and the world, machination came easily.[25]

After Vespasiano climbed through the window, he plied Innocentia with poetry. He recited Ariosto and verses of his own—to
good effect; ere long, love was mutual.

Things moved fast. Vespasiano soon turned to Francesca, asking her to speak on his behalf to the stepfather. As she told the
court:

> He asked me to talk to Messer and tell him that he wanted Inno-
> centia as his wife. I told him I did not want to speak to him, but
> he [Vespasiano] asked me so many times that I spoke to Messer
> Giovanni Battista and told him. He told me that he did not wish
> to put faith in women's words and that he wanted him to speak to
> him himself.[26]

Man-to-man, Vespasiano found parley hard. Like any groom, he
wanted a solid dowry. But, like many parents, Giovanni Battista
hoped to unload a daughter on the cheap. And Innocentia, as stepdaughter, was not even really his. Their testy first exchange, behind locked doors, proved inconclusive.[27] Vespasiano later informed the judge:

> He told me, "This is the only [sic] daughter I have, and this is all
> my property. It isn't much. But if you want her, I will give her to
> you with hose and clothing." And he specified a certain amount
> of money—I don't remember well how much. I told him I would
> mull it over.[28]

When Francesca asked her master what had transpired, she heard
that the cash on offer was worth a bride's gowns and stockings and
a furnished room and that the young man was pondering.[29] Love
or no, Vespasiano wanted a better deal. Innocentia, who may have
overheard, also had word straight from her stepfather that he
balked at giving what her suitor asked.[30] A week later, the young
man came back to bid for a better bargain:

> I told him that it did not profit me to take her the way he wanted
> to give me her. He told me, "*Orsù!* I want to content you. If I have
> a leaf of salad, we will divide it between us." This was in the house
> and I think Francesca overheard this conversation.[31]

Innocentia herself also heard this salad colloquy. What did it mean? Giovanni Battista, clearly, signaled willingness to be more generous. But did he make a bid, and did Vespasiano and he agree? Perhaps. But nothing says so for sure.

Four days later, if we can believe the young man's latter, more abject testimony in court, Innocentia took a quick bold step all her own. In it we see no hint of Francesca's hand. Through Menico, the governess's son, the girl summoned Vespasiano back.[32] Let us hear Vespasiano's account:

> I went to Innocentia's with Menico. As soon as I arrived, she said,
> "I have heard that my father is willing to give me to you as a wife.
> But, lest in the future some impediment arise, if you are content,
> I would want no other husband than you. I would very much like
> you to give me your faith." And so I promised, having already had
> the father's promise, to take her as my wife, and I took her hand.[33]

It was by now late October, perhaps early November.

A fine tale, a handsome image of female initiative and bold action against her parent to take her fate in hand! But perhaps no more than that. It serves historians as a fine example of claims about young women that one might make in court—it sketches plausible boundaries of female agency—but that may be all. Why doubt Vespasiano here? Four reasons. For one thing, Innocentia, who detailed scrupulously the dowry parleys, nowhere in her courtroom quest for redress mentioned this betrothal, hardly the sort of thing to slip the mind. Another reason: only Vespasiano brought up this vow. He mentioned it twice, in his evasive first interrogation and then during his abject third interrogation, when as we shall see, he had turned turtle and recanted assorted slanders against the girl. By then, a fictitious betrothal could have served his harried campaign to patch things up with the stepfather. Third, Innocentia herself recounted a very different, far less decorous wedding promise, later, between the sheets. Admittedly, however, such a version would better serve her legal grievance, making her look less complicit and Vespasiano far less couth. And fourth, even prying Francesca, whose courtroom apologia would have profited by the formal betrothal of Vespasiano's tale, cites no such event. Thus, though Vespasiano's account proves that girls might sometimes do such things, Innocentia herself may never have extracted, on her own, a trothplight.

After Giovanni Battista's salad speech, private betrothal or no, Francesca and Vespasiano decided, without consulting Innocentia, that sex's time had come. We can but guess their motives. His love and lust, surely, but perhaps not only. Vespasiano may have wagered that defloration would loosen Giovanni Battista's knotted purse strings by making marriage to a rival slower, harder, and much more costly. Francesca's first loyalty, herself aside, was to neither master nor Bucchi stepchildren but to her old milk-son. Moreover, ab ovo, the marriage plan had been her hatchling. The plot was easy, for Giovanni Battista spent his Saturday nights away from home.[34] So one Saturday early in November, four or five hours after sundown, with Menico in tow, Vespasiano climbed in through the usual window. When they reached the sala, Innocentia was off tucking her brother into bed.[35] Once the girl entered the sala, the boy sang her a lachrymose dialogue from Ariosto's *Orlando:* "Lips redder than the roses . . ." (Delle vermiglie labre piu che rose [*sic*]). In the poet's verse, the damsel's eyes are humid and her plaint is sweet, and in response, the brave warrior weeps too, and then, on the eve of perilous combat, he comforts her.[36] For what transpired after poetry's poignant sighs and heroic tenderness, Innocentia's words are as good as any:

> Menico wanted to leave and asked Vespasiano to come with him. Francesca told Menico, her son, "Off with you! Go see to your wife and don't bother with Vespasiano. He can go by himself." And to make her son Menico go, she gave him two or three pieces of wood, so big that he could barely carry them. And she gave him bread. So Menico left with the wood and the bread and went out that hole. Vespasiano stayed, and after a bit, Francesca told Vespasiano to go to bed. So Vespasiano went off to Francesca's bed, in a room at the top of the stairs, and then he got ready to sleep in that bed and left me in the sala. Then Francesca called me and said, "Innocentia, come here a bit." And so I went, giving little thought that she was in bed together with Vespasiano. And when I arrived in her room—there was a light on—she said, "Take off your clothes and come to bed."
>
> I didn't want to go, because I was embarrassed because Ves-

pasiano was there and also because I wanted to sleep with Don
Luisso,[37] my brother, who is a boy of six or seven years, in another
room, and I did not want to sleep with her in that bed, because
Don Luisso is a fearful sort. If he had wakened and not found me
in the bed, he would have begun to cry aloud. And she said,
"Come on, come on!" And I said that I did not want to go, that I
was afraid of that man who was there, that he would bother me.
But she said, "Come on! Come on! He's a virgin. He can't do anything at all!" And she got up at once from bed and unpinned and
unlaced me and prevailed upon me to get into bed.

Vespasiano was in the bed, so I got in with my shirt on and
turned my back to him. Vespasiano laid hands on me and kissed
me and touched me and tried to have intercourse with me. I began to raise my voice, saying I did not want to and Francesca said,
"Let her go to sleep!" He left me alone and did nothing more to
me. And in the morning, he got up and at the tenth hour [ca.
5 A.M.] went out the well-side hole.[38]

But neither conspirator gave up easily. Francesca told Innocentia that she wanted the two to sleep together again.[39] Meanwhile,
on assorted pretexts, the young man kept turning up laden with
cash, apples, pears, and further poems.[40] A week later, Saturday
again, he reappeared at night. Innocentia was still next door at the
boardinghouse, reading, probably to Lucretia, house-mistress,
from her *Book of Virgins*. Returning through the hole, she found
milk-son and milk-mother downstairs by the fire, alone together,
for Luisso had gone to sleep.[41] Francesca said the boy would soon
be leaving, so the girl ascended to the sala. But then the other two
came up, and Francesca ordered Vespasiano off to bed. Innocentia protested: Francesca had said he would leave. Vespasiano replied that the late hour persuaded him to stay. When the two had
lain down in the stair-head room, Innocentia was still undressing
to join her brother when Francesca called, "Come here. I want you
to come sleep here." No, she replied; her stepfather would come.
"Do not worry," said Francesca. "Your father will not come." But
Vespasiano would pester her! The lad reassured her: "Come! I
promise you, I won't say anything." Francesca said, "He is an honest man. Come! Come! The other time, he didn't do anything to
you." The girl climbed in, protesting that she did not wish to lie

in the middle. She wanted the nurse in center bed. "I want Vespasiano to be in the middle," said the servant. So Innocentia, semi-innocent, lay down in her shift and fleas. And then, as we know, at Francesca's hands and urging, she lay there naked.[42]

This time things went differently. At first, it was like the first round: Innocentia turned her back; Vespasiano reached for her; Francesca said, "Let her sleep!" But then, hearing Luisso cry, the older woman padded off to join him. Innocentia had almost settled into sleep when Vespasiano mounted her. She screamed and fought hard, legs tight-locked, but he forced his knees between her thighs and then she lost. It really hurt, she later told the court. Vespasiano, having finished, fetched his shirt from the bed's end and mopped up.[43] Two or three more times he had her; it always hurt, she always screamed. After the second bout, he told her, "Do not worry, my girl, for it will turn out well for you. I want to marry you."[44] This then, this blurted, ham-handed declaration, so typical of forensic defloration tales, was the real betrothal promise—at least according to Innocentia. Its mention argues, but does not prove, that, despite Vespasiano's version of events, there had been no prior solemn handshake. Of the young man's feelings on this night we know nothing, and little more of the girl's save that, the next morning, she was too embarrassed to check the sheets for blood. Mortified, she wanted Francesca not to remake the bed.[45] The servant looked. Of course.[46]

In the morning, after Vespasiano had climbed out the window, Luisso said, "What was wrong last night, that you were screaming?" It was the pains, Francesca told him. Luisso objected; he had heard her talking to Vespasiano. He would go tell Giovanni Battista. Francesca, calling him a scamp, made as if to cuff him but then sweet-talked him and bribed his silence with prunes.[47]

Prunes or no, Innocentia's secret was not easily corralled. Madonna Lucretia, reading companion of the *Book of Virgins,* from her boardinghouse had heard the screams. She asked Francesca about them, adding she knew Vespasiano had been there. "Pains!" the servant said. A transparent, flimsy lie. Lucretia then approached Innocentia: "Watch out, you little rascal! I'm going to tell Messer Giovanni Battista, your stepfather."[48] (She never did.) After the midday meal, with Menico, Vespasiano returned. Innocentia did not want to let him in, but, betraying her yet once more,

Francesca opened the door. Now, Vespasiano told the girl, she should love him more than ever.[49] The two young men then conversed in Latin. Then Vespasiano told Innocentia that, while Menico was there, she should not mention what had happened. The girl snarled back that she did not want his blandishments.[50] Leaving Menico behind, Vespasiano departed. Then came Paula, Francesca's daughter. In Innocentia's earshot, Francesca announced that Innocentia and Vespasiano had just slept together; Paula snapped back that if word got out, her mother would be jailed, whipped, and burned, adding that she herself would in no way lend a helpful hand.[51] Paula was right enough about the first two perils; the unlikely stake was just an added flourish.

Despite these indiscretions, the leaky secret was still worth guarding. Vespasiano strove to keep it under wraps; if he had intended to bargain Innocentia's lost virginity for a better dowry, he never followed through. Her pique or his timidity derailed his plan, if plan there ever was. Then, a few weeks later, as Christmas loomed, Innocentia came under pressure from several sides, for her stepfather wanted her to confess in church. The conspirators, Vespasiano and Francesca, joined forces to steer her words. Francesca feared spillage: not only the sex but also the female magic.[52] The servant told Innocentia that she would warn Vespasiano. She did so; Vespasiano then told the girl: "Be careful, if you confess, not to say that I deflowered you. Don't tell the confessor if he does not ask you. And if he does, tell him, but don't tell him my name." [53]

Innocentia did confess, at Sant'Agostino, near home. We know not what she said. Then, around Christmas itself, she moved to another house. In court, she gave no reason. Giovanni Battista seems not yet to have sniffed out the sexual encounters under his roof, so Innocentia may have provoked the move to flee the liaison. Certainly, she told the magistrates that Vespasiano had harassed her with touching, kissing, and attempts, in vain, at forced intercourse.[54] Both Francesca and Vespasiano asserted rather that the two had spent further nights together. Whatever the cause, with her departure the archivist forfeited his handy window. Vespasiano mourned his lost access. Using twelve-year-old Alessandro as messenger, he sent the girl a letter. In it, he asked indulgence for a seven-day absence from Rome, urged her to find an excuse to return to her former house, warned her to keep their secret, and then instructed her to burn the message.[55]

It was all too much to handle. Innocentia needed adult counsel. After a few days, she took the letter, unburnt, to Giovanni Battista's brother-in-law, who read it and questioned her so hard that in the end the whole tale spilled out.[56] Since Giovanni Battista never testified in the eventual trial, we do not know how long it was before he heard what his kinsman had learned, but it cannot have been long. Word of the deflowering anything but smoothed the road to marriage.

Rather, between Christmas and early March, relations between the suitor and the Bucchi household unraveled. Something went awry. Francesca, the machinator, paying treason's price, lost her job; she moved out and took refuge with her daughter.[57] Vespasiano so riled Innocentia that when he sent another letter (this time Menico's brother-in-law was messenger), to spite her lover she sent it back.[58] But she was not too cross to memorize some of the poem packaged with it.[59] Four stanzas, twenty-nine lines. However trite and flat, the verses struck a chord:

> Donna che eccede tutti in questa aetade
> Di costumi di gratie et di belezze [sic]
>
> . . . .
>
> Tal virtù tal valor tal gentilezza
> Passi d'ogni splendor d'ogni vaghezza.[60]

> Woman who exceeds all in this age of ours
> In customs, grace, and beauty
>
> . . . .
>
> Such virtue, such valor, such gentleness
> surpasses every splendor, every charm.

Innocentia, for all her pained ambivalence, may have felt pride, solace, and wry satisfaction when she read how Vespasiano, cut off from access to her, suffered the usual torments of amorous frustration:

> De lassa donna hormai le risa el gioco
> et da orecchie i miei miseri accenti

se non di Roma mi voglio partire
Non già per vivere mai ma per morire

Misero qual fu giamai si gran Cordoglio
che rimedio far' possa al dolor mio?

O woman, give up laughter and play
and give ear to my woeful plaint.
If you do not, I will leave Rome,
not indeed to live, but to die.

Oh poor me, has there ever been so great a grief!
What could ever remedy my pain?

Despite bathos, this poetry had a pragmatic bent. Vespasiano's Muse, for all her lyricism, had a hard nose and an eye for the main chance. She urged the girl to use all her wits to return to the handy house with the well-side window:

Torna ti prego a quel sacrato loco
che fu principio di questo tormento
et leva del mio petto questo foco
che fa che sempre grida e mi lamenti.

And then, in the final lines:

A ritornar' di gratia trova scusa
Oh Dolce anima mia dove sei chiusa

Return, I pray, to that sacred place
that was the beginning of this torment
and lift from my heart this fire
that makes me always wail and cry.
. . . .
Please find an excuse to return,
O sweet soul of mine, [from] where you are now shut in.

That Innocentia nimbly tucked such flowery language into her memory is just one more sign of the caliber of her literacy and of the intelligence that first attracted Vespasiano to her.

Renaissance literature is full of stories where poetry and blan-
dishment come first and rough sex follows. Ben Jonson, in *Volpone,*
a heavy spoof, plays the usual pattern backward; his absurd Italian
villain, having failed with fancy promises, expostulates, "I should
have done the act and then have parleyed. Yield, or I'll force
thee."[61] Bandello's touching story of the peasant Giulia, who, suffering rape, drowns herself, portrays the cad as full of honeyed
words. The same is true of one of Marguérite de Navarre's many
near-rape narratives, her tale of Amador and Florida, where the
lover, feigning deathly sickness, flips from tenderness to force
without a hiccup.[62] There, too, the irony is patent. Vespasiano's er-
ratic treatment of the girl has much in common, in its abrupt aggression, with the literary model. But he also breaks the pattern,
for, oddly, poetry brackets his violence, both before and after. Is
some tenderness the reason for the later lyrics, or are new ob-
stacles, the great love-lyrical topos, the stimulus for his later rhetoric of devotion, torment, and frustration?

Poetry and passion notwithstanding, something—the girl's removal, her confusion, her spite, her stepfather's ire, the absence of
a better offer on the dowry front—then quenched the Muse, the
lover's ardor, and the commitment to a wedding. Word came that
Vespasiano had lost interest.[63] To Giovanni Battista, the lad's de-
fection urged stern measures.

And so it was that, in the second week of March, Vespasiano
found himself in jail. The charge was *stuprum,* not plain rape but
defloration. The plaintiff's goal, as usual, was marriage or hefty
compensation to fund a generous dowry for a later match.[64] In
court, all witnesses knew the stakes and played the usual games.

In her dealings with the law, Francesca played as fast and loose
with truth as she already had with Giovanni Battista, Innocentia,
Luisso, and Lucretia. To her, to break faith came easily. To say this
is not to censure her but to place her, with many other female underlings, in a social zone where the rewards of honesty and honor
were few and costly, often readily outbid by betrayal's profits. Long
traditions, in both art and oral culture, imputed to female servants
a seductive trickery that invited sly alliances in chicanery with
their betters. *Novelle* by Bandello, a painting by Giulio Romano,
and much other love lore featured the lowly *mezzana,* the woman
go-between, who, for fun and profit, eased the path to illicit sex.[65]

Catalogue Francesca's lies and tricks. Against Giovanni Battista, she contrived his daughter's defloration. She also counterfeited his door key and kept his house open at all hours to male traffic. And she taught his daughter illicit magic and then suborned the Christmas confession he commanded. As for Innocentia, Francesca played her false, in large and petty ways, with lies, flimsy promises, and sheer blarney—remember the fleas!—and with petty betrayals as in letting Vespasiano in against her will or peeking at the sheets. She also, with Vespasiano, coached her in falsehood at holy confession. Her fibs to Luisso and to Lucretia about Innocentia's pains were quite in character, as was her expedient bribery with prunes. Again and again in this story, Francesca improvised, jury-rigging solutions on the fly. Her whole seduction campaign amalgamated plots with whims.

The same glib, shifty expediency marked Francesca's dealings with the court. Summoned, she dragged her feet, claiming sickness. Once before the magistrates—on 23 March, ten days after Innocentia—and jailed in Tor di Nona, she played for leniency. She had come voluntarily: "I came here on my own, Saturday evening, if I remember right. I was not arrested in any way, and I came to testify because a warrant came." [66] She also made a bid for sympathy, citing both her illness and her Christian resolve to do right, in view of Easter's coming:

> Because I wanted to confess and take communion the way Christians do this Easter and not to have my soul burdened, I came here on my own to say everything that I know about this affair, for I, if it please God, want to confess and take communion. [67]

Note several traits of Francesca's rhetoric. Like many Romans before the court, in a weak position she conflated magistrates and priests; one sort of confession melded with the other. Such language, though most striking during torture, could surface whenever a witness or defendant felt on shaky ground. Judicial and divine grace had much in common, and both rewarded a penitential posture of supplication and confession. In enacting piety, Francesca thus did more than play for approbation. She also slipped into a style of bargaining appropriate to the weak when power held the moral high ground. [68]

In court, despite her pious protestations, of course Francesca lied: sex, yes, but all Vespasiano's doing. Alerted by screams, she had come running and caught the two in bed, in the act, the girl still shrieking. Scandalized, she berated them, but they reassured her on the spot; it was all quite decently sanctioned by betrothal: "Both of them said, 'We want to get married.'"[69] Then came various nights of sex, tolerated by her because, after promises, sex is nearly normal.

> After that he came in secret I know not how many other times
> to sleep with Innocentia, and he always said he intended to take
> her to wife, and since he had deflowered her, I let him come and
> sleep with her because I thought he was going to marry her as he
> had promised, and the father often found Vespasiano and said
> nothing.[70]

Francesca, in this testimony, strove to extricate herself from any active role in Innocentia's debacle. In her version, all initiative had been Vespasiano's, from first love onward. When asked to intervene with Giovanni Battista, she had resisted:

> He told me that I should speak to Messer and tell him that he
> wanted Innocentia as a wife and I told him I did not want to
> speak, and he said it again and again until finally I spoke about
> it to Messer Giovanni Battista.[71]

Before the judge, Francesca served her own self well. What about the others? Her words did little harm to Giovanni Battista's and Innocentia's campaign for redress, for she portrayed Innocentia as a virtuous virgin who, once betrothed, had only done the normal thing. As for her milk-son, she did Vespasiano some good at first by recasting the seduction as devoid of trickery or undue violence, but then, under accusation of procuring, she shifted the blame toward him: "It is not true that I was a go-between to have Innocentia deflowered by Vespasiano. He forced her with the trick of pretending to intend to marry her."[72] These words also undercut the lad's campaign to escape the marriage or to clinch a better dowry. Francesca's testimony pushed him toward matrimony, as fait accompli, for his promise and subsequent cohabita-

tion already shackled him in the eyes of recent canon law and custom. Technically, since the Council of Trent (1563), surreptitious
marriage on private promise had been out of bounds, but old ways
long lived on.[73] Citing the benign normality of the courtship and
the reality of the marriage, Francesca strove to perfume the fishy
motives and gild the lugubrious effects of her procuring on Vespasiano's behalf.

Innocentia's own performance showed great poise. She testified
on 11 March in her stepfather's house.[74] The manuscript of her
deposition runs six pages, 1,246 words in all, without the trace of
a single interjection by the court. The young woman may not have
poured forth her speech in unbroken spate; to catch up, the notary
may have halted her now and then. In any case, she spoke for fifteen or so minutes, unprompted. Interestingly, says the label on
the file, the case was not her stepfather's but hers; accordingly, she
began very formally, in proper legal language: "I am bearing a
complaint against the said Vespasiano because by force he deflowered me and I will tell you in what way."[75] She then told the whole
story in clear, chronological order and great detail, ending with a
recital of his poem. In conclusion, she began her peroration—
"And this is how Vespasiano, by means of Francesca, deflowered
me"—then, as an afterthought and missed debating point, added
her trouble urinating.[76] Innocentia then summed up the pertinent
essentials of her legal brief:

> And several times Vespasiano, according to what he told me,
> asked my stepfather for my hand, and he told me that my stepfa-
> ther also said so [was in agreement]. And this was before he had
> sex with me. And my stepfather told me that he did not want to
> give him [Vespasiano] as much as he desired for a dowry. And
> then, later, Vespasiano let him know that he no longer desired me
> as a wife, and this was after he had sex with me. And that is how
> it happened.
> For which reason. [*Quare*] [77]

Innocentia's last word poses a puzzle. It stands alone, below the
body of her deposition, and ends with the trailing flourish that signals abbreviation, for it is probably the beginning of the missing
Latin formula "For which reason I bring complaint." Most likely it

is a scribal notation; Innocentia probably never used the Latin phrase. Still, given her intelligence, her literacy, and her family's station, she may have been capable of doing so.[78]

Innocentia's testimony may well have had legal coaching. Certainly, Giovanni Battista, who had several things at stake—his reputation, his purse, the girl's safe future—would have been keen to offer his own counsel, and probably that of lawyers. We know that he had taken an active interest in Francesca's testimony, visiting her at her daughter's house and urging her to come to court, and as we shall see shortly, he also helped craft the denouement. Furthermore, Innocentia, in her recitation, hewed to the conventions of defloration narrative.[79] Like most ex-virgins in court, she recited the stock tale of violence, struggle, pain, and harm—for days she could not urinate without hurting. As was normal in such narratives, she detailed damage to her body but passed in silence over inner feelings not germane to law. Only missing from this defloration narrative were the usual bloody sheets. As sometimes happened with seduction narratives, she shot far sharper barbs at the female betrayer, here Francesca, than at the man she still hoped to marry.[80] To improve her case, Innocentia may also have lied a bit. There was little sex, she averred, one night only.[81] Unlikely! Both Vespasiano and, especially, Francesca did themselves no good in court by admitting, as they did, to several nights of copulation. Innocentia thus, to exalt her virtue, minimized her collusion and subsequent compliance.

The logic of Innocentia's position is curious; the harder she bore down on Vespasiano, the more readily could her stepfather unload her to him on the cheap. Her testimony thus promoted a wedding, precious to a woman no longer virgin, but not prosperity—unless the young man greased his escape with abundant cash. It is therefore hard to say how much her plaint represented her own desires and how much it reflected those of stingy Giovanni Battista. Mere stepfather and guardian, not her father, and now a widower, the man was no longer beholden to her dead mother's solicitude.

Although conventional in its litany of wrongs, Innocentia's testimony was also strikingly original. It stands out not only for its quirky story but also for its rhetoric. Almost never in forensic tales of abandoned maidens does one encounter four stanzas of lyric poetry. Innocentia's recitation may have been a moving moment for the judge, the notary, and the girl herself. As the abandoned girl recites her lover's fragile, treacherous praise, the modern reader will find the spectacle bittersweet. But sentiment should not blind us to these verses' legal function. Their inclusion, plotted by Innocentia or her counselors, was hardly spontaneous, for as we shall see, the rhymes were both probatory and canonically binding.

Vespasiano, in prison, gave off contradictory signals. It is not clear if he still hoped to duck the match or if, once jailed, he reverted to the scheme of marriage with a decent dowry. His remarks cut both ways because to whitewash the seduction he blackened the girl as a trollop, hardly how one paints a likely wife, but from the start he also trumpeted the betrothal, allegedly at the girl's behest, as warranty of his own right sexual conduct. The latter tactic, a concession or confection, signaled his opting for a marriage, even perhaps a cheaply dowered one. Meanwhile, in Francesca's and Vespasiano's testimonies, there are signs of a parallel legal campaign on his behalf waged elsewhere in town, probably in the court of the *vicario,* Rome's acting bishop. At Francesca's home, before her arrest, a vicariate notary and his assistant had grilled her; when Giovanni Battista came to visit, the two, hastily folding papers, scurried off.[82] In his final testimony, Vespasiano mentions and disavows legal depositions by kinsmen, friends, and a procurator. No such testimony appears in the surviving records of the governor's court.[83] A defensive trial on his part before another tribunal is therefore likely. Its object, clearly, was to parry Giovanni Battista, probably by tarnishing the girl's repute. The larger goal is unclear. To open his cell? To escape a wedding? To extort more money? As the trial went on, he shifted postures, at times abruptly; let us follow him, by stages.

Vespasiano, already a prisoner, was examined briefly on 13 March, two days after Innocentia. He recounted the courtship and cited a betrothal. He then moldered for three weeks before, on 1 April, the court recalled him and asked whether he had written poems before having sex. He conceded intercourse at once, three nights' worth, and parried with his proposal, the stepfather's promise, and the noble sentiments of his poems.

Before I had sex with Innocentia, there were firm promises with
the father about giving her to me as wife. I gave her some son-
nets, handwritten, that said how I, as her lover, would never have
abandoned her.[84]

The court asked whether she was a virgin. Vespasiano took refuge
in the usual male ploy: the girl had had no virtue to lose.

I had sex with Innocentia the way you do with other women. I
saw no difference between her and other women. I don't know
what defloration is; I have never deflowered anybody.[85]

And then, in midslander, in midsentence, suddenly, the lad
cracked.

I want to talk to Messer Bernardino [Coto, the judge] to finish
this business and not rot here in jail. I have to say some things
to him.[86]

What unmanned Vespasiano in court? His betrothal, if it ever
really happened, and his poetry! Innocentia's good memory had
pinned him to a legal mat. As he himself acknowledged, his verses
forswore abandonment. By canon law until the Council of Trent
and then afterward by slow-fading custom, sex plus *verba de futuro*
had sufficed to clinch a marriage; the words that she knew by
heart, rough pentameter promising fidelity, bound the suitor to
the girl and to her miserly stepfather. After all, had he not written:

Di rihaver lo spirito farai cose
Per sin' che gira il ciel maravigliose

To reclaim my spirit, I will do things
So long as the marvelous heavens spin.

As requested, Judge Coto did indeed visit Vespasiano in jail. In
the usual way of premodern courts, he brokered an extrajudicial
settlement. That, after all, was what laws and courts were often
for.[87] And the boy's capitulation was what the charge of *stuprum* had

aimed at. Giovanni Battista came too, to shape and seal his victory. There, under the judge's eyes, he reaffirmed to Vespasiano the promises he had made during the dowry negotiations.[88] Trapped, Vespasiano capitulated to his scudo-pinching conditions. "That is how I want her," Vespasiano was constrained to tell the court.[89] To salve the familial name, Giovanni Battista surely also laid down further terms. So, two days after the jailhouse parleys, Vespasiano returned to court to eat what crow he could. Everything he and his friends, kin, and lawyer had ever said "to the detriment and dishonor of Innocentia, my consort," was altogether false. "I revoke them and annul them and call them ill said, for I had her as a virgin and I deflowered her as my wife."[90] She had given all the usual signs of defloration: the screams, the blood. Interestingly, in confessing, Vespasiano still lied to protect Francesca, his *paesana*, insisting he had done it all himself after sending her away. Vespasiano had always, he averred, honored Innocentia as his wife. Poor fellow, he had to settle for Giovanni Battista's measly dowry!

Vespasiano returned to court once more, briefly, on 5 April. As was usual Roman practice, the court asked him to ratify his prior confession and to add anything he wished. It was at this point that the young man described in full his alleged betrothal at Innocentia's behest, mentioned only briefly two days earlier. At the end of his recital of this pact with the girl, of the defloration, and of his negotiations with her stepfather in jail, Vespasiano added a puzzling phrase: "And at this Francesca was present."[91] This tantalizing allusion to a corroborating witness invites two readings. The first, referring back several sentences and beyond the topics of sex and the prison treaty, is, by virtue of the stretch, syntactically far less plausible: Francesca had seen the private betrothal. But, we ask, if she had done so, why had she herself not cited this precious exculpatory fact in court? The second reading sits better with both syntax and with the strategies of courtroom speech: Francesca had been present at the prison negotiations. This latter reading conjures up a three-way settlement in which Vespasiano contrived to spare not only his future father-in-law but his wet nurse, on whose behalf he would hide her tricks in bed. This version offers a beguiling fantasy of triangular bargains. But its problems are manifest. Why would Giovanni Battista bandage the legal wounds of a woman of low status who had dealt him false? Why would he even allow her presence at the moment of his victory? And why would Vespasiano, before the very judge who had seen his promise, ever care to adduce a corroborating witness of weak gender, low class, and manifestly bad character? Thus, syntax notwithstanding, the former reading is the likelier: Francesca had attended the former betrothal, if indeed it ever happened. As often with microhistory, the story's thread becomes a skein of puzzles.

At the end of this, his final session in court, the magistrates released Vespasiano from active-witness solitary into the general prison space and set the usual three-day term for preparing his defense. But nowhere in the records of the tribunal is there any trace of a sentence, of a defense, or of any other formal steps. Most likely, despite the portentous formalities of the transcript, the judicial process soon just folded without the closure of a full trial. The court, after all, had already done its proper social work: mediation and brokered settlement.

Despite its murky moments, this pretty tale is full of lessons for the anthropology of early modern Europe. It shows something of how courtship worked and how men, and especially how women, played the game of life. It also illustrates ways of using literacy to win a reluctant wife or husband. It is a tale of intersecting strategies; each player picked moves with care. As so often with old Italian trials, all protagonists, even the losers, seem canny, not least the court itself. In the end, only Francesca came out badly, unemployed and unhoused. Giovanni Battista unloaded a stepdaughter on the cheap; Innocentia won a reasonably affectionate, if sometimes callous and shifty, husband; Vespasiano took a literate and self-possessed, if weakly dowered, wife. The judge brokered a good settlement. There was comedic closure fit for Shakespeare. Few Roman trials ended so nearly happily.

As this book's introduction says, the brilliant anthropologist and sociologist Pierre Bourdieu in his youth played rugby skillfully.[92] Scornful of autobiographic scholars, he might dismiss the link, but his days on the playing field may have led him to embrace and elaborate a notion put forward by the philosopher Merleau-Ponty: life has much in common with sports.[93] As on the field, things happen so fast that we seldom see everything coming at us. Like athletes in the stadium, on the field of life we act with a half-informed, reflexive semirationality. But life is more complex than

playing ball; we are, Bourdieu notes, on many fields at once. Our
social instincts, which he calls *habitus,* allow us to navigate with partial information and semicomprehension. Bourdieu's *habitus* is
both individual and collective, both semivoluntary and semideter-
mined. It bundles together patterns of perception and judgment—of the costs, benefits, and other effects of actions. According to Bourdieu, we neither blunder blindly nor calculate our
gambits with the precision of an intuitive chess champion, much
less his nemesis, the intuition-free fast computer. Rather, we make
our moves with the half-informed, half-conscious rationality of a
seasoned player of the game of life. Bourdieu calls the requisite
knowledge a "sense of the game."[94] Though it lacks predictive
power, Bourdieu's scheme is nicely suggestive, for it alerts historians to semiconscious, reflex-driven strategic play. In the affair of
Innocentia, our five major protagonists—the judge included—and
all their partners make best sense if seen as playing the games of
friendship, courtship, seduction, matchmaking, litigation, and mediation in just such a fashion.

If, as Bourdieu says, we often play on many fields at once, things
turn interesting when fields join awkwardly. At such moments, our
thoughts and reflexes take unexpected and sometimes nimble
turns. Warring impulses and dramatic improvisations reveal the
edges of our roles and the tensions inside our culture. Clashing
imperatives and discordant roles make for irony. In short, queer
junctures and wry moments make for good stories and for microhistory, for they offer up instructive surprises. Think of our tale.
The judge and the stepfather simply play the customary games.
The girl, however, juggles companionable female conspiracy, pious
readership of encomia to virginity, poetry-laced courtship, rape
victimhood and sexual shame, stepdaughterhood, sisterly solicitude for Luisso, lovelorn abandonment, and poised testimony in
court. Francesca is wet nurse, governess, *paesana* boon gossip, conspirator, matchmaker, bawd, amateur conjurer, mother of grown
offspring, and half-hearted fugitive from justice. Vespasiano is a
suitor, teacher, benefactor, besotted lover, slipshod poet, transparent sneak, and sexual thug. In court, he swaggers and cringes in a
single breath. The characters play out their moves on a fieldscape
shaped by culture; religion, love lore, sexual honor, dowry custom,

family roles, and canon and criminal law all set bounds and rules for love, lust, connivance, litigation, and brokered settlement.

Look, for instance, at Francesca. For a while she could pursue the game of matchmaker without undue tensions because in her eyes the interests of Giovanni Battista, Innocentia, and Vespasiano converged on an honorable wedding. But, when she conspired with Vespasiano to bed the girl, she broke faith with the other two and undercut her old role as Innocentia's confidante. From then on, dishonest broker, she had to play three games not easily reconciled: to keep secrets from her boss, to placate a justly bitter and mistrustful girl, and to serve her milk-son's lust and his marriage hopes. We cannot see her well enough to know how nimbly she juggled. When it came time to testify in court, her strategies were clearer. There, Francesca served not only herself but her old employer's marriage plan: she praised the girl and cited a makeshift bed-betrothal that pinned the suitor. By concealing Vespasiano's violence, she protected him as well but in the end, conceding his guile, left him in the lurch.

For modern readers, Vespasiano is the hardest to decipher. Many who hear this story find him downright loathsome: in raping Innocentia, he violates our deeply held values. Sexual violence, to our eyes, betrays deep contempt for the physical and emotional integrity of its victim. Though it pains our sensibilities, we should however try to ensconce Vespasiano's manifest abuses of Innocentia in the values and usages of his own time. Rape was a rather minor crime back then, seldom prosecuted unless it caused defloration.[95] Early modern Italy read it as a crime that struck more at a woman's social self and her family's reputation than at her psychic integrity.[96] Nevertheless, Vespasiano's sexual violence, deceit, and forensic slander, even in 1570 Rome, sat oddly with the exalted, worshipful attitudes of his poetry, with the gift of a pious encomium to the virgin life, and with enthusiasm for the girl's literacy. Wry contrasts indeed! Can Bourdieu help sort the confusion out? Perhaps—if the field of courtship invited a mix of tender thuggery, if the field of piety was strewn with absentminded potholes of indulgence, and if, as countless trials attest, the field of litigation allowed and rewarded perjury.

Innocentia is also full of puzzles. Pious Carthusian notwithstanding, she climbed into Francesca's crowded bed, not just once but twice. Hurt and angry, she still memorized her suitor's poem. Abused in trust and body, she sought her abuser's hand in marriage. That last gambit, at least, was standard practice for the time, since it salved honor and settled accounts more swiftly, simply, and cheaply than would another match. Innocentia, naive at home but astute in court, in this respect served Giovanni Battista's needs.

Bourdieu's sociology urges historians to seek actors' reasons but to demand of them not a whit more rationality than we readers bring to the dilemmas of our own daily lives. In his view, courtship, seduction, and legal maneuvering are all "practices" more given to ragged rhythms than to rules. As for raggedness, some years back, the *Scientific American* ran a fascinating article by some theoreticians of chaos.[97] They had been making little piles of sand, adding a grain at a time, and tallying the pattern of slides and mini-avalanches. A few slides were big, some were middling, and most, of course, were tiny; interestingly, there was no predicting which would happen when. The growing sandpiles flickered, much like a guttering candle, at once regular and bounded in the large and random in the small. The authors evoked assorted parallels in nature: series of avalanches, earthquakes, and forest fires, for instance, or the blooming and extinction of living species. In matters such as courtship, family politics, and litigation, Bourdieu's "practice," though not altogether chaotic, has much the nature of the purling of a stream or the flutter of a flame or, for that matter, of a game of rugby, for it is at once patterned and bounded in the large and yet unpredictable in its details. Neither the participants nor we can foresee the moves, but all the athletes and fans know the general patterns of the play, the shape of the pitch, and the location of the goals.

This reflection brings us back to microhistory, with its charms and discontents. Microhistory magnifies both knowledge and bafflement. With affairs of the heart, as with those of state, often, the more one knows, the more one knows one does not know. The sleuthing glass reveals fascinating details, each one of which raises further questions about what went on in the sala, the jail, or between the sheets. Time, like a splendid fractal diagram, no matter how much you magnify the image never flattens out and simplifies. Microhistory courts bafflement in a second way as well, for it of-

ten goes for the quirky moments; there, ironies of situation provoke reflexes less easily scripted and more open to inspired choice
or panicky improvisation. Odd junctures push habitual practice
toward its edges. They invite creation. Together, the ironies, the
mysteries, and the surprising twists not only tickle the reader's
imagination but also portray a culture's suppleness and stretch.

This story came to my eyes with student help. One summer, between her third and fourth years of university, with a letter of support from me, Linda Traverso talked her way into the Archivio di
Stato. To her and my amazement, they let her call down volumes.
She found Vespasiano's trial and transcribed it. The next winter,
for their class project in my seminar, she and her good friend Raffaele Girardo, both fine linguists, translated Linda's find for the
other students, edited it, and wrote it up. I have since gone back to
the archive to check details; Linda did her work well. It is poetic
justice—not lame Vespasiano but solid Ariosto—that, having col-
laborated on this wry sixteenth-century romance, my students
married; they have four very lively boys. My two linguist editors
did well in life; all three of us still wonder how things went, after
so odd a start, for Vespasiano and his Innocentia.

SUMMING UP

THE WORLD IN A GRAIN OF SAND

*Famously, the poet Blake saw the world in a grain of sand. "Ah, yes," said a witty
scholar, commenting aloud on a work of mine to a meeting, "but what is a heap of
microhistories? A pile of sand!" Once I had stopped laughing, I scrambled for
counterarguments. I confess, I now forget them. This, I hope, is what I said:*

*Back to the textuality of text! Let us define text widely, covering the whole
of expression: words, images, gestures, gifts, blows, and all other actions that bear*

meaning. And then, having stretched out our intellectual arms to grab so much of culture, let us read our haul closely, attentively, cleverly. As we do so, we will intuit meaning or, like an archeologist meticulously toothbrushing compacted ground, patiently rescue it from the past's detritus. It is fascinating work. As meanings are multiple in kind, so are our strategies. Here are four.

INTERTEXTUAL MEANING

No text stands alone. Historians, reading closely, should listen for the texts out back, behind the ones at hand. Behind Vespasiano's abject retraction before the judge, we can hear his done-deal, in jail, with Innocentia's stepfather. Cintia's cajoling letters to Lelio draw on an entire realm of epistolary language, some of it amorous or fraternal and some hortatory and conspiratorial. Behind Alessio's tale is Panta in her courtyard, sniffing at the impertinence of the young teases at the convent window and drawing on a universe of female moral talk about youngsters' conduct. Notary Schala, drawing up his pigeon document, mixes legal language with the learned prose of medicine. Cultural history, by retrieving meaning, stalks these transfers and transformations.

INTRATEXTUAL MEANING

Texts make dialogue not only with one another but also with themselves. A good close reading therefore looks for structure and for movement, smooth or fractured—whence the fascination of maniacal close reading, as when, for instance, we follow Giovanni Battista Savelli's recitation of the noses his wife's infidelity cut off: first his, then her brother's, and then his entire clan's. And so, likewise, tracing a textual break, we ponder the odd placement of Innocentia's claim in her defloration narrative that she had pain in urination; her seeming afterthought suggests paternal coaching. Conversations, tense parleys, and slanging matches—verbal exchanges all—in effect are texts with several authors. They also reward dissection: Pallantieri's pact making in the Gramar kitchen, for instance, or servant Stefano's speech to Ludovico Savelli about who, for whose sake, killed which lover. These are grains of sand that contain, if not the world, at least wide provinces of arresting terrain.

METONYMY

As a rhetorical device, metonymy deals in signs, not symbols. Words and objects stand in for something bigger; they signify directly, concretely. Sixteenth-century lay culture, like its medieval predecessor, often dealt that way with meaning. Think of Lucretia Casasanta's dropped handkerchief, embodiment of her alliance with the beadle. Remember too Fabritio Giustini's fatal flung egg, not a symbol, but the flying distillation of his mortal hostility. Ascanio's bitten finger, Vespasiano's love gifts, Pallantieri's proffered burnt finger in the Gramar kitchen and his gift of pigeons at Lucretia's childbed, and the door of Vittoria Savelli's chamber, locked upon her and her lover's corpses—all these carried heavy semiotic loads. They weighed more than do symbols. Accordingly, as readers, we dwell on them. In their own time, they were markers, hulking boulders on meaning's landscape. Our own renderings therefore respect them and ponder them long and thoughtfully.

NEGOTIATIONS

Microhistory studies more than language. A second cherished concern is the minor politics of fine-grained structures: a castle household, for instance, or group of female wards of nuns, a noble family, a poison plot, a courting couple, or a sunset dinner party. Negotiations do have their common coin of bids and threats and settlements, but their ploys and ceremonies, everywhere, partake of culture. Renaissance Italian deals and dealings were not the same as ours. They offer a fine illustration of the past's pastness. We have watched the poison plotters build their alliances, seen the Savelli brothers-in-law make their edgy peace, weighed Pallantieri's ploys for stealing sex, followed the sly machinations of Francesca the governess as she tries to engineer a marriage, and charted the play of gender, age, and status as the Giustini battled over Vittoria's will. In almost all these stories, we have kept a sharp eye to the women, who, despite restrictions on their gender, so often seem canny players with real clout. Microhistory scans negotiations for minutiae, the turning points and subtle bargains that shaped and settled them. They illustrate the form and edges of an age's agency.

IN SUM

As I have said before, as a reader and observer of the past, hearken to the Italian wizard of microhistory Carlo Ginzburg, who quotes the German art historian Aby Warburg, who purloined the expression from the ancient Athenian sculptor Praxiteles, who really knew: God is in the details.

NOTES

❧❧

INTRODUCTION

1. Archivio di Stato di Roma, Governatore, Tribunale Criminale, Constituti 61, fall 1558 to winter 1559, fol. 46v.

   For the sake of brevity, I have omitted almost all the original Latin and Italian passages translated in this book. For scholars' and students' convenience, I will post them on my Web site at York University, Toronto, Canada.

CHAPTER ONE

1. This chapter has benefited from the advice and service of Dottoressa Fiora Bellini, of Architetto Giorgio Tarquini, and of the late Père Jean Coste, skilled historical geographer of Lazio, the Roman hinterland.

2. N. Ratti, *Della famiglia Sforza* (Rome, 1794–95). As a related clan, the Savelli figure in the book.

3. Mario Caravale and Alberto Caracciolo, *Lo stato pontificio da Martino V a Pio IX* (Turin: UTET, 1978), pp. 5–8.

4. Cretone village and castle would pass to the rising Borghese family in 1656. Jean Coste, "Castello o casale? Documenti su Cretone in Sabina," *Lunario Romano: Seicento e Settecento nel Lazio,* 1981, pp. 361–71. See p. 362 for the Borghese.

229

5. The Savelli held Cretone by the fifteenth century: ibid., p. 362. In 1594, Cretone had only ten families and some twenty-five or thirty souls: ibid., p. 364. Under the Borghese, it gradually recovered. For the Savelli, see Volker Reinhardt, ed., *Le grandi famiglie italiane* (Vicenza: Neri Pozza, 1996), pp. 541–46. Originally published as *Die grossen Familien Italiens* (Stuttgart: Alfred Kröner Verlag, 1992). Pompeo Litta, *Famiglie celebri d'Italia* (Milan and Turin, 1819–83), has the family tree. Christoph Weber, *Genealogien zur Papstgeschichte*, 4 vols. (Stuttgart: Anton Hiersemann, 1999–2001), omits the Cretone branch.

6. Archivio di Stato di Roma (henceforth ASR), Collegio di Notai Capitolini, busta 1515, fol. 112r, 10 Mar. 1558. In a document about his sister's betrothal, Giovanni Battista, still a minor, is older than seventeen but not yet twenty.

7. Ibid., fol. 193r, 19 Mar. 1559.

8. Ibid., busta 1516, fol. 57r, 8 Feb. 1558.

9. Ibid., busta 1518, fol. 617r–v, 1 Oct. 1559; fols. 750v–751r, 12 Dec. 1560.

10. ASR, Governatore, Tribunale Criminale, Processi, busta 85 (1563), fol. 10v, Diamante. Henceforth, because most notes cite the same trial, for this source I will give only the folio number and the name of the witness. Vittoria's five servants were Silea, the nurse and *massara* (head serving woman); Diamante; Diamante's sister Temperanza; Ottavia; and Attilia.

11. Coste, "Documenti su Cretone," pp. 361–71.

12. Fol. 15v, Silea 2: "they kept familiar company with each other" (*si bazzicavano*). Silea testified twice: first, in the evening, malarial and incoherent; second, in the morning, far better collected. In these notes the two times appear as Silea 1 and Silea 2. No other witness testified twice.

13. Fol. 4r–v, Gentilesca.

14. Fol. 12r, Diamante.

15. Fol. 15v, Silea 2.

16. Architect Giorgio Tarquini pointed out that the blueprints show that the annex has no foundation. The older section, he noted, still shows traces of a fifteenth-century fire and of subsequent restoration, renovation, and early Renaissance decoration, particularly in the frescoed sala.

17. For her widowhood: fol. 12v, the court. Maddalena calls her *una vecchia*, "an old woman": fol. 6v. For the list of maids: fol. 10v, Diamante. For the two beds: fol. 12v, Silea 1.

18. Fol. 9v, Cecco (Francesco), who reports on where Giovanni Battista was sleeping, was not a castle denizen.

19. For his use of the window: fol. 3v, Loreto; fols. 9v, 10r, Cecco; fol. 12r, Diamante; fol. 15v, Silea 2.

20. Matteo Bandello, day 1, story 9: A great cask blocked the cellar door. "But

love, who has more eyes than Argus, when the woman pondered letting Lattantio in, lent her one of his" (*Novelle* [n.p.: Armando Curcio Editore, n.d.], p. 44, my translation). Any edition of Bandello will serve.

21. Fol. 12r, Diamante, who did not know, she said, if the lovers had ever before used the room.

22. On the fraternal hugs, which Silea claimed in court to have misread: fol. 15v, Silea 2.

23. Cecco, a villager, reports Giacobo's account (fol. 10r). Giacobo himself fled and did not testify. Cecco, an outsider, reported hearsay.

24. Fol. 15v, Silea 2.

25. For the trundle bed: fol. 9v, Cecco.

26. Fol. 3r, Loreto, relaying Giacobo's account of Domenico's account of Troiano's words. Bedclothes: *panni*. Are these blankets or hangings? The cape: *burrichio*.

27. Fol. 9v, Cecco.

28. Fol. 10r, Cecco, reporting Giacobo's account. Cecco's account, as usual, should be taken with care.

29. Fol. 15v, Silea 2. Cecco collapses Giovanni Battista's two nights at Vittoria's portal into one. Relaying hearsay from Giacobo, he is less credible: fol. 9v.

30. Prospero Farinaccio, *Opera Criminalia,* pt. I, tome I, *Consilia, seu responsa* (Venice, 1602), p. 39: "A husband killing an adulterer caught with his wife is not punished by the ordinary penalty *on assassins* nor by any other punishment which afflicts the body, whether the adulterer is of vile condition, or whether he is not. . . . A husband who kills an adulterer is punished more mildly if three conditions concur: first, if the adulterer is caught in the act of adultery or in the act of venery; second, if he is killed in the house of the husband himself and not elsewhere, unless [killed elsewhere] he has had a threefold warning; third, that the husband is not a person of vile condition." Pt. II, tome I (Venice, 1604), p. 197: "That a father or a husband who kills a daughter or a wife caught in adultery, and the adulterer himself, should be much excused on account of the just anger and the just grief [*justum dolorem*] by which he is so moved to kill, and when he is excused from ordinary penalties, and when in toto." *Statuta Almae Urbis Romae* (Rome, 1580), p. 108: "In the case of adultery with incest, within the fourth degree of kinship, both she and he are put to death, and no peace is allowed." Eva Cantarella, "Homicides of Honor: The Development of Italian Adultery Law of Two Millennia," in David I. Kertzer and Richard P. Saller, eds., *The Family in Italy from Antiquity to the Present* (New Haven: Yale University Press, 1991), pp. 229–44, argues that in early modern times a husband often could with

impunity kill the lovers even at some leisure. For hot anger in France, see Natalie Zemon Davis, *Fiction in the Archives: Pardon Tales and Their Tellers in Sixteenth-Century France* (Stanford: Stanford University Press, 1987), pp. 36–38.

31. For the "little house": fol. 3r, Loreto. Cecco, fol. 10r, has a different version of these events, entailing one night only of tower climbing. According to him, only after the lord heard that Troiano was up the tower did he send Giacobo down to spy. Cecco's story has improbable elements: how did the spy avoid detection as he moved into position? Also, Cecco, very improbably, portrays Giovanni Battista as standing in the maids' room, listening at his wife's door for sounds of sex. But the maids, in their versions, all claim to have been wakened or roused from bed when he and his servants stormed through their chamber with a blazing torch and weapons drawn.

32. For Giacobo's gun: fol. 15r, Silea 2. Her source is the lord: "For that is how the signore had organized it. And Signor Giovanni Battista told me all of this, as I said above."

33. For the "fourth hour of the night": fol. 4r, Loreto.

34. Fol. 15r, Silea 2, again via Giovanni Battista: "Signore adesso e tempo."

35. Fol. 12r, Diamante, who heard from Temperanza.

36. For dozing off: fol. 10v, Diamante. Diamante puts Temperanza back in bed with her by the time Giovanni Battista struck, but if the story of the stairway chase is true, this is unlikely. The court seems not to have interviewed Temperanza; she may still have been upstairs and missed the killings.

37. Fol. 13r, Silea 1.

38. Fol. 11r, Diamante. She erroneously identifies the armed servant as Giacobo.

39. Fol. 11v, Diamante.

40. Fol. 10v, Cecco.

41. Fol. 13v, Silea 2.

42. Ibid.; also, fol. 14v, Silea 2, for a second version with the same sense: "Stefano, finish killing him! And on my account nobody touch the signora. Leave it to me!"

43. For the dagger: fol. 13v, Silea 2; for wounds to the head, arm, chest, and everywhere: fol. 15r; for Troiano's wounds to the back: fol. 10v, Cecco.

44. Fols. 12v, Silea 1; 13v, Silea 2.

45. Cantarella, "Homicides of Honor," p. 237, for the thirteenth-century *Consuetudines Regni Siciliae,* ruling that the husband who failed to catch his wife in the act could not kill her but could cut off her nose. Cantarella suggests that legal nose cutting had Arab origins.

46. Fol. 11r–v, Diamante; see also fol. 15r, Silea 2, who cites two head blows and confirms the cuts' order.

47. ASR, Governatore, Tribunale Criminale, Processi, busta 34 (sixteenth century), for a father's murder of his daughter in Montelione, in the Sabina district, in the early 1550s.
48. Fol. 13v, Silea 2.
49. Fol. 11v, Diamante.
50. Ibid.
51. Fol. 13v–14r, Silea 2.
52. Fols. 13v, Silea 2; 11v, Diamante.
53. Fol. 11v, Diamante.
54. Fol. 1r–v, Loreto.
55. Ibid.
56. Fol. 15r, Silea 2.
57. Dennis Romano, *Housecraft and Statecraft: Domestic Service in Renaissance Venice, 1400–1600* (Baltimore: Johns Hopkins University Press, 1996), pp. 193 ff. See also chapter 3 below.
58. Fol. 11v, Diamante.
59. Fol. 1r, Loreto: "So I stayed all that day [Tuesday], sometimes in my house, and sometimes in the house of the signore." Yet, the next morning, he still did not know the story. See also fol. 2v: "I, who knew not a thing . . ." and there claimed to have first heard of the honor killing when Ludovico came inside the castle.
60. Fol. 5r, Caterina.
61. For the two hours between Silea and Caterina's conversation and the call to wash the corpses: fol. 5v. So Ludovico must have come soon after Silea's oracular declaration. Note too how Cecco claims not to have heard about the killing until after the burials: fol. 9r.
62. Fol. 1v–2r, Loreto.
63. Fol. 1v, Loreto.
64. Fol. 14r–v, Silea 2.
65. Thomas V. Cohen, "Three Forms of Jeopardy: Honor, Pain, and Truth-Telling in a Sixteenth-Century Italian Courtroom," *Sixteenth Century Journal* 29, no. 4 (1998): 975–98.
66. Fol. 2r, Loreto.
67. There was also female moral language, after the fact, in court. It is less clear what moral language the women used in public, as things came clear. Note Diamante's report, fol. 12r: "The page told me that . . . he could arrange for him [Giovanni Battista] to find Signor Troiano and the signora *a cavallieri* [doing the knight's ride]." Silea, as we shall see, covered her tracks with moral expostulations in her lord's defense.

68. Fols. 5v, Caterina, Maddalena; 6r: Antonia.

69. Fol. 6v, Maddalena: "perche haveva trovati tutti doi a dormire insieme," ambiguously, could mean either "because he had found the two of them sleeping together" (in flagrante delicto) or "because he had found out that the two of them were sleeping together." Diamante used *dormeva con* in the latter sense to describe the liaison since Christmas: fol. 12r.

70. Fol. 6v, Maddalena, who adds that the women acted on Ludovico's instructions.

71. Fol. 6v, Maddalena: "pel dolore che havevo." *Dolore* could also mean "pain," as from the stench, but that is less likely.

72. Fol. 2r, Loreto.

73. Fol. 8r–v, Bernardino: "amazed" *(maravigliato)*.

74. Fol. 7r, Cocorzotto. See Tomasso Astarita, *Village Justice: Community, Family, and Popular Culture in Early Modern Italy* (Baltimore: Johns Hopkins University Press, 1999), pp. 170–202, for villagers' chthonic morality.

75. Fol. 8r–v, Bernardino.

76. Fol. 2r, Loreto.

77. Fol. 2v, Loreto.

78. Fol. 10r–v, Cecco.

79. Fol. 8v, Bernardino. Some who left returned. Stefano remained with his fleeing master.

80. Fol. 2v, Loreto. The church, a nucleus for the original settlement, no longer exists. For its disappearance and extramural location, see Coste, "Documenti su Cretone," p. 362.

81. For the letter patent: fol. 1r. For Pallantieri, see Alberto Aubert, *Paul IV: Politica, Inquisizione e storiografia* (Florence: Le Lettere, 1999), esp. pp. 127–61; and chapter 4 below.

82. Fol. 12v, Silea 1.

83. Fol. 13r, Silea 1.

84. Fol. 13r–v, Silea 2.

85. I have checked the series ASR, Governatore, Tribunale Criminale, Sentenze 2 (1563–64), but only three sentences survive: Constituti 105 and 106 (1563 and 1564) and Investigazioni 80 (1563). Other standard series are lacking for the dates. For instance, Manuali d'Atti has a gap until busta 45 starts on 14 Sept. 1563. Thus, the court's minutiae are harder to trace. Also, for summer 1563, there is no Registro di Sentenze. For this court's records, 1563 was a bad year.

86. Litta, *Famiglie celebri.*

87. Biblioteca Apostolica Vaticana, Ottobon. Lat. 2549, pt. III, D. Iacovacci, "Repertorii di Famiglie," Savelli.

CHAPTER TWO

1. See Daniele Manacorda, ed., *Archeologia urbana a Roma: Il progetto della Crypta Balbi*, vol. 3, *Il giardino del Conservatorio di S. Caterina della Rosa* (Florence: Edizioni all'Insegna del Giglio, 1985), p. 56, for an architect's drawing of the atrocious building never built; ibid., pp. 20–57, for a good history of the site, with maps, drawings, prints, and photographs.

2. Ibid., p. 8, for a picture of the trees and for a ground plan of the complex prior to demolition; ibid., pp. 9–18, for a history of the dig. There had been preliminary soundings in 1961.

3. Ada Gabucci and Leonella Tesei, eds., *Archeologia urbana a Roma: Il progetto della Crypta Balbi*, vol. 4, *Il giardino del Conservatorio di S. Caterina della Rosa, Supplemento* (Florence: Edizioni all'Insegna del Giglio, 1989), pp. 8–10, for the earlier history of the church. Before 1400, Santa Maria had had canons and been called Santo Saturnino. See also Louise Smith Bross, "'She is among all virgins the queen. . . . so worthy a patron . . . for maidens to copy,'" in Barbara Wisch and Diane Cohl Ahl, eds., *Confraternities and the Visual Arts in Renaissance Italy* (Cambridge: Cambridge University Press, 2002), pp. 280–97; this posthumous article is one more sad ghost. Lance G. Lazar, "'E faucibus demonis,' Daughters of Prostitutes, the First Jesuits and the Compagnia delle Vergini Miserabili di Santa Caterina della Rosa," in Wisch and Ahl, *Confraternities*, pp. 259–79.

4. Manacorda, *Giardino*, p. 22, notes that records of a cult of Santa Caterina at the older church trace back to 1409; for the destruction of the last rope walks in 1559, as the new church began to rise: ibid. For a good archeological map of the city block: Gabucci and Tesei, *Giardino, Supplemento*, p. 28; for the history of the *funari*, who go back to the latter fourteenth century: p. 11; the quarter had also been the site of many lime kilns, some of which surfaced in the dig: p. 18.

5. Manacorda, *Giardino*, p. 42, citing Gaetano Moroni, *Dizionario di erudizione storico-ecclesiastica* (Venice, 1842), vol. 17, pp. 16–17, which says that around 1600 there were about twelve nuns and 160 boarders.

6. For Loyola: Sherrill Cohen, *The Evolution of Women's Asylums since 1500: From Refuges for Ex-Prostitutes to Shelters for Battered Women* (New York: Oxford University Press, 1992), p. 20; for a serried chronology of such foundations: pp. 20–21. See also Angela Groppi, "Mercato del lavoro e mercato

dell'assistenza: Le opportunità delle donne nella Roma pontificia," *Memoria,* no. 30 (Mar. 1990): 4–32; Anna Esposito, "Le confraternite del matrimonio: Carità, devozione e bisogni sociali a Roma nel tardo Quattrocento," in L. Fortini, ed., *Un'idea di Roma: Società, arte e cultura tra umanesimo e Rinascimento* (Rome: Roma nel Rinascimento, 1993), pp. 7–51.

7. For both sexes in the original company of Santa Caterina and for the meetings: Mario Scaduto, *Storia della Compagnia di Gesù in Italia,* vol. 4, *L'epoca di Giacomo Laínez, 1556–1565: L'azione* (Rome: Civiltà Cattolica, 1974), p. 645. See also Lazar, *"E faucibus demonis,"* p. 263.

8. Lucia Ferrante, "Patronesse e patroni in un istituzione assistenziale femminile (Bologna, sec. xvii)," in Lucia Ferrante, Maura Palazzi, and Giana Pomata, eds., *Ragnatela di rapporti: Patronage e reti di relazione nella storia delle donne* (Turin: Rosenberg e Sellier, 1988), pp. 59–79, esp. pp. 61–62 for male governance, and pp. 63–69 for elite female auxiliaries.

9. See Sandra Cavallo, *Charity and Power in Early Modern Italy* (Cambridge: Cambridge University Press, 1995), pp. 110–14, for versions of this pattern of social preference in seventeenth-century Turin; S. Cohen, *Evolution of Women's Asylums,* p. 154. See Luisa Ciammitti, "Quanto costa essere normali: La dote nel conservatorio femminile di Santa Maria del Baraccano (1630)," *Quaderni storici* 53 (Aug. 1983): 469–97, esp. p. 469, for the artisanal girls assisted there.

10. Alessandra Camerano, "Assistenza richiesta ed assistenza imposta: Il Conservatorio di S. Caterina della Rosa di Roma," *Quaderni storici* 82 (Apr. 1993): 227–60; ibid., p. 231 n. 17, on how, in 1576, the house had to stop abducting former residents; ibid., p. 233, for sending *sbirri* (policemen). For the upper artisans at Bologna's *conservatorio* of Santa Maria del Baraccano, see ibid., p. 239; Luisa Ciammitti, "Fanciulle, monache, madri: Povertà femminile e previdenza in Bologna nei secoli xvi–xviii," in *Arte e pietà: I patrimoni culturali delle opere pie* (Bologna: Istituto per i Beni Culturali della Regione Emila-Romagna, 1981), p. 470.

11. Camerano, "Assistenza," pp. 232–33.

12. Ibid., p. 229.

13. Ibid. The statutes set the entry age; the album of girls confirms the pattern: Archivio di Stato di Roma (henceforth ASR), Santa Caterina della Rosa, busta 79.

14. Camerano, "Assistenza," p. 240.

15. Manacorda, *Giardino,* p. 33. The present Museo Nazionale Romano Crypta Balbi displays a modern picture reconstructing the event. It uses Gigli's diary for the costume. See figure 8. For the diary, see the next note; see Manacorda, *Giardino,* p. 44, for Gigli's address.

16. Giacinto Gigli, *Diario di Roma* (Rome: Carlo Colombo, 1994), pp. 10–11. In 1640, the processions started up again but took place in May: ibid., p. 331.

17. On the trades at Santa Maria del Baraccano: Ciammitti, "Fanciulle, monache, madri," pp. 476–77.

18. For the size of dowries: Camerano, "Assistenza," p. 231.

19. For enhancing the dowry in seventeenth-century Turin: Cavallo, *Charity and Power,* p. 181.

20. Marina D'Amelia, "La conquista d'una dote: Regole di gioco e scambi femminili alla Confraternita dell'Annunziata (sec. xvii–xviii)," in Ferrante, Palazzi, and Pomata, *Ragnatela di rapporti,* p. 321, counts girls attached to other Roman dowry funds who ended up as nuns. The Annunziata, whose girls lived at home, had 10 percent. San Rocco had 27 percent. The album of girls at the ASR (Santa Caterina della Rosa, busta 79) shows very few eventual nuns. See also Marina D'Amelia, "Economia familiare e sussidi dotali: La politica della confraternita," in Simonetta Cavaciocchi, ed., *La donna nell'economia, sec. xiii–xviii,* Istituto Internazionale di Storia Economica Datini, Prato, ser. 2, vol. 21 (Florence: Le Monnier, 1990), p. 199. See Ciammitti, "Fanciulle, monache, madri," p. 494, on a *conservatorio's* wish that its charges not become nuns; it cost more.

21. Manacorda, *Giardino,* pp. 22–24; Moroni, *Dizionario,* vol. 11 (1846), pp. 135–38. Federico Cesi was the family's second cardinal and endowed Santa Caterina at Loyola's urging. On Cesi strivings to arrive in high society: Carolyn Valone, "Mothers and Sons: Two Paintings for San Bonaventura in Early Modern Rome," *Renaissance Quarterly* 53, no. 1 (Spring 2000): 108–32. For the devotion of the Cesi cardinals to Santa Caterina: Valone, "Mothers and Sons," p. 123.

22. Manacorda, *Giardino,* p. 33.

23. Gabucci and Tesei, *Giardino, Supplemento,* p. 20. The nuns paid rent in the 1550s to one Stefano Centolini, not only for the church but also for "the house and old rooms where our maidens live when they are attached to Santa Caterina."

24. In the same period, the monastery had an old tower, the Torre della Melangola, across the street to the south, demolished for better *clausura.* See ibid., p. 26; Camerano, "Assistenza," pp. 257–58 n. 49.

25. S. Cohen, *Evolution of Women's Asylums,* esp. pp. 142–43. Cohen distinguishes the punitive houses for ex-prostitutes, with their bread and water, tight confinement, and other rigors, from the milder *conservatori.*

26. See chapter 4.

27. Elizabeth S. Cohen, "No Longer Virgins: Self-Presentation by Young

Women of Late Renaissance Rome," in Marilyn Migiel and Juliana Schiesari, eds., *Refiguring Woman: Perspectives on Gender and the Italian Renaissance* (Ithaca: Cornell University Press, 1991), pp. 161–91; Thomas V. Cohen and Elizabeth S. Cohen, *Words and Deeds in Renaissance Rome: Trials before the Papal Magistrates* (Toronto: University of Toronto Press, 1993), pp. 103–33.

28. Sandra Cavallo and Lucia Ferrante, "Donne, famiglie e istituzioni nella Roma del sette-ottocento," *Quaderni storici* 31, no. 2 (Aug. 1996): 429–48, two reviews of the same book. The authors argue for the complexity of relations between charitable organizations and their clientele. They oppose scholars who see paternalism as reducing a population to dependency. For alliances in the hunt for dowry money, charitable and otherwise: D'Amelia, "La conquista d'una dote," pp. 305–43, esp. p. 316 but also passim. For escaping inmates: Camerano, "Assistenza," p. 253. For a positive view of the uses of the *conservatorio* by Roman women in later centuries: Groppi, "Mercato del lavoro e mercato dell'assistenza," p. 18.

29. Manacorda, *Giardino*, p. 544.

30. Ibid., p. 571.

31. Ibid., p. 577.

32. Ibid., p. 47.

33. For snails: ibid., p. 371; for a bird, rabbit, and dragon: p. 273; for dragons: p. 357; for putti: p. 361; for houses and landscapes: p. 373; for the colors: pp. 255, 396–401. For a bird: Gabucci and Tesei, *Giardino, Supplemento*, p. 255.

34. For the names: Manacorda, *Giardino*, p. 437; for the objects: pp. 425–38.

35. For the bones and for the ages of the various kinds of animals: Gabucci and Tesei, *Giardino, Supplemento*, p. 197. Very few poultry bones were found. As for Rome's traditional *porchetta*, the pigs were mostly young. The *conservatorio* statutes tell us the seasons in which the dishes were served.

36. Mention of Alessio's story appears in Maria Elena Vasaio, "Il tessuto della virtù: Le zitelle di S Eufemia e di S Caterina dei Funari nella Controriforma," *Memoria* 11–12 (1984): 53–64. Lazar, *"E faucibus daemonis,"* p. 268, cites her report. I found Alessio's story first, in 1984, and passed it to Vasaio for her article.

37. For the bishop of Mondovì: Moroni, *Dizionario*, vol. 46 (1847), p. 89.

38. Ibid., vol. 39 (1846), pp. 135–36; for Lomellino's friendship with the Jesuits: Scaduto, *Lainez*, vol. 4, p. 493.

39. For examples of how the Baraccano in Bologna tested, and often rejected, prospective husbands for its girls: Ciammitti, "Quanto costa essere normali," pp. 482–84.

40. ASR, Governatore, Tribunale Criminale, Processi, busta 48, case 7, fol. 278r–v; henceforth, as all quotations are from the same manuscript, I will just give folio numbers. Searches in other archival series have turned up no traces of Alessio's trial.

41. For Sigismonda's marriage and her abbess aunt: fol. 278v.

42. For the interpellation about Elena and Chiara: ibid.

43. On this general arrangement in such Roman institutions: Cavallo and Ferrante, "Donne, famiglie e istituzioni," p. 437. For the general pattern: D'Amelia, "La conquista d'una dote," p. 323. For this pattern, by 1475, for the Annunziata's dowry recipients: Esposito, "Le confraternite del matrimonio," p. 13 and 13n. For the same arrangement at Bologna's Baraccano: Ciammitti, "Quanto costa essere normali," p. 472.

44. For the names of dataries: Moroni, *Dizionario*, vol. 19 (1843), p. 134.

45. Ibid., vol. 38 (1846), p. 301, article on Luigi Lippomano. For Lippomano's close relations with Loyola and the Jesuits: Mario Scaduto, *Storia della Compagnia di Gesù in Italia*, vol. 3, *L'epoca di Giacomo Laínez, 1556–1565: Il governo* (Rome: Civiltà Cattolica, 1964), p. 490. For Lippomano's very early alliance with the Jesuits in Venice in 1542: Leopold von Ranke, *Storia dei papi* (Florence: Sansoni, 1965), p. 159. For his career and tomb at Santa Caterina: *Dictionnaire de Spiritualité*, vol. 9 (Paris: Beauchesne, 1976), p. 858.

46. Fol. 279r: "la Badessa le haveva gridato."

47. Camerano, "Assistenza," p. 228.

48. I have been unable to trace the abbot. The Martinenghi were a titled family from Brescia. Scaduto, *Laínez*, vol. 3, p. 228, mentions a Girolamo, active in the curia in 1558.

49. Lazar, "E faucibus daemonis," p. 268 and 277–82, for the girls' usual activities. He cites an early-seventeenth-century observer who mentions singing and reading as well.

50. Fol. 280v. Lazar, "E faucibus deamonis," pp. 268–69, reports, from the manuscript collection of capsule biographies (ASR, Santa Caterina della Rosa, busta 79) that girls who married had stayed on average "9.8" years. Given that most who joined were between ten and twelve, many would have married between twenty and twenty-two, just as Alessio says.

51. Fol. 276v.

52. Fol. 278r.

53. Fol. 276v.

54. Fol. 280v.

55. On higher dowries for nuns in Rome than for girls of the artisanal class in

the seventeenth and eighteenth centuries: D'Amelia, "La conquista d'una dote," pp. 310–11. See also D'Amelia, "Economia familiare e sussidi dotali," p. 199.

56. Fol. 278r.

57. Moroni, *Dizionario*, vol. 66 (1854), pp. 163–64. Luigi Simonetta, bishop of Pesaro, would become datary in 1561.

58. Cavallo, *Charity and Power*, pp. 153–82, and esp. pp. 153–59, for aristocratic women involved in charities for poor women and the work's fruits for them. On the emotional and sociopolitical benefits of patronage for upper-class women: S. Cohen, *Evolution of Women's Asylums*, pp. 122–23. On visiting and inspecting by congregations' noble women: Ferrante, "Patronesse e patroni," pp. 62–69.

59. For the Sanguigni: Teodoro Amayden, *Storia delle famiglie romane*, vol. 2 (Rome: Collegio Araldico, [after 1906]; repr., Rome: Edizioni Romane Colosseum, n.d.), pp. 185–86. For Costanza Salviati: Pierre Hurtubise, *Une famille témoin: Les Salviati* (Vatican City: Biblioteca Apostolica Vaticana, 1985), p. 254 and, for a family tree, p. 499. For Giulia Colonna: Alfonso Ceccarelli, "Historia di Casa Cesarina," unpublished family history, ASR, fondo Sforza-Cesarini, busta 89, item 12, fol. 23v.

60. Fol. 279r–v.

61. Fol. 280v.

62. Christoph Weber, *Legati e governatori dello stato pontificio, 1550–1809* (Rome: Ministero per i Beni Culturali e Ambientali, 1994), p. 359.

63. For music as part of the girls' instruction in later centuries: Camerano, "Assistenza," pp. 250–51.

64. Italian historians of gender have stressed female initiative in matrimonial politics. Cavallo and Ferrante, "Donne, famiglie e istituzioni," p. 429, argue, for a later period, that the women and their families, in dealing with institutions of public assistance, were far from passive. D'Amelia, "La conquista d'una dote," passim, stresses female alliances in the pursuit of dowries, marriages, and berths in nunneries.

65. Manacorda, *Giardino*, p. 437.

66. ASR, Santa Caterina della Rosa, busta 79. There is no Sigismonda among the shards in Manacorda's volume.

CHAPTER THREE

1. I thank Jane Bestor, Sandra Cavallo, Robert Davis, Charles Donahue, Simona Feci, Thomas Kuehn, Laurie Nussdorfer, Carolyn Valone, and the

York University seminar on social history and anthropology for their comments and suggestions.

2. Rhys Isaac, *The Transformation of Virginia* (Chapel Hill: University of North Carolina Press, 1982), pp. 323–57, esp. pp. 350–56, propounds dramaturgy as a model for cultural history.

3. For the strengths and weaknesses of microhistory, see Samuel K. Cohn Jr., *Women in the Streets: Essays on Sex and Power in Renaissance Italy* (Baltimore: Johns Hopkins University Press, 1996), pp. 2–3. For a defense, see Edward Muir, "Introduction: Observing Trifles," in E. Muir and G. Ruggiero, eds., *Microhistory and the Lost Peoples of Europe* (Baltimore: John Hopkins University Press, 1991), pp. vii–xxi.

4. A guide to the witnesses cited:

   Acts I and II, the story of Vittoria's testament
   Members of the Giustini family
   The male alliance
   · The brothers: Pompeo, Cosmo, and Fabritio Giustini
   · The male servants: Stefano, Gano
   · The witnesses to the will: Giuliano Blandino, a family friend; Giovannni Battista Marioni, a business associate; Gennaro di Violante and Bartolomeo di Antonio di Taddeo, servants of the Giustini brothers; Etienne de Montréal; Francesco di Giustiniano; Angelo di Tivoli
   The female alliance
   · The sisters: Silvia and Cecilia Giustini
   · Silvia's female servants: Clementia, Francesca, Lucretia
   Tiberio Alberini, husband of Cecilia, a neutral party
   Bernardino del Conte, the notary
   Act III, the courtyard battle
   The Giustini fraternal alliance
   · The brothers: Pompeo, Cosmo, and Fabritio
   · Giustini servants: Francesco di Dotti; François, the stable boy; Angelo di Nobili, the butler
   · A Giustini guest: Marcantonio di Cantalmaggio
   Ascanio and his servant Giuliano
   Neutrals: Lorenzo Quarra, Agostino Bonamore, Jacobo dello Stincho

5. Teodoro Amayden, *La storia delle famiglie romane,* vol. 1 (Rome: Collegio Araldico, [after 1906]; repr., Rome: Edizioni Romane Colosseum, n.d.),

pp. 453–54 (Amayden's manuscript dates from before 1625). I thank
Egmont Lee for information on the Giustini in Città di Castello. Pio Pec-
chiai, *Roma nel Cinquecento* (Bologna: Licinio Cappelli, 1948), p. 280, calls
Geronimo one of "due illustri giureconsulti" consulted about taxes in 1523.
Geronimo was then thirty or so, young for glory.

6. Archivio di Stato di Roma (henceforth ASR), Collegio di Notai Capitolini
    (henceforth Not. Cap.) 620, fol. 277v, 21 July 1547. Geronimo buys the rent
    rights of a chapel of Santa Maria Maggiore.

7. For Geronima's birth family: ibid., 618, fol. 186v, 22 Apr. 1541; also ibid., 619,
    fol. 110r, 22 Apr. 1541. For the antiquity of the Fabii: Amayden, *Famiglie ro-
    mane*, pp. 384–87.

8. Otterio Pio Conti, *Elenco dei defensores e degli avvocati concistoriali dall'anno 598 al 1905
    con discorso preliminare* (Rome: Tipografia Vaticana, 1905), p. 44.

9. For the two vineyards at Porta Latina, south of Rome: Not. Cap. 620, fol.
    308v, 3 Oct. 1547, Geronimo's will. For the vineyard outside Porta del
    Popolo: ibid., 621, fol. 55r. Geronimo had sold a fourth vineyard, part of his
    wife's dowry, to Cardinal Salviati for 2,500 ducats, according to his will:
    ibid., 620, fol. 309r.

10. Vincenzo Forcella, *Feste in Roma nel pontificato di Paolo III* (Rome: Tipografia
    Artigianelli, 1885), p. 55.

11. Shortly before his death, Geronimo bought Castel de Leo e della Torricella,
    outside the Porta Appia, for just under 9,000 scudi. It cost as much as two
    daughters' dowries: Not. Cap. 621, fol. 277r–v, 21 July 1547. The sellers were
    members of the noble family Margani. For the location: ibid., 622, fol. 134r.
    Other notarial acts trace this *casale* as it passes first to Ascanio and then to
    Cosmo. Camillo de Astalli rents it. See ibid., 621, fol. 48r, 23 Sept. 1553; also
    fol. 313; 622, fols. 134, 183r–v. Geronimo owned a second farm, Casal Ro-
    tondo, also outside the Porta Appia. For Casal Rotondo's passage from hand
    to Giustini hand: ibid., 621, fols. 48r, 55r, 198r, 202r. In 1548, Geronimo
    willed it to Cosmo, who ceded it to Ascanio, who ceded it to Pietro Paolo in
    November 1552. We do not learn its price. There was a third estate, Casal
    Lucchese, which was smaller than Castel de Leo and lay west of Rome, at Tre
    Capanne. Pietro Paolo sold it to his aunt Lucretia for only 1,500 gold scudi,
    perhaps a shadow price, masking a familial loan behind a *censo* (mortgage).
    See ibid., 621, fol. 313r, 9 Oct. 1555.

12. Ibid., 620, fol. 309r, 3 Oct. 1547, Geronimo's will. He passes the storage pits
    to his widow. They lay near Santa Maria della Consolazione, below the
    Capitoline Hill.

13. Ibid. The sale's proceeds, 300 ducats, funded his widow's dowry.

14. Ibid., fol. 308v, 3 Oct. 1547, Geronimo's will.

15. Ibid., 621, fol. 202r, 13 Nov. 1552. The palace stood by San Simeone, in Rione Ponte. Pietro Paolo, the heir, trades the palace to Ascanio in exchange for their father's house and Castel de Leo. The governor of Rome is a tenant.

16. Ibid., fol. 198, 12 Sept. 1552. Ascanio cedes this "domum magnam." In May 1547, Geronimo had paid 1,000 scudi for another house, with two shops, in the Via Papale (today Governo Vecchio), abutting his property on the Via di Parione but around the corner: ibid., 620, fol. 219r–v, 5 May 1547. It is not clear if he joined the two dwellings.

17. Ibid., 621, fol. 48r, 23 Sept. 1551, mentions the shops. Here Cosmo cedes the house to Ascanio, though Pompeo lives there. Ascanio cedes to Pietro Paolo the same paternal house "across the street from Saint Thomas's church": ibid., fol. 207v, 13 Sept. 1552.

18. Lucretia's house faced Cardinal Balduino del Monte's. See ibid., 621, fol. 405r, 7 Apr. 1554, where Pompeo takes it over after his aunt's death. The del Monte palace, on the Bufalini map of 1551, lies on the west side of the Via di Parione, south of the first cross street, Via della Fossa. Lucretia's house across the way, eventually Pompeo's, thus faces west. For the three shops: ibid., fol. 359r, 27 Jan. 1554, Lucretia's will. From separate acts we know that one Giustini witness, a tailor, lived "in sight of" both houses, so they were very close: ibid., fol. 313, Geronimo's will; ibid., fol. 360v, Lucretia's will.

19. Ibid., 620, fol. 615, 9 Feb. 1550. Pompeo sells busts in the Pace church and other valuables to Mario Frangipani for 500 gold scudi. For Giustini public offices, see the inventory, at the Capitoline Archive: Magni, *Archivio della Camera Capitolina, Protocolli,* fols. 448, 719, 915, 949, 1153, 1158, 1192, 2071. For burial at Santa Maria della Pace: Not. Cap. 621, fol. 307r, Geronimo's will; 622, fol. 127r, Vittoria's will. According to Geronimo's will, Santa Maria del Popolo, at Rome's northern gate, was a second Giustini burial church. Lucretia's will offered her heirs a choice of two churches. See Not. Cap. 621, fol. 358r.

20. Geronimo's will specifies a dowry of 4,500 ducats for Cecilia, from the income of his rents, if other assets fell short: Not. Cap. 621, fol. 308r–v. It makes the same arrangements for Vittoria, should she marry and should funds be short. Geronimo bought Ascanio the sinecure of *scriptor apostolicus* for 1,937 scudi: ibid., fol. 309v.

21. For the will's chosen epitaph, "Hic jacet Hieronymus de Justinis de Castello advocatus consistorialis et pro se et suis faciendis curavit": ibid., 620, fol. 307r. See also Amayden, *Famiglie romane,* p. 454, or the tomb itself, where the

actual epitaph lacks the proud affirmation of assiduity: "Hic jacet Hieronymus Justinus de Castello advocatus consitorialis. Vixit annos LV menses IX
Obiit XX Junii MDXLVIII."

22. When Silvia married, probably just before 12 Nov. 1543, she was a minor, not
yet twenty. At her father's death, five years later, she thus might have been
twenty-three or twenty-four. Silvia's waiver of inheritance in exchange for
dowry: Not. Cap. 619, fols. 285r–291v, 12 Nov. 1543. For her legal minority:
fol. 285v; for her husband's: fol. 291v.

23. Ibid., 620, fol. 309r, 3 Oct. 1547.

24. Ibid., fol. 361r, 17 Apr. 1548. The physician, Lancellotti, two years later arbi-
trates the division of Geronimo's property: ibid., fol. 615r, 9 Feb. 1550. This
document revokes the first will but does not replace it. I can find no second
full will revising terms and doubt there was one. Later notarial acts show
that all five sons did receive substantial lands, houses, rents, and sinecures.

25. We do not know the ages of the eldest sons, but consistent lists of sons in
their father's will prove birth order: ibid., 620, fol. 309r. All notarial papers
list the sons in the same order. For the family's esteem for and trust in del
Conte: Archivio Secreto Vaticano (henceforth ASV), Archivio della Valle–
del Bufalo 182, letter of Cosimo and Fabritio, 24 Apr. 1554.

26. ASR, Governatore, Tribunale Criminale, Constituti 52 (henceforth Constituti 52), fol. 227r, 1 Sept. 1557. "A hundred" is figurative. Ascanio listed as
well other noble gaming partners: Cencio Capizucchi and Innocenzio del
Bufalo. See ASR, Governatore, Tribunale Criminale, Processi (henceforth
G.P.), busta 31, case 1 (1557), fol. 224v. G.P. 20.4 (1555), fol. 378r, shows Ascanio playing with, and cheating, the noble Filippo della Valle, a kinsman of
his sister's husband, and many other victims.

27. Constituti 52, fol. 227r. See also ibid., fol. 226v: "I have played with ten
thousand gentlemen, with whom I have always lost." In court, Ascanio blusters and whines.

28. Ascanio tells the court: "Another time, [we] were playing *primiera*, Pompeo
and I and Antonio [Cagnetto, the perennial witness?], our house agent. In
the early morning, we played at dice and I won up to a hundred scudi. After
the midday meal, we took to playing *primiera*, and Pompeo won more than
four hundred scudi from me, and, out of money, I sent for Giuliano, the
wholesaler across the way. He brought me eighty silver scudi he owed me,
and I know not how many gold ones. We began to play, and I won mine
back, and I won a good hundred scudi of his. All these scudi were *battaglini*.
["little battles": probably new-minted gold scudi, unworn and not clipped,
with the archangel's sword unsheathed. Alan M. Stahl of the American Nu-

mismatic Society suggested this reading.] When we were playing, Pompeo did not want anyone to come watch. He chased them all away when we played. Pompeo wanted to wager some jewels and necklaces. I didn't want to play anymore. So he got angry" (ibid., fol. 225v). See also ibid., fol. 227v. Under the judge's pressure, Ascanio admits to five cards in his hand on another occasion, but claims inadvertence. The Giuliano [Blandino] who lent money figures in assorted Giustini papers and also witnesses Vittoria's will and stays with her at her death and burial: G.P. 31.1, fols. 36r–37r. He reports his shock and grief.

29. Ascanio's version continues: "In the morning [after my big winnings], I went to find him [Pompeo] in bed. He told me that a servant named Francesco Tanci had seen me with five cards in hand. I said that he [Tanci] was lying through his gullet, and that he was accustomed to having a tip every time his master won, and this time he didn't get one. Pompeo then said that he wanted to go to the governor, who was then Messer Girolametto. He went to find all the persons who wished me ill and had played with me. There was Cencio Dolce [author of the later printed libel and of whom more follows, later in the chapter]. They examined me about it, saying I had played with five cards, but before Messer Girolametto, the governor, and before Antonio Motula, the governor, and before Messer Antonio de Belli, *iudice compromissario* [the compromise judge], [Pompeo] got just the [small] honor that he deserved" (Constituti 52, fols. 225v–226r). "Messer Girolametto" was Girolamo Federici, in office from 21 Jan. to 5 July 1555. See Niccolò del Re, *Monsignore governatore di Roma* (Rome: Istituto di Studi Romani, 1972), p. 84. Motula does not appear in del Re's list.

30. Ascanio's version: Constituti 52, fols. 223r–v, 226r. Ascanio attributes the warning to Girolametto's predecessor, the bishop of Pavia, in office from 22 Nov. 1551 to 21 Jan. 1555. Del Re, *Governatore,* p. 84. The cart (the brawl) thus comes before the horse (the five-card hand). Yet it seems hard to detach the two incidents. Ascanio may have muddled his governors. Notarial evidence helps date the quarrel. As late as 10 Apr. 1554, Ascanio and Pompeo seem to be doing amicable business, since Ascanio sells Pompeo his share in Lucretia's estate for 400 scudi: Not. Cap. 621, fol. 406v. For the next five years, no notarized act links the two brothers. So we have a *terminus post quem* for the falling out. The fraternal feud would have developed between 10 Apr. 1554 and 5 July 1555, when Governor Federici stepped down. As we shall see, Ascanio had taken an ex-courtesan as wife by 12 Sept. 1552 (Not. Cap. 621, fol. 198). This marriage, while an irritant, could not have been the sole cause of the feud. The brothers came to blows more than once.

246 · NOTES TO PAGES 80–81

Ascanio testified: "He [Pompeo] is tougher and bigger than me, for we have battled several times" (Constituti 52, fol. 221v).

31. Ascanio testifies: "At the time when the bishop of Pavia was governor, Pompeo did it to me one evening, perhaps around the third hour of the night [9 P.M.], for I was without arms and without anything. I went to the bishop of Pavia and governor the same night and I told him everything, the injury and the wound that Pompeo had inflicted on me. The governor sent for him at once and, if I remember, asked him, 'What sort of business is this? You deserve a punishment from me.' I told the governor so much that he said, 'Don't do any more such things, for I will punish both of you, and the first who wounds the other I will make pay a thousand scudi!' if I remember well. He put fear into both of us, saying those words. I don't remember if there was a formal obligation. I am sure that there was no oath, nor anything, but I remember that he put fear into us, saying he wanted to make us pay a big fine, and he made us make peace" (Constituti 52, fol. 223r–v). Ascanio here strives to obscure and belittle the governor's ruling. Much searching has failed to turn up the actual warning text.

32. G.P. 20.4 (1555), fols. 374r–379r. Generally, the governor himself sat in on only the gravest cases; his presence is thus notable. The governor heard two depositions, his notaries four others.

33. Pecchiai, *Roma nel Cinquecento,* pp. 335–36. Pecchiai, following G. Tomassetti, who published the tract in his "Due manifesti del secolo xvi," *Studi e documenti di storia e diritto* 3 (1882): 89–96, fails to ascertain Ascanio's family. The tract's author, Cencio Dolce, nowhere uses the Giustini name. One reads that on two occasions Ascanio had fled a fight with a single adversary. Once, his black servant ran with him. I thank Helen Langdon and Lisa Duncan for these citations.

34. "They cannot stand me and have schemed together, for they would rather see me dead. I can show you letters that show what Pompeo was scheming. And all this on account of a woman I took. They hold that she is my wife. She was a prostitute, but I do not want to say here if she is my wife or not, because I do not want to prejudice myself in other important matters, but I will tell the governor by mouth if he wants to know or Cardinal Carafa, our common master" (G.P. 31.1, fol. 55r–v). Carafa, the pope's energetic cardinal nephew, was Rome's most powerful man.

35. Not. Cap. 621, fol. 198. She then had dowry in Casal Rotondo and in Geronimo's house in Via di Parione. A Neapolitan, she lacked Roman kin.

36. Pecchiai, *Roma nel Cinquecento,* pp. 335–36. The broadside claimed the

courtesan-wife had brought a dowry of 1,300 scudi. It summarized a dotal act registered in Tivoli in Oct. 1555. Laodomia de Rasis Napoletana had credits on the noble Cosmo Pallavicino; clearly, she was a courtesan of means, who furnished her own dowry.

37. Monika Kurzel-Runtscheiner, *Töchter der Venus: Die Kurtisanen Roms im 16 Jahrhundert* (Munich: C. H. Beck, 1995), pp. 235–36, proves that such marriages were not rare but cites some that provoked ferocious familial resistance. Laodomia is not in her book.

38. Caporione [of Parione]: Magni, *Archivio della Camera Capitolina, Protocolli,* fol. 719, 1 Apr. 1563. Consigliere of Parione: ibid., fols. 1153, 1 Oct. 1563; 1158, 1 Apr. 1564.

39. See Marcello Alberini, *Il sacco di Roma,* ed. D. Orano (1901; repr., Rome: Roma nel Rinascimento, 1997), p. 499, for a genealogical table. The table mistakes the date of Tiberio Alberini's marriage to Cecilia.

40. Pompeo is asked why he did not rush to the walls to defend the city against the Spanish army. "Signore, yes, I believe I was at the house of [Pasqua?] the Paduan. I was on horseback in the street and the Paduan, at the window, and I think some other whores—I think Isabella de Luna was among them— asked me why I did not run to the walls" (G.P. 31.1, fols. 53v–54r). For Pasqua the Paduan: Elizabeth S. Cohen and Thomas V. Cohen, *Words and Deeds in Renaissance Rome: Trials before the Papal Magistrates* (Toronto: University of Toronto Press, 1993), pp. 45–64, 91–94. For the traffic of married men of the upper class with courtesans: Kurzel-Runtscheiner, *Töchter der Venus,* p. 100; for the famous Isabella de Luna: ibid., passim, using the index.

41. Dante, *Inferno,* 30.32.

42. As the court puts the matter to Cecilia: "Does she know that the aforesaid Pompeo, who has been examined, when his aunt Lucretia was dead in bed, put some other person in the said bed with the curtains closed and had the notary register and make a will to his [i.e., Pompeo's] liking?" (G.P. 31.1, fol. 16v).

43. Not. Cap. 620, fol. 307r, Geronimo's will. See also, e.g., ibid., 621, fol. 48r, 23 Sept. 1551, where Lucretia appears as *tutrix et curatrix* of Cosmo, and ibid., fol. 188r, as *tutrix* of Cosmo and Fabritio. Although Geronimo's wife, in his will, shares with Lucretia joint discretion over charitable bequests, she never figures in subsequent documents.

44. Ibid., 621, fols. 358r–360r.

45. Ibid., 620, fols. 319r, 361v, 615r (*procuratore,* not witness); ibid., 621, fols. 127r, 188r, 198v, 208r, 313r, 359r, 360v, 404v, 421r.

46. Cecilia: "I know that she wrote it in her own hand first and I have that writing in my hands. Messer Bernardino sent to me asking for it and I did not want to give it to him" (G.P. 31.1, fol. 16v).

47. "Enrico de Tucchis noverco consanguineo" (Not. Cap. 621, fol. 359r).

48. In conversation, Charles Donahue, historian of medieval law, suggested, first, that a codicil, having the weight of the will itself, should have had just as many witnesses and as much procedure. Second, it would have been strange of Lucretia, already mortally ill, to take such a matter to anyone other than her old associate del Conte. Third, the codicil was therefore probably not fraud but fiction, and del Conte and Pompeo were likely in explicit or tacit collusion, conniving at an imaginary reference. But how, then, Donahue asked, could Pompeo have fended off a suit from the Tucchi heir? Laurie Nussdorfer, on the other hand, in her work on Roman notaries, has, she tells me, seen many codicils from notaries not present for the will itself.

49. Ibid., 620, fol. 317r. This will disinherited the first two sons.

50. Ibid., 621, fol. 202r.

51. For citizenship and office: ibid., 622, fol. 131r. Ibid., 621, fol. 188r, 30 Sept. 1552, records Pietro Paolo's legal majority and a sale of his real estate in Città di Castello to his younger brothers. Conti, *Avvocati concistoriali,* p. 45, dates the title to 1554.

52. Not. Cap. 621, fol. 202r–v, 13 Nov. 1552.

53. For Pietro Paolo's young wife: G.P. 31.1, fol. 7v.

54. Constituti 52, fol. 225r.

55. For Pietro Paolo's public offices: Magni, *Archivio della Camera Capitolina, Protocolli,* 1 July 1556, *síndico* (he is already *advocatus*); 1 Jan. 1569, *riformatore;* 1 Oct. 1570, *conservatore;* 1 Oct. 1573, *consigliere* for Parione. He is then thirty-eight; the chain breaks at life's prime; did he die soon after?

56. Not. Cap. 621, fols. 49r, 55r, 23 Sept. 1551, notes that Cosmo is studying in Padua. By May 1558, he will be a doctor ("magnificus vir doctor iuris utriusque"): ibid., 622, fol. 189r, 26 May 1558. Fabritio would take the doctorate a few months later ("iuris utriusque doctor, nobilis vir"): ibid., fol. 218r, 3 Aug. 1558. ASV, Archivio della Valle–del Bufalo 182, the only letter from Cosmo and Fabritio, shows both already students there in Apr. 1554.

57. Not. Cap. 622, fol. 475r, 2 Oct. 1561, where Cosmo is first called "reverendus dominus Cosmus."

58. For the move: ibid., fol. 233r, 2 Sept. 1558. Ibid., fol. 218r, 3 Aug. 1558, finds Fabritio alive, exchanging assets with Cosmo, who sells two Gubbio merchants credits on land sales in Città di Castello. One year later, Pompeo passes Ascanio one-fourth of the late Fabritio's estate: ibid., fol. 135r,

4 Aug. 1559. Fabritio had probably been dead some months, for probate took time. We will return to Pompeo's transfer. Gubbio is near Città di Castello.

59. For Silvia's wedding: ibid., 619, fols. 285r–291v, 12 Nov. 1543. Geronimo's will: ibid., 620, fol. 307v.

60. Stanley Chojnacki, "The Power of Love: Wives and Husbands in Late Medieval Venice," in Mary Erler and Maryanne Kowaleski, eds., *Women and Power in the Middle Ages* (Athens: University of Georgia Press, 1988), p. 130, comments that, in wills, fathers often enhanced dowries. Geronimo claimed that Silvia's dowry, too generous for her station, required papal dispensation: Not. Cap. 619, fol. 285r, 12 Nov. 1543.

61. G.P. 31.1, fol. 9r. Clementia, a twenty-seven-year-old widow, had one daughter. For the names of Silvia Giustini's offspring: Christoph Weber, *Genealogien zur Papstgeschichte*, vol. 1 (Stuttgart: Anton Hiersemann, 1999), p. 351, where, erroneously, she appears as "Livia."

62. For Silvia's signature: Not. Cap. 619, fols. 289v, 291v, 12 Nov. and 20 Nov. 1543.

63. ASV, Archivio della Valle–del Bufalo 182, Silvia's letters (henceforth simply Silvia). For the evil eye: letter 8, 25 May 1559. For news of politics: letter 6, 19 Feb. 1559.

64. Lucretia gives Cecilia 100 extra scudi for her hope chest; she leaves none for Vittoria: Not. Cap. 621, fol. 360r.

65. G.P. 31.1, fol. 16v.

66. For the genealogical table: Alberini, *Sacco,* p. 499. Note the wrong date for Tiberio's marriage to Cecilia.

67. Richard Trexler, "The Nuns of Florence," in his *Power and Dependence in Renaissance Florence,* vol. 2, *The Women of Renaissance Florence* (Binghamton, N.Y.: Medieval and Renaissance Texts and Studies, 1993), p. 21 (originally published in *Annales, E.S.C.,* 27ème année, 1972, pp. 1329–50), argues that fifteenth-century Florentines usually chose daughters for the nunnery by age six. See also Anthony Molho, *Marriage Alliance in Late Medieval Florence* (Cambridge: Cambridge University Press, 1994), pp. 175, 177.

68. Geronimo's will: Not. Cap. 620, fol. 308r.

69. Ibid.

70. In the 1550s, San Lorenzo in Panisperna boarded adolescent girls: G.P. 31.1, fol. 27v. For their debauchery by Pallantieri's ally Bartolomeo Camerario: G.P. 44.10 (1558). Geronimo's will mentions the convent of Castellane nuns at Montecitorio: Not. Cap. 620, fol. 308v. For the history of the vanished nunnery: Ferruccio Lombardi, *Roma: Le chiese scomparse* (Rome: Fratelli Palombi, 1996), p. 136. In her own will, Vittoria left twenty-five scudi to

Aurelia, a tertiary there who had taught her: Not. Cap. 616, fol. 127r. Vittoria thus patronized two congregations. For Pietro Paolo's collusion with Pompeo in urging Vittoria to move to the Castellane nunnery: Cecilia's testimony, G.P. 31.1, fol. 15v. For Ascanio's opposition: Silvia's testimony, ibid., fol. 8v. For struggles between daughters who would marry and male kin who would make them nuns: Giulia Calvi, *Il contratto morale: Madri e figli nella Toscana moderna* (Rome and Bari: Laterza, 1994), pp. 178–94.

71. G.P. 31.1, fol. 7r–v.

72. In matters of inheritance, the *ius commune,* the default position in the absence of statutes, like ancient Roman law, privileged agnates—children of a father—of whatever sex. For ancient inheritance by sisters from intestate brothers: Jane F. Gardner, *Women in Roman Law and Society* (Bloomington and Indianapolis: University of Indiana Press, 1986), pp. 190–92. Local statutes could overrule the *ius commune.* Those of Rome did so sometimes, in males' interests. The earlier Roman statutes are silent on succession to an intestate sister. For those of 1362: Camillo Re, *Statuti della città di Roma* (Rome: Tipografia della Pace, 1880), article 98, "De successoribus ab intestato," p. 63. There only the death of a father or grandfather figures. But the 1580 statutes, part I, article 146, "De successione fratrum," expressly exclude sisters from inheriting from an intestate brother. However, the place of sisters upon an intestate sister's death long remained contentious. See Joannes Baptista Fenzonius, *Annotationes in statuta, sive ius municipale Romanae urbis* (Rome: ex typographis A. Phasi, 1636), pp. 313–15: "Whether this statute . . . holds in the case of a defunct sister is a very difficult question." The persistence of this "very difficult question" would hardly have pacified the four brothers' minds at Vittoria's looming end. I thank Laurie Nussdorfer for finding these texts for me, and Thomas Kuehn, Charles Donahue, and Jane Bestor for elucidating them. To Jane Bestor, special thanks for the passage from Fenzonius.

73. For suites of rooms in rich Romans' houses: Patricia Waddy, *Sixteenth-Century Roman Palaces* (Cambridge: MIT Press, 1990), pp. 3–13. For houses in general: Deborah Nelson Wilde, "Housing and Urban Development in Sixteenth Century Rome: The Properties of the Arciconfraternita della SS.ma Annunziata" (Ph.D. diss., New York University, 1989).

74. G.P. 31.1, fol. 30r, Fabritio.

75. Ibid. Fabritio and his brothers wish to hide their hand in Ascanio's exclusion. This line thus is dubious.

76. Ibid., fol. 20r, Pompeo: "I went in on the commission of my brothers, who lacked the nerve to tell her to make a will."

77. Ibid., fol. 29r, Fabritio: "With the consent of all . . . Pompeo began to speak."
78. Ibid., fol. 16r: Cecilia says it is the room where Lucretia died.
79. For Clementia's age and widowhood: ibid., fol. 9r. Her daughter figures in Vittoria's will.
80. Ibid., fol. 7v, Silvia. Silvia is not yet in the room, but since she attributes such words to Vittoria sometime in her sickness, I quote them here as self-diagnosis. Silvia averred that the pain's cause was melancholy, from forced entry into the nunnery.
81. For Pompeo's lean: ibid., fol. 27r, Francesca. For the *lettiera*: Peter Thornton, *The Italian Renaissance Interior* (New York: Abrams, 1991), pp. 113–20. I surmise that Pompeo sat down because he stays in the room for a long time.
82. G.P. 31.1, fol. 20r–v, Pompeo. I have enhanced the scant punctuation and capitalization in Italian passages to make meaning clear. I have not changed the grammar. Geronimo's will indeed antedated his final illness. I have found no maternal will. It may have lodged with the Fabii, her birth family.
83. Ibid., fol. 9v, Clementia.
84. Ibid.
85. Ibid. This exchange may have come later that evening.
86. Ibid., fol. 26v, Clementia.
87. Ibid., for Clementia's words and Pompeo's.
88. For the help with the clothing (*panno*): ibid., fol. 9v, Clementia.
89. For their presence: ibid., fols. 27r, Francesca; 23r, Lucretia.
90. For Vittoria's reaching arms: ibid., fol. 3v, Silvia.
91. For the whole scene: ibid., fol. 35, Silvia. For Vittoria's distress: also ibid., fols. 23r, 27r, Lucretia and Francesca, Silvia's servants who came with her. Fabritio, who was not there, testified that Silvia "began to shriek, as was her wont": ibid., fol. 29r.
92. For Silvia's words: ibid., fol. 3r, Silvia. For "Let her rest!" not quoted here: ibid., fol. 23v, Lucretia.
93. For his standing up: ibid., fol. 3v, Silvia.
94. Ibid., fol. 10r, Clementia. Cf. ibid., fol. 3v, Silvia: "What do you mean, assassinate? I am not a man to assassinate anybody."
95. Ibid., fol. 10r, Clementia.
96. Ibid., fol. 26r, Clementia. Lucretia repeats this self-damning outburst of Pompeo's: ibid., fol. 23v. Silvia herself also cites the same words: ibid., fol. 3v. Fabritio, ibid., fol. 29r, offers the words in parentheses; they burnish Pompeo and tarnish Silvia. He claims to have heard the words as he entered the room.
97. Ibid., fol. 26r, Clementia.

98. For running in to quell the fight: ibid., fols. 14r, Cecila; 29r, Fabritio.

99. Cosmo says only that Silvia's servant summoned them: ibid., fol. 31r–v.

100. Ibid., fol. 14r, Cecilia.

101. Ibid., fols. 3v–4r, Silvia.

102. Ibid., fol. 14r, Cecilia. For the same words: ibid., fol. 4r, Silvia.

103. Ibid., fol. 4r, Silvia. Silvia claims Cosmo also restrained Pompeo, but in error, for Cosmo came only when she was back downstairs. Ibid., fol. 31v, Cosmo: "We went in the door and found that Silvia and Pompeo were shouting at one another downstairs."

104. Ibid., fols. 23r, Lucretia; 4r, Silvia.

105. For grabbing Silvia's arm: ibid., fols. 23r, Lucretia; 25v, Clementia; 29v, Fabritio.

106. Ibid., fol. 4r, Silvia. To go uncovered signaled a courtesan. For tears on the stairs: ibid., fol. 14v, Cecilia.

107. Ibid., fol. 4r, Silvia.

108. Fifty paces: I jogged Silvia's run, counting steps.

109. Ibid., fols. 4v, Silvia; 10v, Clementia; 21r, Pompeo; 27r, Francesca the servant; all for Pompeo's running after Silvia and fetching her back. Silvia dwelt at the eastern end of the della Valle palace complex, near the modern Largo Argentina, about a seven-minute walk from Pompeo's house. I thank Kathleen Christian for Silvia's location in the complex of della Valle palaces.

110. Ibid., fol. 31v, Cosmo, on waiting for the coach. He says it is the night's second hour (ca. 9 P.M.).

111. Ibid., fol. 4v, Silvia.

112. For the coach's return and the hour: ibid., fol. 31v, Cosmo.

113. Ibid., fol. 4v, Silvia.

114. Ibid., fols. 4v, Silvia; 31v, Cosmo.

115. Ibid., fol. 31v, Cosmo, on who was there.

116. Ibid.; see also ibid., fol. 29v, Fabritio.

117. Ibid., fol. 10v, Clementia.

118. Ibid., fols. 4v–5r, Silvia. What betokened this gesture, which Silvia found memorable? Anger barely contained?

119. Ibid., fols. 4v–5r, Silvia; 14v, Cecilia. In court (fol. 50v), Tiberio Alberini confirms Cecilia's willingness to call the notary but insists she did so only so that Vittoria would be left in peace. Tiberio probably wanted a slice of the inheritance.

120. Ibid., fol. 30v, Fabritio, who says this conversation took place while Silvia and Pompeo fought in the sala.

121. For the whole slap sequence: ibid., fol. 21r, Pompeo. Pompeo's partisans re-

call readily Silvia's transgressive words: ibid., fols. 29v, Fabritio; 31v, Cosmo. Silvia reluctantly concedes: "Perhaps I said something" to provoke the slap (fol. 5v). Caught in the middle, Tiberio Alberini concedes half of Silvia's reproach: "You are assassinating her! Oh, this is a piece of skulduggery!" (fol. 51v). Pompeo concedes the hand to dagger but, he insists, only to quell his sister's insults (fol. 21v). Many reported this slap, a grave offense: fols. 5v, Silvia; 10v, Clementia; 21r, Pompeo; 29r–v, Lucretia; 29v, Fabritio; 32r, Cosmo; 51v, Tiberio Alberini.

122. Ibid., fol. 14r, Cecilia, on her own intervention; ibid., fol. 5r, Silvia, on how Alberini and her brothers restrained Pompeo.

123. Ibid., fol. 32r, Cosmo.

124. For the exchange: ibid., fol. 21r, Pompeo.

125. The Alberini palace stood on the lower Corso.

126. For departures and bed: ibid., fol. 21v, Pompeo.

127. Ibid., fol. 15r, Cecilia.

128. Ibid., fol. 5v, Silvia.

129. Ibid.

130. On del Conte's domicile: ibid., fol. 18v, Pompeo. Ibid., fol. 37v, del Conte, that Pietro Paolo sent for him.

131. Trexler distinguishes "contract" and "sacrifice," two principles that, he posits, dominated Florentine moral and political discourse. See Richard Trexler, *The Public Life of Renaissance Florence* (New York: Academic Press: 1980), pp. 19, 33, and passim.

132. G.P. 31.1, fol. 6v, Silvia. Ascanio, if out of town, perhaps stayed at his house in Tivoli.

133. For Clementia's intervention and the apothecary's arrival: ibid., fol. 6r, Silvia.

134. For the exchange: ibid., fol. 15r, Cecilia.

135. Ibid., fol. 52r, Tiberio. This sharp retort, more calculating than other words attributed to Cecilia, comes secondhand from a report by her husband, who of course had a strong sense of his own stake in his wife's inclusion.

136. Ibid., fol. 6r–v, Silvia.

137. For this exchange: ibid., fol. 15r–v, Cecilia.

138. Ibid., fol. 23v, Lucretia. This may be hearsay, as is much of Lucretia's testimony. A servant, she was privy to few of the conversations. She may have assembled her version later, at Silvia's house.

139. Ibid., fol. 34r. Blandino, the merchant, says he has known the Giustini since 1544. He lives near Pietro Paolo. We have met him in these notes lending money to Ascanio for the latter's gambling. He also witnesses Not. Cap. 621,

fols. 188r, 421r, and Not. Cap. 622, fols. 134v, 183r, 191v, 203r–v, 233v. Most of these papers involve Cosmo. Cosmo brings Blandino and informs him in the garden, beforehand, of the need for a will.

140. For the exchange: G.P. 31.1, fols. 332v–333r, Cosmo.

141. For Bernardino's and Vittoria's exchange: ibid., fol. 33r, Cosmo.

142. Vittoria's will survives: Not. Cap. 622, fol. 127r–v.

143. The grain merchant Giovanni Battista Marioni would later be involved in the sale of Giustini assets in Città di Castello. See ibid., fols. 218v, 3 Aug. 1558; 222v, 19 Aug. 1558.

144. G.P. 31.1, fol. 15v, Cecilia. The precise timing of these words uttered before Bernardino is unclear.

145. Giuliano Blandino, witness, describes the person who objected as a red-visaged notary of the *vicario* (Rome acting bishop for local ecclesiastical affairs) and adds that he does not know him. This is probably Etienne de Montréal, for it is evident from Blandino's clear testimony that only one bystander protested: ibid., fol. 35v.

146. For the question about Ascanio: ibid., fol. 42r, Giovanni Battista Marioni of Gubbio, witness.

147. For the exchange with Cecilia: ibid., fol. 18v, Pompeo. Francesco di Giustiniano (of Montefiascone) and Pompeo's servant Bartolomeo di Taddeo, witnesses, confirm Cecilia's intervention: ibid., fols. 40r, 41r.

148. For Cecilia's and Vittoria's exchange: ibid., fols. 33v, Cosmo; 39r, Bernardino del Conte.

149. For Vittoria's rejection of Ascanio: ibid., fol. 41r, Bartolomeo di Taddeo, servant of Pompeo, witness; ibid., fol. 42r, Giovanni Battista Marioni, the merchant from Gubbio, witness. Bernardino del Conte makes clear that Etienne de Montréal's exclamation provoked Cecilia's protest, Pompeo's intervention, and Vittoria's reassertion of her rejection of Ascanio: ibid., fol. 39r.

150. For his own words and for Bernardino del Conte's resuming work: ibid., fol. 39v, Etienne de Montréal.

151. For his words calling all to notice and for Pompeo's alleged silence: ibid., fol. 39r, Bernardino del Conte, the notary.

152. For Bernardino's words of notice and for the list of heirs: ibid., fol. 35v, Giuliano Blandino, witness.

153. For Vittoria's final question and contentment: ibid., fols. 35v–36r, Giuliano Blandino, witness. For Pietro Paolo's departure: ibid., fol. 37v, del Conte.

154. Ibid., fol. 22r, Pompeo. Francesco di Giustiniano, a witness, confirms this

expression of contentment; another witness, Pompeo's servant, uses words almost identical to Pompeo's, as if they had colluded: ibid., fols. 40r, 41r.

155. For the clyster: ibid., fol. 40r, Francesco di Giustiniani, witness.

156. Cosmo describes how Bernardino del Conte sat in the antechamber writing the names of witnesses, who then dispersed: ibid., fol. 33v.

157. Bernardino del Conte, the notary, affirms that Vittoria died some three hours after she made her will: ibid., fol. 37r. Cosmo puts her death at the eighteenth or nineteenth hour, Roman afternoon: fol. 33v. The servant Lucretia puts the death "around the midday meal": fol. 23r. Other witnesses concur: fol. 43r. Though many must have grieved, we hear of feelings only from the old family friend Blandino: "I went to Mass and after Mass I passed by the house and found that she had lost the power of speech, and because of that I was dismayed, having left her well and in her right mind, and I stayed until she breathed her last and saw her opened up [for autopsy] and I stayed in the church until she was buried" (fol. 36r).

158. The court, suspecting poison, asks about the appearance of the corpse: ibid., fol. 7v, Silvia.

159. For patterns of piety, charity, and gender roles: Cohn, *Women in the Streets,* esp. chaps. 3–5. For female control of property: Samuel K. Cohn Jr., *The Cult of Remembrance and the Black Death* (Baltimore: Johns Hopkins University Press, 1992), pp. 197–201. For female wealth and power and for sentiments in wills: Chojnacki, "The Power of Love," pp. 126–48. For mothers' major role in the passage of property: Stanley Chojnacki, "The Most Serious Duty: Motherhood, Gender, and Patrician Culture in Renaissance Venice," in Marilyn Migiel and Juliana Schiesari, eds., *Refiguring Woman: Perspectives on Gender and the Italian Renaissance* (Ithaca: Cornell University Press, 1991), pp. 133–54, esp. pp. 143–44. For the passage of funds by bilateral inheritance into dowries: Joanne Ferraro, *Family and Public Life in Brescia, 1580–1650* (Cambridge and New York: Cambridge University Press, 1993), pp. 121–30. For female legacies and inheritance pathways: James S. Grubb, *Provincial Families of the Renaissance: Public and Private Life in the Veneto* (Baltimore: Johns Hopkins University Press, 1996), pp. 17, 28; and for the kinds of funerals chosen: pp. 68–69. For wills as a clue to female friendships and patronage: Dennis Romano, *Patricians and Popolani: The Social Foundations of the Venetian Renaissance State* (Baltimore: Johns Hopkins University Press, 1987), pp. 133–40. For using wills to bind servants to a family: Dennis Romano, *Housecraft and Statecraft: Domestic Service in Renaissance Venice, 1400–1600* (Baltimore: Johns Hopkins University Press, 1996), pp. 196–97.

160. ASV, Archivio della Valle–del Bufalo 182. We have no letters from Cecilia, but Silvia's to her husband are full of Giustini news and family politics. There is much scholarly debate on the nature of wives' alliances to families of birth and marriage. The classic argument for a main attachment to the natal family is in Christiane Klapisch-Zuber, *Women, Family, and Ritual in Renaissance Italy*, trans. Lydia G. Cochrane (Chicago: University of Chicago Press, 1985). See esp. chaps. 6 and 10. For more nuanced bilateralism: Sharon T. Strocchia, "Death Rites and the Ritual Family in Renaissance Florence," in Marce Tetel, Ronald G. Witt, and Rona Goffen, eds., *Life and Death in Fifteenth-Century Florence* (Durham, N.C.: Duke University Press, 1989), pp. 120–45.

161. For female violence in the pursuit of honor: Cohen and Cohen, *Words and Deeds*, pp. 90–94; Elizabeth S. Cohen, "Honor and Gender in the Streets of Early Modern Rome," *Journal of Interdisciplinary History* 22, no. 4 (1992): 597–625.

162. For the hour: Constituti 52, fol. 221, Ascanio. See also G.P. 31.1, fol. 45r. The sources for what follows are many. I will cite only the most useful.

163. The six males at the dinner were Pompeo, Fabritio, and Cosmo Giustini, Marcantonio Cantalmaggio, and Bartolomeo and Daniele Ferentilli, the latter two of whom I have not found in the Giustini papers: G.P. 31.1, fol. 45r, Cosmo and Fabritio's servant Angelo di Nobili.

164. Cantalmaggio joined his fellow townsman G. B. Marioni, witness to Vittoria's will, in negotiations around the sale of the Castello lands of the Giustini. See Not. Cap. 622, fols. 218v, 3 Aug. 1558; 222v, 19 Aug. 1558.

165. I infer François's hesitation at the door from his statement on opening to "Ascanio . . . , whom I do not know too well" (G.P. 31.1, fol. 47v). See Tomassetti, "Due manifesti," p. 94, for Ascanio's "schiauo, o servitor negro," not named, with him at a brawl. We do know that Giuliano had a father named Vincenzo and came from Tivoli, facts that tilt him away from Africa but do not rule it out: G.P. 33.15, fol. 1r.

166. For the meal's approaching end: G.P. 31.1, fols. 43r, 44r.

167. For Ascanio's words: ibid., fol. 43r, Cantalmaggio.

168. Ibid., fols. 43v–44r, Fabritio; cf. also ibid., fols. 43r, Cantalmaggio; 45r, Angelo di Nobili, butler of Cosmo and Fabritio.

169. For his exchange with Ascanio: ibid., fol. 44r, Fabritio.

170. For Cosmo's movements and words: Constituti 52, fol. 221v, Ascanio.

171. For Ascanio's change in manner and his words about the fraud: G.P. 31.1, fol. 44r–v, Fabritio. Other witnesses, including Ascanio himself, confirm the al-

legation about Lucretia's will: ibid., fol. 43r, Cantalmaggio; Constituti 52, fol. 221v, Ascanio.

172. Many witnesses attest that Pompeo was unarmed. For testimony friendly to Pompeo: G.P. 31.1, fols. 43r, 44v, 45r, 47v. Ascanio confirms the fact: Constituti 52, fol. 221v.

173. For Pompeo, unarmed, challenging Ascanio: G.P. 31.1, fol. 44v, Fabritio. For the charge that Ascanio is raising a ruckus: G.P. 33.15, fol. 1r, Giuliano, Ascanio's servant.

174. From here to Pompeo's taking a sword I follow Cantalmaggio's version, detailed and less partisan than the versions of the brothers and their servants: G.P. 31.1, fol. 43r–v.

175. This exchange is an amalgam of four accounts, two from either side. Two favor Pompeo: ibid., fols. 43v, Cantalmaggio; 145r, Angelo di Nobili, Cosmo and Fabritio's servant. Two favor Ascanio: Constituti 52, fol. 221v, Ascanio; G.P. 33.15, fol. 1r, Giuliano, Ascanio's servant, who alone offers "You know I have never considered you a brother and never will!" Giuliano's testimony throughout, so loyal to Ascanio and so different from all other versions, is thereby dubious.

176. For the finger biting: G.P. 31.1, fols. 45r, 46r, 47v, the servants Angelo di Nobili; Francesco di Dotti; and François the stable boy.

177. Ibid., fol. 43v. This version comes from the guest, Cantalmaggio. Pompeo's gross insult to Ascanio appears in many other testimonies. See ibid., fols. 44v, Fabritio; 45r, Angelo di Nobili; 47v, François. On the other hand, amour propre or shame deterred Ascanio from recounting this blow to his honor: Constituti 52, fol. 221v: "And there were many shameful words between him and me and he insulted me with very bad words." He says no more.

178. Did he draw the dagger? Ascanio denies it: Constituti 52, fol. 221v. Fabritio says he drew: G.P. 31.1, fol. 44v. Cantalmaggio, unfortunately, does not say, but his silence argues against a draw: G.P. 31.1, fol. 43v.

179. For Ascanio's words and lunge: G.P. 31.1, fol. 46v, Francesco di Dotti, servant. This account, loyal to Pompeo, includes the bitten finger but omits the obscene rejoinder.

180. G.P. 31.1, fol. 43v, Cantalmaggio; also fol. 46v, Francesco di Dotti. Ascanio's testimony, on the other hand, would have Cantalmaggio holding him after Pompeo had gone and armed himself. No one else confirms this.

181. For the well and the naked sword: G.P. 33.15, fol. 1r, Giuliano, Ascanio's servant. Pompeo's backers confirm this sequence: G.P. 31.1, fols. 43v, 44v, 45r, 46v, as on 53r does Pompeo himself.

182. For fetching a sword from the garden: G.P. 33.15, fol. 1v, Giuliano, Ascanio's servant.

183. For this exchange: G.P. 33.15, fol. 1v, unreliable testimony of Giuliano, Ascanio's servant.

184. Some versions call the weapon a *partigianone*. The *corsesca*'s blade was almond shaped, the *partigianone*'s asymmetrical, bellying like a half-moon.

185. For this disposition of the forces: G.P. 33.15, fols. 1v, 2r, Giuliano, Ascanio's servant. He claims implausibly that six or seven armed servants attacked his master but grants that only the Frenchman pressed him hard. François himself relates his part in the fight at G.P. 31.1, fol. 47v.

186. For the door and Ascanio's taunt: G.P. 31.1, fol. 44v, Fabritio. Two other witnesses confirm that Ascanio called his brother out to fight in the street: ibid., fol. 47v, François and Francesco di Dotti, servants. "Traitor" appears in di Dotti's version.

187. For the fallen cape: Constituti 52, fol. 221v, Ascanio.

188. For the opened door: ibid.

189. Ascanio claims fifteen battle axes arrayed against him: ibid., fol. 223v. Lorenzo Quarra, a neutral witness, cites "one or two": G.P. 33.15, fol. 3r.

190. Cohen and Cohen, *Words and Deeds,* pp. 135–57.

191. G.P. 33.15, fol. 3r, Lorenzo Quarra, an intervenor.

192. For the soldiers' words: ibid., fols. 3r, Lorenzo Quarra; 4v–5r, Agostino Bonamore, druggist.

193. For Fabritio's warning off the soldiers: G.P. 31.1, fol. 45r, Angelo di Nobili. Angelo could err here. Was Fabritio really telling François to keep out of the fight?

194. Ibid., fol. 53v, Pompeo: "Those fellows who were with Ascanio wanted to hit my brother, in his gown." Ibid., fol. 47r, Francesco di Dotti, servant, confirms the aimed blow.

195. On breaking up the fight: ibid., fol. 43v, Cantalmaggio. Ascanio claims the fight lasted half an hour. Lorenzo Quarra, less partisan, wagers it lasted a mere recited "credo," i.e., a few minutes: G.P. 33.15, fol. 3v.

196. For fetching the cape: G.P. 31.1, fol. 53v, Lorenzo Quarra, neutral witness.

197. For Ascanio's refusing an escort: G.P. 33.15, fol. 5r, Agostino Bonamore, neutral witness.

198. For the words by Sant'Agostino: G.P. 31.1, fol. 43v, Cantalmaggio.

199. Ibid.

200. For mock battles: Gregory Hanlon, "Les rituels de l'aggression au XVIIe siècle," *Annales, E.S.C.,* 40ème année, no. 2 (Mar.–Apr. 1985): 244–68. Italian fights were more sanguinary than French pantomimes.

201. On the use of criminal courts for domestic ends: Nicole Castan, "The Arbitration of Disputes under the *Ancien Régime*," in John Bossy, ed., *Disputes and Settlements: Law and Human Relations in the West* (Cambridge: Cambridge University Press, 1983), pp. 219–20.
202. Lacking the text of Ascanio's denunciation, I infer its contents from the court's questions to witnesses and from the wording of Pompeo's sentence.
203. For repayment of Ascanio's loan of 110 scudi to Capizucchi in 1555: Not. Cap. 621, fol. 535r, 1 June 1559. For Pompeo on Capizucchi's partisanship for Ascanio: G.P. 31.1, fol. 18r. For Ascanio's claim of his backing: Constituti 52, fol. 227r. For the relationship of the di Fabii and the Giustini mother: Not. Cap. 619, fol. 115, 22 Apr. 1541.
204. G.P. 31.1, fol. 8v.
205. Ibid., fols. 13r–16v.
206. Ibid., fols. 17r–22v.
207. Ibid., fols. 43r–47v. The *processo* is not cleanly chronological.
208. Ibid., fols. 23r–28r.
209. Ibid., fols. 37r–42v.
210. Ibid., fols. 28v–31r.
211. Ibid., fol. 50r.
212. The cover pages of the trials call them defendants: G.P. 31.1, fols. 1v, 2v; 33.15, fol. 1r.
213. Constituti 52, fols. 220r–224v.
214. G.P. 31.1, fols. 53r–54r.
215. Ibid., fols. 54v–55v.
216. Ibid.
217. The cover of G.P. 31.1, fol. 2v, is labeled "In the case of an alleged falsity of a will in Rome." Atti di Cancelleria, busta 6 (unbound sentences), 7 Oct. 1557, sentence of Pompeo, indicates the major charges but only alludes to others.
218. Silvia, letters 1–4: 8 Jan. 1558, 3 July 1558, 13 Aug. 1558, 29 Aug. 1558, no pagination.
219. For Cosmo, addressed as doctor of both (canon and civil) laws: Not. Cap. 622, fol. 189r, 26 May 1558. For Fabritio's first appearance with the title: ibid., fol. 218r–v, 3 Aug. 1558.
220. Ibid., fol. 475r, 2 Oct. 1561, numbers the servants. Ibid., fol. 233r–v, 2 Sept. 1558, mentions the mule and sets room and board for household and beast at 300 scudi annually. The rent, that first year, just canceled a debt.
221. Ibid., fols. 205v, 22 June 1558; 218v, 3 Aug. 1558.
222. ASR, Governatore, Tribunale Criminale, atti 6, Sentences, busta 20 (1558), sentence 10.

223. ASV, Archivio della Valle–del Bufalo 182, Pompeo's sole letter.

224. Silvia, letter 5, 19 Jan. 1559.

225. ASR, Governatore, Tribunale Criminale, Atti di Cancelleria, busta 6, Sentences, busta 20 (1558).

226. Silvia, letter 11, 13 June 1559. Pompeo does not want Cosmo told of Fabritio's banishment, for fear Cosmo will go to Gubbio to see him. Not. Cap. 622, fols. 314r and 332r, a single act of 28 June 1559, interleaved by others, shows him already dead.

227. Silvia, letter 6, 19 Feb. 1559.

228. Not. Cap. 1517, fol. 95v, 8 Feb. 1559.

229. Ibid., fols. 97r–102r, 9 Feb. 1559.

230. Ibid., 616, fol. 127r, 18 July 1557.

231. Ibid., 1517, fol. 99r, 9 Feb. 1559.

232. Ibid.

233. Silvia, letter 7, 16 Mar. 1559.

234. Not. Cap. 1517, fols. 206v–207r. I think, but cannot prove, that this is a new will, not that of the month before.

235. Silvia, letter 11, 13 June 1559.

236. Not. Cap. 622, fol. 332r.

237. Not. Cap. 1518, fols. 279, 3 Mar. 1560; 354, 15 May 1560.

238. Ibid., fol. 406r, 6 June 1560.

239. Ibid.

240. Ibid., fol. 719v, 27 Sept. 1560. The act is drawn up in Cardinal Crispi's palace.

241. Archivio di Stato di Mantova, Archivio Gonzaga, busta 890, fol. 82v. I thank the generosity of Giampiero Brunelli for this extract from his data base of military men and for all my other information on Pompeo Giustini's subsequent career and death.

242. For the legal actions, see the introduction to the agreement: Not. Cap. 1519, fols. 420r–422v, 4 June 1561.

243. Ibid., 14 June 1561.

244. Ibid., fols. 446–47, 21 June 1561.

245. Ibid., fol. 528v, 24 July 1561. Laodomia is still at the convent, where the act is drawn up.

246. Ibid., fols. 635r–636r, 30 Aug. 1561.

247. Ibid., fol. 636r.

248. Not. Cap. 1520, fols. 472v–473r, 12 July 1562.

249. ASV, Archivio della Valle–del Bufalo 182, fol. 2r, remark by seventeenth-century compiler of the letters.

250. Magni, *Archivio della Camera Capitolina, Protocolli,* fol. 719.
251. ASV, Armadio 42, busta 20, fol. 287r; information via Giampiero Brunelli.
252. Archivio di Stato di Mantova, Archivio Gonzaga, busta 898, fol. 124r–v; Archivio di Stato di Venezia, Senato, Dispacci, Roma, 2, fol. 48r–v; both via Giampiero Brunelli.
253. Archivio di Stato di Mantova, Archivio Gonzaga, busta 898, fol. 450v, via Giampiero Brunelli.
254. Biblioteca Apostolica Vaticana, Urb. Lat. 1041, Avvisi di Roma, pt. 1, fol. 156r–v, 21 Sept. 1659, via Giampiero Brunelli.
255. Archivio Colonna, II C.D. Ca 38 and 39; Biblioteca Apostolica Vaticana, Urb. Lat. 1042, Avvisi di Roma, fol. 51v, 25 Apr. 1571; both via Giampiero Brunelli.
256. Archivio di Stato di Venezia, Senato, Dispacci, Roma, Sorzano and P. Tiepolo to the Senato, 4 Dec. 1571, via Giampiero Brunelli.
257. Weber, *Genealogien,* vol. 1, p. 351.
258. For the Carnival incident: G.P. 177.3 (1582). For the footstool killing: G.P. 180.19 (1582).
259. See, e.g., Margaret L. King, *Women of the Renaissance* (Chicago: University of Chicago Press, 1991), which sees only pervasive female impotence. For similar bleakness, see Claudia Opitz, "Life in the Late Middle Ages," in Georges Duby and Michelle Perrot, general eds., *A History of Women in the West,* vol. 2, *Silences of the Middle Ages,* ed. Christiane Klapisch-Zuber (Cambridge: Belknap Press of Harvard University Press, 1992), p. 283: "in middle-class families the husband functioned as the sole enforcer of social norms and controls." These works have far too constricted a notion of the agency available to underlings of all sorts. For a more balanced view, see Calvi, *Contratto morale;* Chojnacki, "The Power of Love"; and the entire oeuvre of Natalie Z. Davis. See also Thomas Kuehn, *Law, Family, and Women: Toward a Legal Anthropology of Renaissance Italy* (Chicago: University of Chicago Press, 1991), which modifies the view that Italian law always tilted against females.
260. Romano, *Housecraft,* pp. 193–207, discusses the complex ties that often bound masters and servants. For the privileged milk-mothers like Clementia, see p. 200. For the participation of male servants in their masters' violence, see p. 205.
261. Isaac, *Transformation of Virginia,* p. 357.

CHAPTER FOUR

1. Archivio di Stato di Roma (henceforth ASR), Governatore, Tribunale Criminale, Processi (sixteenth century), busta 36, entire. Henceforth, for

this manuscript I will simply give folio numbers, as most of this chapter comes out of this one, very long trial of 446 folia.

    Lucretia (fol. 16v) and Livia (fol. 17v) first appear as in jail on 12 Oct., Faustina on 17 Oct. 1557. Cristoforo first testifies on 12 Oct. and is already in jail (fol. 20v).

2. Biblioteca Apostolica Vaticana, Urb. Lat. 1038, Avvisi di Roma, fol. 272v, 9 Oct. 1557, reporting the arrest, cited suspicions of corruption: "he will explain how one can in a few years buy houses and build at great expense, buy an apostolic protonotariate, a notariate of the Camera, a knighthood, properties in the hometown, and other things."

3. Alberto Aubert, *Paolo IV: Politica, Inquisizione e storiografia* (Florence: Le Lettere, 1999), p. 47 n. 5, citing Vatican manuscripts; Paolo Grandi, "Il processo Pallantieri" (master's thesis, University of Bologna, 1981), p. 40. I owe Signore Grandi great thanks for a personal copy of his thesis. Fols. 341v–342r, Pallantieri.

4. Grandi, "Il processo Pallantieri," p. 38, for the near miss at the *fiscalato* in 1549.

5. Fol. 368v gives verbatim the memo to Julius III for the *fiscale*'s post.

6. Fol. 364r–v, Pallantieri.

7. Grandi, "Il processo Pallantieri," pp. 40–41.

8. ASR, Governatore, Tribunale Criminale, Processi, busta 56 (1560), fol. 34r, Cardinal Crispo.

9. Fol. 60r–v, Pallantieri. Since the Inquisition sat on Thursdays, the conversation probably took place on 30 Sept., because one week later Pallantieri was in jail.

10. Fol. 58v, Pallantieri, punctuation added for clarity.

11. For the birth: Grandi, "Il processo Pallantieri," p. 20; for the legal studies: p. 33.

12. For the wife's name: fol. 3v, Merulo.

13. Fol. 3r, Merulo: "In the time I have been with Messer Alessandro, he has never had his wife here in Rome." Merulo had served Pallantieri since 1544.

14. Fol. 61r, Pallantieri; Christoph Weber, *Legati e governatori dello stato pontificio (1550–1809)* (Rome: Ministero per i Beni Culturali ed Ambientali, 1994), p. 964, helps clinch the date through details on Baccio Valori, his boss.

15. Fol. 426v, Pallantieri: he was *luogotenente* to Cardinal di Trani; Grandi, "Il processo Pallantieri," p. 36, calls him *procuratore generale* and then *luogotenente in criminalibus* to *uditore Parisio,* not yet a cardinal.

16. For both cities: fol. 61r, Pallantieri.

17. For the future cardinal as patron: fol. 61r, Pallantieri; for the reason for the

jailing: Grandi, "Il processo Pallantieri," pp. 28–29 (but with an error in the date: 1554 for 1534) and p. 36.

18. Fol. 364r, Pallantieri.

19. Fol. 61r, Pallantieri.

20. Fol. 62v, Pallantieri. In this capacity, he served first the future Cardinal Parisio and then the future Cardinal Cicada.

21. Grandi, "Il processo Pallantieri," pp. 37–38; fol. 347r, Pallantieri.

22. Fol. 347v, Pallantieri; and for Ascoli: fol. 62r, Pallantieri.

23. For getting the job: fol. 62r, Pallantieri; for the castle: fol. 404r (the grateful town wanted to erect a statue in his honor for reclaiming their castle, he claims); for the threat to appeal to higher authorities against his conduct: fol. 425r–v, Pallantieri; for judicial review: fol. 30v, Merulo; for sexual matters: fol. 398v, Aurelini; for judicial review of sexual matters: fol. 406v, Pallantieri.

24. For Ulm: fol. 388r, Pallantieri; for his return from the Netherlands in 1548: fols. 2r, Merulo, and 128r, Lucretia; see also Pallantieri: fols. 62v, 388r, and 419v–420r, the latter for the mission's duration.

25. For the sense of blockage as a married man: fols. 363v–364r, Pallantieri.

26. Fol. 363v, Pallantieri. Pallantieri was willing to call the *fiscalato* a *prelatura* (prelacy), as if it too were a cleric's position, though it in fact was not: "[The pope's brother, Del Monte,] had spoken to me about that other prelacy than the *fiscale's* job, since I could not be a prelate, for I had a wife" (fols. 363v–364r).

27. For Genoa and Siena: fol. 363v, Pallantieri. The pope was upset at the prospect, Pallantieri claimed, and said, "I do not want you to leave, for I want to make you *fiscale* in Rome."

28. For the job of *luogotenente in criminalibus* for the governor: fol. 3r, Merulo; fols. 55r, 118v, both Pallantieri.

29. On his discussions about the *fiscalato* with Farnese, the pope's cardinal nephew (acting chief minister), before he went to Flanders: fol. 367v, Pallantieri. See also Grandi, "Il processo Pallantieri," p. 38. For his memorandum to Julius III seeking the *fiscalato,* in full: fol. 368v.

30. Fol. 55r, Pallantieri.

31. For Camerino: Grandi, "Il processo Pallantieri," p. 39; for Ravenna: fol. 2r, Merulo; for Ravenna and Spoleto: fol. 347r, Pallantieri; for Todi: fols. 62v–63r, Pallantieri.

32. For the whole scam in Tuscanella: ASR, Governatore, Tribunale Criminale, Processi (sixteenth century), busta 33, case 27. For the line about profiting a scudo on each grain purchase: ibid., fol. 86v. Since grain sold in Rome that

year for four scudi a *rubbio,* such a cut, if real, would have yielded one-quarter of the price, so the claim is too strong. The witness Mansueto, fol. 68r, lays out the whole scam.

33. Fols. 351v–352r, Pallantieri. The second-person pronouns are generally the formal *voi* but once slip to the familiar *tu,* conveying cozy relations with the pope.

34. Fol. 82r, Pallantieri.

35. Fol. 311r, Pallantieri.

36. Fol. 100r, Pallantieri.

37. Fol. 212r, Pallantieri.

38. For Lucretia's appearances in court in Pallantieri's absence: fols. 15r–16v, 12 Oct. 1557; fol. 31r, 21 Oct. 1557; fols. 88–90, 22 Nov. 1557.

39. Fols. 116r–129r, 28 Nov. 1557; fol. 143r, 1 Dec. 1557, the time of the torture.

40. Fol. 143r–v, Lucretia and the court.

41. Elizabeth S. Cohen, "The Trials of Artemisia Gentileschi: A Rape as History," *Sixteenth Century Journal* 31, no. 1 (2000): 47–75.

42. Thomas V. Cohen, "Three Forms of Jeopardy: Honor, Pain, and Truth-Telling in a Sixteenth-Century Italian Courtroom," *Sixteenth Century Journal* 29, no. 4 (1998): 975–98.

43. Fol. 17v, Cristoforo, for the father's profession and location, for his arrival in the Holy City one year after the 1527 sack, and for the date of his marriage: "about two years, or a year and a half, before Pope Clement died." The pope died in Sept. 1534.

44. Fol. 16r, Lucretia. The logic of several testimonies sets the date of Adriana's death at 24 Nov. 1556. See Cristoforo, fol. 19v; Faustina, fol. 25r; and the chronology of baby Helena, born just before the death, below.

45. Fol. 17v, Cristoforo.

46. Fol. 17r, Cristoforo.

47. Fol. 17r and passim, Cristoforo.

48. By deduction from the location of Pallantieri's house across the street. For the latter: "It is near Pasquino, before you arrive at Pasquino, on the right side, in a street" (fol. 313v, Merulo). Merulo must be approaching the statue, in his mind, from the south because the street ended and still ends at Pasquino.

49. Fol. 19r, Cristoforo, by deduction. He puts her age at thirteen or fourteen when, at Christmas 1548 (by other deductions), she spent a week at Pallantieri's house.

50. The court, in Oct. 1557, labels her as sixteen years old: fol. 24r.

51. By deductions. Fol. 110v: Pallantieri in court asked Livia how she could re-

member circumstances around the birth of Orazio in (by further deductions) Aug. 1548 if she then was only five or six years old. Moreover, Livia,
fol. 8v: "I am the youngest, and I am fifteen, going on sixteen."

52. Fol. 81r, Pallantieri: "[T]he wife . . . taught certain little girls and little boys."

53. Fol. 10v, Livia, describing escaping Pallantieri's attentions by reading in the
kitchen: "I was alone there in the kitchen, reading a book."

54. The girls' names need not have come straight from books, as most were
common in Rome. Lucretia, the famous victim of King Tarquin's rape, appears in Livy, and Livia, Augustus Caesar's wife, is in Suetonius. Faustina,
Marcus Aurelius's consort, is in neither book, but her surviving statues are
abundant. Martia's name is more rare in sixteenth-century Rome. It hearkens to the name of Mars. The only notable classical exemplar, one Marcia,
the concubine of the horrid emperor Commodus, is by career doubly shady,
and so a very dubious model. Furthermore, though the Renaissance often
substituted *t* for *c,* her etymology is in fact different, and Adriana, the girls'
mother, did teach school and should have known. I thank my colleague
Jonathan Edmondson for counsel here.

55. Fol. 139r, Faustina: "I and my sister never went out except, with my family,
to the Seven Churches." This pilgrimage, new in the sixteenth century, visited five basilicas: Saint Peter's, Saint John Lateran, San Paolo fuori le Mura,
Santa Maria Maggiore, and San Lorenzo fueri le Mura. It also stopped at the
catacomb church of San Sebastiano and at Santa Croce in Gerusalemme.

56. Fol. 106v, Livia.

57. Fol. 127r, Lucretia.

58. Fols. 109v–110, Livia: "They never came, except sometimes they came to
the shop to talk with Messer. They never came upstairs to Madonna. And
Messer knew them; they were those men who were living in Lucretia's
house." About the German acquaintances of Cristoforo, see, e.g., fol. 106v,
Livia: "Nobody came to our house except those who came to the shop to buy
lutes and cords, and I could not name anybody because I did not know
them."

59. Fol. 126v, Lucretia.

60. Fol. 126r–v, Lucretia; ibid., for Stefano's other three teachers.

61. For the friar, a kinsman of the mother's: fol. 124v, Lucretia; for the priest: fol.
128r, Lucretia.

62. Fol. 127v, Lucretia. She adds that his partner never came upstairs. See also
Faustina, fol. 139v, for his name: "There was no one except a cloth merchant
who gave us work, named Ambrosio, who came for awhile."

63. Fols. 139v–140r, Faustina: "Women did come to bring us work, but men

never came." Faustina mentions the young son of one female customer, who asked that they make his shirt look nice.

64. Fol. 139v, Faustina: "I saw him sometimes from the blinds, in the street, but I never talked with him."

65. For the two years in the first house and for 1544 as the beginning of their acquaintance: fol. 2v, Merulo.

66. Fols. 63v, Pallantieri; 349v, Pallantieri.

67. For the investigation of Onorio Savelli's crimes: ASR, Governatore, Tribunale Criminale, Processi, busta 116 (1566).

68. Fol. 63r, Pallantieri. Pallantieri claims in court he had protested to the pope that the relationship was too close, given god-kinship, free house, and services rendered, to let him go, "for I was god-kinsman of the signore and had lived here in Rome in his house and done him many favors." Pallantieri asserts that Julius replied that even if Angelo came back to life, he would still send him.

69. Fol. 3r, Merulo. Merulo remained in Pallantieri's employ in the 1560s.

70. Fol. 351r, Pallantieri.

71. Fol. 348r–v, Pallantieri: "And there once saw fit to take pleasure in my house Pope Paul III, of blessed memory, with all his court, a great favor to me, even if it cost me several hundred scudi."

72. Fol. 6v, Merulo: "From the beginning of our living in that house—we weren't there six months—Messer Alessandro began to pay court to the women in the house of Messer Cristoforo." Fol. 128r, Lucretia: "Shortly before he began to look at me, at his house, he arrived from Flanders."

73. Fol. 12r, Lucretia.

74. Fol. 12r–v, Lucretia; also fol. 116v, Lucretia.

75. Fol. 12v, Lucretia. The expression *fare le baie,* "to kid around," "to joke," is here distinctly sexual; Lucretia and her sisters use it throughout the trial to denote heavy flirtation.

76. Fol. 12v, Lucretia. In fact, unless Pallantieri started flirting a year sooner than I calculate, these conversations probably lasted only about four months.

77. Fol. 13r, Lucretia.

78. Ibid.

79. Fol. 13r–v, Lucretia.

80. Fol. 18v, Cristoforo. Or so he says. Cristoforo is an evasive witness.

81. Fol. 116v, Lucretia.

82. Ibid.

83. Fol. 13v, Lucretia. Lucretia, fol. 116v, mentions kisses.

84. Fol. 145v, Giacomina, Helena's wet nurse, for Pallantieri's appearance: "He is a big man with a long, whitish beard, a brusque expression, and a long purple robe." For Helena and for this description, see her story below. For wearing cape and sword, Merulo, in response to a question about Pallantieri's love expeditions, states, "I have seen him indeed go out alone at night, with sword and cape" (fol. 5v). Lucretia herself assumed that Pallantieri was a priest: "You go dressed as a priest" (fol. 128r).

85. Fol. 117v, Lucretia; for the second rape attempt: fol. 13v.

86. Fols. 13v–14r, Lucretia. For this chronology, see also fol. 117r, Lucretia.

87. Fol. 117r–v, Lucretia.

88. Fol. 14r, Lucretia.

89. Ibid.

90. Ibid.: "And my mother opened the door, for he said, 'What do you want me to do? Given what I can do, if you do not open for me, you will not have anything.'" The passage continues in a similar vein on fol. 14v.

91. For pregnancy at the end of one month: fol. 14r, Lucretia; see also fol. 117v, Lucretia.

92. Fol. 14v, Lucretia.

93. Fol. 117v, Lucretia.

94. Ibid. Lucretia adds, "My mother had spoken with my father many times beforehand."

95. Ibid.

96. Fol. 14v, Lucretia.

97. Fols. 117v–118r, Lucretia. I am using two accounts, from separate depositions. They are very similar but vary somewhat in the distribution of sharp detail. The burnt finger transaction must have happened, for Livia too refers to it in her testimony. Livia calls up the incident as express proof of her veracity: "I will give you another sign [of memory]. That day that you came was Christmas Eve, and you had burned your finger and had some varnish put on it" (fols. 110v–111r).

98. Fols. 117v–118r, Lucretia.

99. Fol. 10v, Livia: "I saw her, for she took her clothing and he took her away and went down the stairs."

100. Fols. 18v–19r, Cristoforo. Among his other fibs, Cristoforo puts this negotiation before the child's conception.

101. For three days: fol. 14v, Lucretia; for four or five: fol. 11r, Lucretia; for a week: fols. 19r, Cristoforo, and 27v, Faustina.

102. Fol. 14v, Lucretia.

103. Fol. 27v, Faustina.

104. Fols. 14v, 118r, Lucretia.

105. Fol. 14v, Lucretia: "And after that he came in the night to our house and had sex with me, continuing the practice, and when he came there he gave caresses to my other sisters." Translation here is tricky, as *faceva careze* could just mean "he was nice." Nevertheless, context here, subsequent tales, and the girls' habitual use of the term to mean sexual touching all argue for my translation.

106. Fol. 5v, Merulo: "I have seen him indeed go out alone at night, with sword and cape, and I think he went there, and he stayed four or five hours each time. . . . I waited for him, and I waited upstairs in the house."

107. Fol. 110r–v, Livia.

108. Fol. 110v, Livia.

109. Fol. 15r, Lucretia.

110. Fols. 15r, 118r–v, Lucretia.

111. For this incident: fol. 128v, Lucretia. Lucretia puts his age at two months and slots the event into the Vacant See of Paul III. Paul died on 10 Nov. 1549, when the boy was two and a half months old.

112. Fol. 121v, Lucretia.

113. Fols. 128v–129r, Pallantieri and Lucretia.

114. Fol. 118v, Lucretia.

115. For the high status of flying fowl like pigeons in food's hierarchy: Allan J. Grieco, "Food and Social Classes in Late Medieval and Renaissance Italy," in Jean-Louis Flandrin and Alessandro Montanari, eds., *Food: A Culinary History from Antiquity to the Present* (New York: Columbia University Press, 1999), pp. 302–12 (French and Italian editions, Paris and Rome, 1996).

116. Fol. 118v, Lucretia.

117. Fol. 15r, Lucretia.

118. Ibid.: "He kept up his practice with me for more than a year in all, until about three months before I married."

119. We know the rough date by inference; Pallantieri was by then *luogotenente in criminalibus,* a judicial office he acquired in the Vacant See of Paul III (10 Nov. 1549–8 Feb. 1550). For his office: fol. 128v, Lucretia. Furthermore, Cristoforo, fol. 19r, remarks that it was the *anno santo,* 1550, a jubilee year. Lucretia had two children by 1552, so we cannot place her wedding very late in 1550.

120. Fol. 118v, Lucretia.

121. Grandi, "Il processo Pallantieri," p. 164.

122. Fols. 118v–120r (fol. 119 never existed), Lucretia: "And so the *amicitia* [relationship] ended." *Amicitia* is hard to translate, for in sexual matters it meant

not only "friendship" but any steady partnership, whatever the accompanying sentiments.

123. Fol. 88v, Cristoforo.

124. Fol. 26r, Faustina.

125. Ibid.: "She had the dowry from the Confraternity of the Annunziata and also a little bit from Messer Alessandro, although at the time he was angry at my mother because she would not consent that he have sex with me." We never learn the dowry subsidy from the Annunziata.

126. Fol. 15r–v, Lucretia.

127. Fol. 122v, Lucretia.

128. Fol. 123r, Lucretia.

129. Fol. 109r, Lucretia.

130. For the visit: fol. 15v, Lucretia. More on this visit and on continued contact with her sisters below, in Faustina's and Livia's stories.

131. Fol. 124v, Lucretia: "This Messer Alberto slept with me after my husband went away. It's been five months. Before that we did not sleep together [i.e., spend the night], but for a year now he has had carnal knowledge of me but did not sleep there [i.e., in her house]."

132. Fols. 123r–124v, Lucretia and Pallantieri.

133. Fol. 80r: Pallantieri claims the mother is a servant.

134. Fols. 80r–v, Pallantieri and the court.

135. Fol. 81r, Pallantieri: "Then I kept him in the house of a woman whose name I do not remember, but the husband is a process server of the governor, and then, if I am right, I kept him in the house of a Maestro Bartolomeo, who lives by the Customs House."

136. Fol. 75v: Pallantieri calls her eighty years old.

137. Fols. 7r, 8r, Merulo: "She ceded it for benefits received and for the love she bore that boy." Agostino Merulo's attestation of her affection could be just an apologia for his master's shady legal actions.

138. For Fiorina and the inn: fols. 7v–8r, Merulo; 21v, Fiorina; for Fiorina's responsibility while the boy was with a nurse: fol. 9v, Livia.

139. Fol. 21r–v, Fiorina.

140. Fol. 21v, Fiorina.

141. For his age and weaning: fol. 9r, Livia.

142. Fol. 81r–v, Pallantieri: "Because the wife, so far as one could see, taught certain little girls and little boys, so that she teach Orazio too and bring him up." For his learning to read at the Gramar house: fol. 9r, Livia.

143. Fols. 83v–84r, Pallantieri. At the time, people sometimes called mucous diarrhea "worms."

144. Pallantieri explains that the pope let him have a special dispensation from the rules when he leased Fiorina's inn: "He did me the favor, having learned of the gifts of this boy" (fol. 76r).

145. Fol. 5r, Merulo; fol. 25r, Faustina. Inference from other details rules out the Feast of Catherine of Siena, which leaves the Feast of Catherine of Alexandria.

146. Fol. 24r, Faustina: "He kept him as his son and has done so and does do and it's been about a year." Pallantieri seems to put the move before Adriana's death: "I put him there in the house [Pallantieri's], where he has been ever since, except after the death of Maestro Cristoforo's wife" (fol. 81v). The implication here is that he went back to Cristoforo's house briefly when his grandmother died.

147. Fol. 393r, Johanna the laundress.

148. Fol. 18r, Cristoforo: "He went to his house to be schooled with his sons." Carlo, the eldest, was twenty-nine or thirty. See also fol. 4r, Merulo.

149. Fol. 8r, Merulo.

150. Fol. 18r, Cristoforo; fol. 4r, Merulo. For Camerario's exploitation of young women: ASR, Governatore, Tribunale Criminale, Processi, busta 44, case 10, summer 1558.

151. Fol. 82r, Pallantieri.

152. For the gossip: fols. 28v–29v, Mattea, wife of a bookseller who lived by San Lorenzo in Damaso, just down the street.

153. Fols. 141v–142r, Faustina. Cristoforo told Adriana, who told Pallantieri, who told Faustina. So this must have happened late, during Faustina's liaison.

154. For the claim and words: fol. 26v, Faustina.

155. Fols. 26v–27r, Faustina.

156. Fol. 27r–v, Faustina. The passage also refers to Livia, more recently.

157. Fol. 24v, Faustina.

158. Fol. 24r–v, Faustina.

159. Fol. 15v, Lucretia.

160. Ibid.

161. Fols. 24v–25r, Faustina.

162. Fols. 27v–28r, Faustina.

163. Fol. 10r, Livia.

164. Fol. 19v, Cristforo.

165. Fol. 27v, Faustina.

166. Fol. 91r, Faustina.

167. Fol. 90r–v, Lucretia.

168. Fol. 19v, Cristoforo.

169. Fol. 36r, Faustina.

170. Fol. 25r, Faustina.

171. Ibid.: "The child was born, for I was in the ninth month, and during the birth I was very sick and the child could not be born, and so he died. And to receive him at the birth nobody was there except my mother and my sister Martia."

172. Fol. 25r, Faustina.

173. Ibid.: "Messer Alessandro continued seeing me and came to the house while I was still in bed. After I was cured and out of bed, he had sex with me many times."

174. Fol. 27v, Faustina.

175. Fols. 89v–90r, Lucretia.

176. Fol. 136v, Faustina.

177. Fol. 25r, Faustina.

178. Fol. 136v, Faustina.

179. Fols. 25r, 136v, Faustina.

180. Fols. 19v, Cristoforo; 25r, Faustina.

181. Fol. 25r–v, Faustina.

182. Fol. 25v, Faustina.

183. Fols. 108v, Livia; 123v, Lucretia; 25v–26r, Faustina.

184. Fols. 15r, Lucretia; 27v, Faustina.

185. Fol. 127r, Lucretia.

186. Fol. 25v, Faustina. This is the same monastery that figures in chapter 3, the story of Vittoria Giustini. Cristoforo says the letter was a d[ett]a instanza mia, that is, in his name (fol. 20r).

187. Fol. 141r, Faustina.

188. Fol. 25v, Faustina.

189. Fols. 25v–26r, Faustina.

190. Fol. 26r, Faustina.

191. Ibid.

192. Fol. 10v, Livia.

193. Ibid.

194. Ibid.

195. For Cristoforo sending Faustina back by coach: fol. 11r, Livia.

196. Fol. 91r–v, Faustina.

197. Three scudi: fol. 11r, Livia; twenty-eight giulii: fol. 20r, Cristoforo; Faustina is not sure if the fee is twenty-seven or twenty-eight giulii: fol. 25v.

198. Fol. 144v, Livia.

199. Ibid.
200. Fols. 37v–38r, Socio; 2r, Merulo; and for his career: 25r, Paolo Vittorio.
201. Fol. 188r: The line is from a transcript of Pallantieri's intercepted letter, included with the trial. For "an old fellow": fol. 20v, Paolo Vittorio.
202. Fol. 41r, Socio.
203. Fol. 42r, Socio.
204. Fols. 94v–95r, Faustina. Socio (fol. 19v) and Lucretia (fols. 15v–16r) confirm this mission of Socio's.
205. Fol. 42r–v, Socio.
206. Fol. 95r, Socio.
207. Fols. 42r–43r, Socio. Italians did not give children the names of living kin.
208. Fol. 95v, Socio.
209. Fol. 43r, Socio.
210. Ibid.
211. Ibid.
212. Fol. 95v, Socio.
213. Fol. 145v, Giacomina.
214. For the amount: fol. 20r, Cristoforo; for the tidings: fol. 95v, Socio.
215. Fol. 20r, Cristoforo.
216. Fol. 106r, Livia and Pallantieri.
217. Fol. 121r, Lucretia.
218. Fol. 108v, Livia.
219. Fol. 140r, Faustina.
220. Fol. 108r–v, Livia; for the open door: fol. 140r, Faustina.
221. Fol. 140r, Faustina.
222. Ibid.: "I never saw him enter but Messer Alessandro did tell me that he went in."
223. Fol. 109r, Livia.
224. Fol. 27r, Faustina.
225. Fol. 9v, Livia. See also fols. 16v–17r, Livia; 27r, Faustina, who claims to have stayed close, in earlier times, to keep Pallantieri off.
226. Fols. 108v, Livia; 16r, Lucretia. The date of moving is by inference from the month of marriage, in June, "three months later." See fol. 8v, Livia.
227. Fol. 5r, Merulo.
228. Fols. 17v, Cristoforo; 8v, Livia.
229. Fol. 121v, Lucretia.
230. Fols. 95v–96r, Livia.
231. Aubert, *Paolo IV,* pp. 32–36, 43–48, 127–61, and passim.
232. For the sodomy: fols. 398r–399v, 407v–412v.

233. Grandi, "Il processo Pallantieri," pp. 55–56.

234. Ibid., p. 57.

235. Ibid., p. 81.

236. Ibid., p. 85.

237. Ibid., p. 219.

238. Ibid., pp. 178–79. Biblioteca Casanatense, MS 2314, "Esecuzione di Giustizia in Roma sotto i Papi Sisto V, Pio V, Urbano VIII, Innocenzenio X, Clemente XI: Relazione della prigionia e morte del fiscal Palentieri nel pap[a]to di felicis memorie papae Pio V," fols. 160r–175v, is colorful but not accurate on most points; it has Pallantieri hanged, not beheaded.

CHAPTER FIVE

1. This chapter has benefited from the encouragement, criticism, and kind counsel of David Gentilcore, Greg Hanlon, and Nancy Siraisi.

2. Archivio di Stato di Roma, Governatore, Tribunale Criminale, Processi (sixteenth century), busta 180, case 7 (1582), fols. 395r–396r. Henceforth, since all citations come from the same manuscript, I will use just folio numbers.

3. Giovanna Fiume, "Il sordo macello dei mariti: Un processo per veneficio nella Palermo di fine Settecento," in Lucia Ferrante, Maura Palazzi, and Gianna Pomata, eds., *Ragnatela di rapporti: Patronage e reti di relazione nella storia delle donne* (Turin: Rosenberg e Sellier, 1988), pp. 435–53, for a great chain of husband killings, all using louse-killing ointment as the fatal remedy to unhappy marriages.

4. Gene Brucker, *Giovanni and Lusanna: Love and Marriage in Renaissance Florence* (Berkeley and Los Angeles: University of California Press, 1986), pp. 29–33, 49, for the lovers' promise and the suspicious death of the inconvenient husband; pp. 72–73, for the ban and the possibility of Roman dispensation.

5. Cesarina Casanova and Giovanni Tocci, eds., *Storia di Forlì*, vol. 3 ([Forlì?]: Nuova Alfa Editoriale, 1989), pp. 14–15; Sigismondo Marchesi, *Supplemento istorico dell'antica città di Forlì in cui si descrive la provincia di Romagna* (Forlì: al segno di S. Antonio Abbate, 1678; repr., Bologna: Forni, [1968]), pp. 609–11, 613–14, and passim.

6. *Catholic Encyclopedia*, s.v. "Nuncio"; Konrad Eubel, *Hierarchia Catholica medii et recentioris aevi*, vol. 3 (Regensberg: Monasterii sumptibus et typis librariae Regensbergianae, 1935), pp. 183, 200.

7. Eubel, *Hierarchia Catholica*, vol. 3, p. 200, says that Giovanni Ruffo held Cadiz from 8 Sept. 1523 to 6 Sept. 1525, and that Geronimo, Giovanni Ruffo's nephew, took Cadiz from his uncle and held it until 25 Oct. 1564. Geronimo

was called back to Italy in 1529 "to settle matters in Forlì" and in 1536 became *secretarius apostolicus*. He was at Trent in 1546–47 and resigned his see in
1564. For a Teodoli family tree: Christoph Weber, *Genealogien zur Papstgeschichte*, vol. 2 (Stuttgart: Anton Hiersemann, 1999), p. 935.

8. For this *vigna* (vineyard) and its replacement by the Altemps *vigna* under
   Pius IV: David R. Coffin, *The Villa in the Life of Renaissance Rome* (Princeton:
   Princeton University Press, 1979), pp. 174–75. For a 1632 painting of the
   palace: Richard Krautheimer, *The Rome of Alexander VII, 1655–1667* (Princeton:
   Princeton University Press, 1985), p. 22. The palace already appears on the
   Bufalini map of 1551.

9. Giulio Silvestrelli, *Città, castelli e terre della regione romana*, 2 vols. (Rome: Multi-
   grafica, 1970), vol. 1, pp. 310–11, 369, for San Vito and Ceciliano, sold to a
   Monsignore Teodoli, presumably Geronimo. Weber, *Genealogien zur Papstgeschichte*, vol. 2, p. 935, shows two plausible candidates for the bishop's dynastic largess named Teodolo Teodoli. The first appears as a son of the
   bishop's brother, Francesco. This elder Teodolo died without issue. The
   second Teodolo, eldest son of our Cavaliere Giacomo, took the title of
   marchese di San Vito in 1591. Weber may have misattributed the first
   Teodolo's parentage, for a veteran servant of the palace, who should have
   known, calls him the bishop's son: fol. 378r, Tomasso d'Avignone.

10. Silvestrelli, *Città, castelli e terre*, vol. 1, p. 369, gives the purchase date as 1572.
    Christoph Weber, *Legati e governatori dello Stato Pontificio* (Rome: Ministero per
    i Beni Culturali e Ambientali, 1994), p. 945, often more accurate, cites 1570
    for the title of conte di Ceciliano.

11. For the cardinal and for the family: Gaetano Moroni, *Dizionario di erudizione
    storico-ecclesiastico*, vol. 74 (Venice, 1855), p. 18; for the architect: *Indice biografico
    italiano* (Munich: Sauer, 1997), s.v.

12. Krautheimer, *Alexander VII*, p. 22; for the eighteenth-century revival of the
    line after it died out in Rome: Giovanni Battista Crollalanza, *Dizionario
    storico-blasonico delle famiglie nobili e notabili italiane*, vol. 3 (Bologna: Forni, n.d.),
    p. 49.

13. Weber, *Genealogien zur Papstgeschichte*, vol. 2, p. 935. Giovanni Ruffo Teodoli
    was thus a great-uncle.

14. Fol. 397v.

15. Fol. 378r.

16. For letters from Lelio at Ceciliano: fol. 380r, Domenico Gagliardelli, the
    physician; an envelope from Cintia to Lelio gives Ceciliano as his address:
    fol. 406v.

17. Fol. 374r, Alessandro Ruspoli, banker's son, for the stipend.

18. Fol. 371r: Cintia cites letters from Giacomo's brothers. Weber's family tree (*Genealogien zur Papstgeschichte,* vol. 2) shows three brothers, the eldest of them the first Teodolo, who, if he was indeed the bishop's bastard, would have been a cousin.

19. Fol. 375r: Felice calls Mario her *genero* (son-in-law).

20. Pompeo Litta, *Famiglie celebri d'Italia* (Milan and Turin, 1819–83), p. 114, pl. viii, "Orsini"; Weber, *Genealogien zur Papstgeschichte,* vol. 2, p. 935, marks Cornelia as Giacomo's third child.

21. Litta, *Famiglie celebri,* p. 114, pl. viii.

22. Fol. 393v, Cintia, letter 1.

23. Crollalanza, *Dizionario storico-blasonico,* vol. 2, p. 54; Marchesi, *Antica città di Forlì,* passim, for the Maldenti. For a modern photograph of the medieval palace façade: www.queen.it/città/Forlì/ monum/palazzi/Malden.htm.

24. For the Forlì ancestry of the maid who testifies: fol. 376v.

25. Fol. 379v, Domenico Gagliardelli, the physician, had known Lelio Perleoni "for three or so years, for he was living in the house of the aforesaid Signor Giacomo and of his wife, Felice." Gagliardelli had been attached to the Teodoli palace; that fact makes the couple's palace lodging more plausible but not yet sure.

26. Giorgina Masson, *Courtesans of the Italian Renaissance* (New York: Saint Martin's Press, 1975); Monica Kürzel-Runtscheiner, *Töchter der Venus: Die Kurtisanen im 16. Jahrhundert* (Munich: Beck, 1995). The latter work, more scholarly than Masson's, makes much use of archival records. Elizabeth S. Cohen, whose current research on prostitution reaches down the social scale and later in the century, has not uncovered any information on Cintia Antelma.

27. Fol. 370r, Cintia. Fol. 370r: in Sept. 1582, Cintia says that the affair had begun eighteen months before—thus, in the spring of 1581. Fol. 367v: however, Domenico Costa, her brother, testifies to only a year.

28. Fol. 370v, Cintia.

29. Fol. 367v, Domenico Costa. I have not been able to trace this Otterio. Courtesans and other prostitutes very often had steady lovers with exclusive or partial rights to their bodies.

30. For Perleoni citizens of Venice: www/digilander.101.it/marci57/tassini/ppp.html. The Web site, a survey of Venetian monuments, refers to Foscarini, *Della letteratura veneziana,* but gives no more exact citation.

31. See www/geocities.com.Paris/Louvre/3987/Genova/famiglia_fregoso.htm. Unfortunately, the site makes no reference to an authority in print.

32. Fol. 379v, Domenico Gagliardelli, physician; fol. 390v: the court asked if Lelio lived continually with and served Felice; fol. 367v: Domenico Costa,

asked about Cintia's quarters, stated, "Lelio Perleoni da Rimini was always in my sister's house, for the cavaliere's sake, and was as at home as am I"; for reading letters: fol. 371r, Cintia.

33. For Lelio's fights with other gentlemen: fol. 375r, Felice.

34. Fol. 379v, Domenico Gagliardelli.

35. For Domenico Costa's two testimonies: fols. 367r–369v, 373r–v.

36. Fol. 379v, Cintia.

37. Fols. 367v–368r, Domenico Costa: "Lelio came at five or six hours of the night [11 or 12 P.M.] to my sister's house."

38. Fol. 383v, Cintia. Note that Cintia has motive to lie about rummagings in her papers, to duck the pact found in her letter box.

39. Fol. 393r–v, Cintia to Lelio, 24 June 1581 (letter 1).

40. The court understands "C.A.T." that way (fol. 387r) and glosses the initials: "signed 'most affectionate sister C.A.T.' and in other letters 'most affectionate as a sister C.A.T.,' which words mean nothing other than Cintia Antelma Teodoli."

41. The scudo, the standard Roman gold coin, could, however, also be an accounting measure applied to other assets. Thus, we do not know that Lelio had bullion in hand. Fifty scudi was enough for an artisan's daughter's dowry or perhaps his year's income.

42. The Felice here, male or female, cannot be Giacomo's wife, Cintia's rival.

43. Fol. 392r, Cintia to Lelio, 11 Sept. 1581 (letter 2).

44. Fol. 368v, Domenico Costa: "Two or three times I heard them call one another sister and brother. That is, Lelio called Cintia sister, and Cintia called him brother."

45. Fol. 387r–v, Cintia: ." . two months before he had the fight with Signor Giorgio, kinsman of the cavaliere, and some others." But the fight in question probably took place in late spring or early summer 1582, and as we have seen, the letter of Sept. 1581 uses fraternal address.

46. For who fought: fol. 375r, Felice.

47. Fol. 394r, Lelio to Cintia, undated (letter 3).

48. Fol. 399r–v, Lelio to Felice, 17 June 1582 (letter 4).

49. I cannot find Rocha's name in this or similar spelling (Rocca, Larocca) in any works on Rome.

50. Fol. 398r–v, Lelio to Giacomo, undated (letter 5).

51. Fol. 397r, Mario Orsini to the court, 1 Sept. 1582 (letter 6).

52. Fols. 375v–376r.

53. We have no record of an earlier testimony by Felice. The fragmentation of

trial records makes it impossible to say for sure that she never deposed before 27 Sept. 1582.

54. For the earlier arrests: fols. 370v, 386v.

55. Fol. 371r, Cintia: "and for other needs," she adds.

56. Fol. 386v.

57. We can tell that Giacomo is dead by Sept., for he appears consistently throughout the documents as *quondam* (the late), while Lelio has no such label.

58. See chapter 4.

59. Fols. 377r–378r.

60. Nancy Siraisi, "Anatomizing the Past: Physicians and History in Renaissance Culture," *Renaissance Quarterly* 103, no. 1 (Spring 2000): 1–30, discusses the fifteenth-century rise of the historical narrative of illness as a medical literary mode. Here, instead, we have a narrative of a medical test.

61. Thomas V. Cohen, "A Long Day in Monte Rotondo: The Politics of Jeopardy in a Village Rising (1558)," *Comparative Studies in Society and History* 33 (1991): 639–68; Thomas V. Cohen, "Three Forms of Jeopardy: Honor, Pain, and Truth-Telling in a Sixteenth-Century Italian Courtroom," *Sixteenth Century Journal* 29, no. 4 (1998): 975–98. See also chapter 4.

62. Catherine Crawford, "Legalizing Medicine: Early Modern Legal Systems and the Growth of Medico-Legal Knowledge," in Michael Clark and Catherine Crawford, eds., *Legal Medicine in History* (Cambridge: Cambridge University Press, 1994), pp. 89–115, esp. pp. 91–94; Katharine Park, *Doctors and Medicine in Early Renaissance Florence* (Princeton: Princeton University Press, 1985), pp. 87–99, for the many roles, forensic among them, of doctors in communal pay and, p. 89, for their substantial wages, and pp. 131, 133, for the search for fame through *consilia* (essays on cases); Guido Ruggiero, "The Cooperation of Physicians and the State in the Control of Violence in Renaissance Venice," *Journal of the History of Medicine* 33 (1978): 156–66. Ruggiero, pp. 160–62, notes that as here in Rome, the scribe, not the physicians, set the reports' forms.

63. I thank David Gentilcore and Silvia Rienzi for this important fact and the reference that follows: Prosperus Mandosius, *Theatron in quo maximorum Cristiani orbis pontificum archiatros Prosper Mandosius nobilis romanus Ordinis Sancti Stephani Eques spectandos exhibit* (Rome: Pagliarini, 1784), pp. 137–39, with its own pagination but bound with Gaetano Marini, *Degli archiatri pontefici* (Rome: Pagliarini, 1784). In all, Clement appointed thirteen *archiatri*, more

than many popes. Gismondo Brumano's name might also appear as "Sigis-
mundus Brumanus."

64. For the corpses of the condemned: Andrea Carlino, *Books of the Body*, tr. John
Tedeschi and Anne C. Tedeschi (Chicago: University of Chicago Press,
1999), pp. 182–89 and passim; Katharine Park, "The Criminal and the
Saintly Body: Autopsy and Dissection in Renaissance Italy," *Renaissance Quarterly* 47, no. 1 (Spring 1994): 1–33; Katharine Park, "The Life of the Corpse:
Division and Dissection in Late Medieval Europe," *Journal of the History of
Medicine and Allied Sciences* 50 (1995): 111–32; Giovanna Ferrari, "Public Anatomy Lessons and the Carnival in Bologna," *Past and Present* 117 (Nov. 1987):
50–106 passim. For experiments on living convicts: Walter Artelt, "Die ältesten Nachrichten über die Sektion menschlicher Leichen im mittelalter-
lichen Abendland," *Abhandlungen zur Geschichte der Medizin und der Naturwis-
senschaften,* Heft 34 (Berlin, 1940; repr., Nendeln, Lichtenstein: Kraus,
1969), pp. 3–25, and for a tall story from the Italian chronicler Salimbene di
Adam about a homicidal experiment by Frederick II, see esp. pp. 5–6. For
the possibility that Gabriello Fallopio tried poisons out on convicts: Ferrari,
"Public Anatomy Lessons," p. 60n. For the rumor that Andreas Vesalius did
human vivisection, or almost, such was his haste to cut: Park, "The Criminal and the Saintly Body," p. 19, and for Fallopio's letting a criminal wager
his life against two draughts of opium, and when he lost, dissecting his
unlucky body, see p. 20. For a summary of a French surgeon's account of a
successful experiment to prove inefficacious a poison antidote, the well-
known bezoar stone, that he carried out on the king's behalf upon a
condemned cook, who, thanks to the cure's uselessness, died horribly: Wal-
lace B. Hamby, *Ambroise Paré: Surgeon of the Renaissance* (Saint Louis: Warren H.
Green, 1967), pp. 128–29.

65. Roger French, *Dissection and Vivisection in the European Renaissance* (Brookfield,
Vt.: Aldershot, 1999), pp. 193–214, and, for live animals, esp. pp. 190–200,
205–9. For William Harvey's use of vivisection to establish circulation of
the blood and for Paracelsan objections to its cruelty: Laurence Brockliss
and Colin Jones, *The Medical World of Early Modern France* (Oxford: Clarendon
Press, 1997), pp. 139, 141n. For Vesalius's use of three dead humans and six
live dogs to illustrate twenty-six lectures: Andrew Cunningham, "The
Kinds of Anatomy," *Medical History* 19 (1975): 1–19, esp. p. 4; also Ferrari,
"Public Anatomy Lessons," pp. 62–64, for the same numbers. See Paula
Findlen, *Possessing Nature* (Berkeley and Los Angeles: University of California Press, 1994), pp. 210–12, for how the avid naturalist Aldrovandi dis-
sected all his many captive beasts, exotics included, except his lucky monkey,

whom he merely made drunk; p. 216, for flamingos cut by members of the Roman scientific academy Dei Lincei; p. 279, for feeding the antidote theriac to a cock and then trying assorted poisons on the bird. On Cardano's preference, when he lacked a human, for apes and cows: Nancy Siraisi, *The Clock and the Mirror: Girolamo Cardano and Renaissance Medicine* (Princeton: Princeton University Press, 1997), p. 105. On the early use of pigs by the school of Salerno, in the twelfth century, before regular human dissection: Nancy Siraisi, *Medieval and Early Renaissance Medicine* (Chicago: University of Chicago Press, 1990), p. 86.

66. Barbara J. Shapiro, *A Culture of Fact: England, 1550–1720* (Ithaca: Cornell University Press, 1999), pp. 8–9, reminds us that in early modern Continental Roman law, the concept of *factum* had long been central to evidence's definition. The term "fact" itself came from law's idiom. The easy coexistence of legal and medical senses of evidence in Brumano's report is thus less surprising. The pigeon report owed much to a long history of legal empiricism.

67. Sante Ardoino [Santis Ardoyni Pisaurensis], *Opus de venenis* (Basel: Zuinnger, 1562); Hieronymus Mercurialis, *De morbis venenosis et venenis . . . ,* bound with Iohannis Chrosczieyioskij, *De morbis puerorum* (Venice and Padua: apud Paulum Meietum, 1588); Ambroise Paré, *The Collected Works of Ambroise Paré, Translated Out of the Latin by Thomas Johnson; From the First English Edition, London, 1534* (Pound Ridge, N.Y.: Mildford House, 1968), book 21, pp. 776–810. For Cardano: Siraisi, *The Clock and the Mirror.* On the history of poison itself, modern commentaries can be flimsy and sensationalistic, as with Louis Lewin, *Die Gifte in der Weltgeschichte* (Berlin: Springer, 1920; repr., Hildesheim: Gerstenbert, 1971). Esther Fischer-Homberger, *Medizin vor Gericht* (Bern, Stuttgart, and Vienna: Verlag Hans Huber, 1983), pp. 364–95, is more solid, but pedestrian. Fiume, "Il sordo macello dei mariti," does elegant anthropology on female motivation for eighteenth-century Sicilian husband murders. On poisons and their supposed antidotes: David Gentilcore, *Healers and Healing in Early Modern Italy* (Manchester and New York: Manchester University Press, 1998), pp. 96–124. For Spain: Michael R. McVaugh, *Medicine before the Plague: Practitioners and Their Patients in the Crown of Aragon, 1285–1345* (Cambridge: Cambridge University Press, 1993), p. 59. Lynn Thorndike, *The History of Magic and Experimental Science,* vol. 5 (New York: Columbia University Press, 1941), pp. 472–87, is just a Whiggish summary of treatises.

68. As for the identity of Lelio's poisons themselves, neither their colors nor their actions tell us much. They are unlikely to have been forms of arsenic, which was, despite many rivals, the commonest premodern poison. In the sixteenth century, arsenic usually appeared as a red (realgar, the disulfide)

or yellow (orpiment, the trisulfide) compound. Only white arsenic (the tri-oxide) killed; it was present as a contaminant in the other, harmless forms but, until the seventeenth century, not readily separated; it took patient sub-limation to smoke it out. In Italy in 1582, the white could already be had but was expensive; plentiful arsenic appeared some eight decades later. Note, moreover, that Lelio's white powder was not the most deadly for the pi-geons. For the economic history of early modern arsenic: Kari Konkola, "More Than a Coincidence: The Arrival of Arsenic and the Disappearance of Plague in Early Modern Europe," *Journal of the History of Medicine and Allied Sciences* 47 (1992): 186–209.

69. R. W. Serjeantson, "Testimony and Proof in Early Modern England," *Studies in the History and Philosophy of Science* 30, no. 2 (1999): 195–236, argues that the premodern world saw "testimony" as offering a lesser truth than what writ-ten authorities furnished. It served mere fact, not theory. See p. 206, where human testimony is merely contingent and probable, not binding. Thus, the three-pigeon result, even though a lab report, was good for a specific, not a general, fact. On the other hand, while insufficient to establish a law of na-ture, the pigeon test, along with other evidence, clearly built a case against Cintia Antelma. Though merely probable, it afforded *probatio* (proof). For another discussion of the role of medical testimony in judicial decision of an alleged poison case: Andrée Courtemanche, "The Judge, the Doctor, and the Poisoner: Medical Expertise in Manosquin Judicial Rituals at the End of the Fourteenth Century," in Joelle Rollo-Koster, ed., *Medieval and Early Mod-ern Ritual: Formalized Behavior in Europe, China, and Japan* (Leiden: Brill, 2002), pp. 105–23. In that case, the physician saw a husband's corpse and cleared the wife.

70. For an overview of the interaction of medicine and law: Catherine Craw-ford, "Legalizing Medicine: Early Modern Legal Systems and the Growth of Medico-Legal Knowledge," in Michael Clark and Catherine Crawford, eds., *Legal Medicine in History* (Cambridge: Cambridge University Press, 1994), pp. 89–115. See also Fischer-Homberger, *Medizin vor Gericht*, pp. 24–39; Jo-seph Shatzmiller, *Médecine et justice en Provence médiévale: Documents de Manosque, 1262–1348* (Aix-en-Provence: Publications de l'Université de Provence, 1989).

71. Artelt, "Die ältesten Nachrichten über die Sektion," p. 17; Fischer-Homberger, *Medizin vor Gericht*, p. 35; Alessandro Simili, "Bartolomeo da Varignano e la sua perizia giudiziaria," *Riforma medica* 57, no. 2 (1941): 1101–6 and, for the Latin text of the report of the two physicians and three sur-geons in the case, p. 1102.

72. Darrel W. Amundsen and Gary B. Ferngren, "The Forensic Role of Physicians in Roman Law," *Bulletin of the History of Medicine* 53, no. 1 (Spring 1979): 39–55, on ancient Roman *periti;* Alessandro Simili, "Sulle origini della medicina legale e peritale," *Riforma medica* 75, no. 3 (1961): 753–56 (cursory, largely on the ancients).

73. For the late-thirteenth-century Bolognese procedure of visits to a patient's bedside by two or more *medici* drawn by lot and by a notary: Simili, "Origini," p. 775. Alessandro Simili, "The Beginnings of Forensic Medicine in Bologna (with Two Unpublished Documents)," in H. Karplus, ed., *International Symposium on Society, Medicine, and Law* (Amsterdam: Elsevier, 1973), pp. 91–100. For the thirteenth- and fourteenth-century Provençal visitation custom, in which the judge, the notary, the bailiff, and five medical men all went together to see the patient: Shatzmiller, *Médecine et justice en Provence médiévale,* p. 38.

74. For Aragonese practices, which usually involved sworn or written testimony in the court itself: McVaugh, *Medicine before the Plague,* pp. 207–18.

75. Ardoino, *Opus de venenis,* p. 106.

76. For the notion of combustion and the Galenic humor, or "complexion," theory on which it rested: Siraisi, *Medieval and Early Renaissance Medicine,* pp. 101–6; for combustion, see also Eric Midelfort, *A History of Madness in Sixteenth-Century Germany* (Stanford: Stanford University Press, 1999), p. 147.

77. Giovanni Battista Codronchi, *Methodus testificandi,* bound with his treatise *De vitiis vocis, libri duo . . . cui accedit . . . methodus testificandi . . .* (Francofurti, apud haeredes Andreae Wecheli etc., 1597); on Codronchi, see Fischer-Homberger, *Medizin vor Gericht,* p. 43, for his career, and also pp. 358–60, 371, 387–88, 395, 444n, and passim.

78. Codronchi, *Methodus testificandi,* pp. 226–27.

CHAPTER SIX

1. My student Linda Traverso discovered this case in Rome and, with the help of Raffaele Girardo, made a first transcription, which I later enhanced and corrected. The two students also made a first translation. Xenia von Tippelskirche, a doctoral candidate at Fiesole, has used the case for several papers, where she has made valuable discoveries about what Innocentia read, generously communicated to me. An earlier version of this chapter has appeared as "Bourdieu in Bed: The Seduction of Innocentia (Rome, 1570)," *Journal of Early Modern History* 7, nos. 1–2 (2003): 55–85.

2. Francesca's grown son and daughter figure in this story.

3. Archivio di Stato di Roma, Governatore, Tribunale Criminale, Processi

(sixteenth century), busta 137, case 5 (1570), fol. 3v: Innocentia. Henceforth, I give only the folio number, as all references are to one document unless otherwise indicated.

4. Fol. 3v, Innocentia. Had Francesca been clothed, the admonition to the girl
would have made little sense.

5. Edward Muir, "Observing Trifles," in Edward Muir and Guido Ruggiero,
eds., *Microhistory and the Lost Peoples of Europe* (Baltimore: Johns Hopkins University Press, 1991), pp. vii–xxviii, defends microhistory and surveys its
evolution. Last-ditch defenses fall back on slow empiricist induction.

6. Thomas Kuehn, "Reading Microhistory: The Example of *Giovanni and Lusanna*," *Journal of Modern History* 61 (Sept. 1989): 514–34; Gene Brucker, *Giovanni and Lusanna: Love and Marriage in Renaissance Florence* (Berkeley and Los Angeles: University of California Press, 1986). The hermeneutic circle twists
especially tight in love and courtship, where behavior took cues from art.
Then, it becomes the harder to unravel "what really happened." See Elizabeth S. Cohen and Thomas V. Cohen, "Camilla the Go-Between: The Politics of Gender in a Roman Household (1559)," *Continuity and Change* 4, no. 1
(1989): 53–77. The locus classicus for the artistry of court testimony is Natalie Zemon Davis, *Fiction in the Archives: Pardon Tales and Their Tellers in Sixteenth-
Century France* (Stanford: Stanford University Press, 1987).

7. David Harlan, "Intellectual History and the Return of Literature," *American
Historical Review* 94, no. 3 (June 1989): 581–609, offers an eloquent defense
of the textualist position.

8. We know only that his house is big. For the Bucchi (Bocchi), see Christoph
Weber, *Legati e governatori dello stato pontificio, 1550–1809* (Rome: Ministero per
i Beni Culturali e Ambientali, 1994), p. 504. The two Bolognese families of
Bucchi and Bocchi were distinct, but manuscript vowels were slippery. I
thank Nicholas Terpstra for Bolognese counsel.

9. Fol. 10r, Innocentia. Isabella was from Modena.

10. For Francesca's prior service with the mother: fol. 1r, Innocentia.

11. For his jobs in Rome: fol. 7r, Vespasiano 1. (I will number Vespasiano's four
sessions in court. In sessions 1 and 2, he was defiant and subverted Innocentia's reputation; in sessions 3 and 4, he was more submissive and rebuilt
her reputation.) His first masters were a *"dottore"* from his village, two
archivists, and a member of the Fosco family, who often served as state officials. See Weber, *Legati e governatori*, p. 676.

12. Fol. 10r, Francesca.

13. Ibid.

14. For this and for the quotation: fol. 7r, Vespasiano 1.

15. Fol. 7v, Vespasiano 1; see also fols. 10r, Francesca; 7r, Vespasiano 1. Alessandro was twelve or so, the son of a widow named Camilla, who, like Innocentia's mother, came from Modena: fol. 5v, Innocentia.

16. For this discovery, I thank Xenia von Tippelskirche. Now Ms. von Tippelskirche has written me, however, that she has doubts about the authorship. If, in her dissertation on female reading, she discovers a different author, my own wry point will remain unchanged.

17. Fol. 10r, Francesca.

18. Ibid.

19. Fols. 12v–13r, Vespasiano 2. Innocentia sometimes disobeyed the command to keep the door locked. Vespasiano reported, "[One time] I came in by the door, for Innocentia came and opened it for me, and I asked her with what key she was opening it, and she answered, 'We have made a counterfeit key because Madonna Francesca has certain friends [*amici*] and at night she opens for them as she likes.'" *Amici* here must be male, as women did not wander the city after dark.

20. For the tattler next door: fol. 12v, Vespasiano 2.

21. For the men's use of the window: fols. 1v, Francesca; 2v, 4r, Innocentia. For Innocentia's visits to neighbors: fol. 2v, Innocentia.

22. Fols. 7v–8r, Vespasiano 1.

23. Fol. 8r, Vespasiano 1.

24. Fol. 5v, Innocentia: "She made me say, without giving it a thought, more than a thousand scurrilous things and rhymes [*filastrochi*], not to mention what she herself was doing." For a similar tale of shared magic: Cohen and Cohen, "Camilla the Go-Between."

25. For the motives for a servant's subversion of a master's rules: Cohen and Cohen, "Camilla the Go-Between"; Dennis Romano, *Housecraft and Statecraft: Domestic Service in Renaissance Venice, 1400–1600* (Baltimore: Johns Hopkins University Press, 1996), pp. 207–22; Cissie Fairchilds, *Domestic Enemies: Servants and Their Masters in Old Regime France* (Baltimore: Johns Hopkins University Press, 1984), where servants seem to have less power.

26. Fol. 10v, Francesca.

27. Ibid. Although Francesca next gives a false description of other events, this report seems likely.

28. Fol. 8r, Vespasiano 1.

29. Fol. 10v, Francesca.

30. Fol. 6v, Innocentia.

31. Fol. 15r, Vespasiano 4. See also fol. 14r, Vespasiano 4, for the salad leaf, but also for a report that it was Innocentia herself who overheard.

32. Fols. 14v–15r, Vespasiano 4.

33. Fol. 15r, Vespasiano 4. Note that in favor of Vespasiano's veracity are the circumstantial details and the mention of Menico, a potential witness. See also fols. 8r, Vespasiano 1; 14r, Vespasiano 3.

34. For his sleeping out on Saturdays: fol. 2v, Innocentia.

35. Fol. 1v, Innocentia.

36. Ibid. Ludovico Ariosto, *Orlando furioso*, 30.37. I thank Julia Hairston for tracking down this passage.

37. Luisso's title "Don" suggests tonsure or minor orders.

38. Fols. 1v–2v, Innocentia.

39. Fol. 2v, Innocentia.

40. For pretexts, apples, pears, and poems: fol. 2v, Innocentia; for the money and for "things to eat": fol. 13r, Vespasiano 2.

41. Fols. 2v–3r, Innocentia. We cannot be sure she was reading the book aloud to her neighbor, but it seems likely. Otherwise, why not read by herself at home? For reading aloud: Roger Chartier, "Texts, Printings, Readings," in Lynn Hunt, ed., *The New Cultural History* (Berkeley and Los Angeles: University of California Press, 1989), pp. 154–75, esp. pp. 165, 170.

42. Fols. 2v–3v, Innocentia.

43. For the location of the shirt, see Innocentia's version on fols. 3v–4r. Vespasiano, on the other hand, implied in court that he had worn the shirt. There are two possible translations: the shirt he was wearing at the instant or, less likely, the shirt that he was wearing that day.

44. Fols. 3v–4r, Innocentia.

45. Fol. 5r, Innocentia.

46. Ibid.; fol. 11r, Francesca.

47. Fol. 4v, Innocentia (probably prunes, not plums, as it was already November).

48. Ibid.

49. Fol. 4r–v, Innocentia.

50. Fol. 4v, Innocentia.

51. Ibid. We cannot tell if Menico was still present.

52. Fol. 5r, Innocentia.

53. Ibid.

54. Fol. 4v, Innocentia: "He came several times by day to my house and kissed me and touched me and tried to force me and I didn't want to."

55. Fol. 5r, Innocentia.

56. Fol. 5v, Innocentia. This brother-in-law seems not to have been an uncle, a

brother of Innocentia's mother, for the girl identifies him solely through his links to her stepfather. He must have been the husband of a Bucchi sister.

57. Fol. 8v, Francesca.

58. Fol. 5v, Innocentia.

59. For the poems recited in court: fol. 6r, Innocentia.

60. Ibid. This remembered poem of Vespasiano's is a bit ragged. As recorded, it had the following rhyme scheme: *ababbcc dedeff ghgigijj klklklmm,* each stanza ending in a couplet. The stanzas thus had seven, six, eight, and eight lines. The rhythmic structure is rough, in no classic pattern, but most lines had four major stresses; a few had five or three.

61. Ben Jonson, *Volpone,* 3.7.256–57.

62. Matteo Bandello, *Novelle,* day 1, story 8 (any edition); Marguérite de Navarre, *Heptaméron,* story 10 (any edition; e.g., P. A. Chilton, tr. [Harmondsworth: Penguin, 1984], p. 141).

63. Fol. 6v, Innocentia.

64. Sandra Cavallo and Simona Cerutti, "Female Honor and the Social Control of Reproduction in Piedmont between 1600 and 1800," in Edward Muir and Guido Ruggiero, eds., *Sex and Gender in Historical Perspective* (Baltimore: Johns Hopkins University Press, 1990), pp. 73–109; Thomas V. Cohen and Elizabeth S. Cohen, *Words and Deeds in Renaissance Rome: Trials before the Papal Magistrates* (Toronto: University of Toronto Press, 1993), pp. 126–33, for compensation money. See also Elizabeth S. Cohen, "The Trials of Artemisia Gentileschi: A Rape as History," *Sixteenth Century Journal* 31, no. 1 (2000): 47–75, esp. 59–60; Georges Vigarello, *A History of Rape: Sexual Violence in France from the 16th to the 20th Century,* tr. Jean Birrel (Cambridge: Polity Press, 2001) (French edition, 1998). Arlette Farge, *Fragile Lives: Violence, Power, and Solidarity in Eighteenth-Century Paris,* tr. Carol Shelton (Cambridge: Harvard University Press, 1993), pp. 26–41, discusses the seductions and seduction narratives of Parisian women of a lower class than Innocentia's, with parallels but signal differences.

65. Cohen and Cohen, "Camilla the Go-Between." See also Bandello, *Novelle,* day 1, story 9 (any edition), for a pair of go-betweens. At the Hermitage, see Giulio Romano's courtesan, seated on her bed with her lover while the old *mezzana* peers in from the open door. James C. Scott, *Domination and the Arts of Resistance: Hidden Transcripts* (New Haven: Yale University Press, 1990), pp. 162–66, discusses the trickster, but more as figment of subaltern imagination than as real player or subject for elite fantasies.

66. Fol. 8v, Francesca.

67. Fols. 8v–9r, Francesca.
68. Thomas V. Cohen, "Three Forms of Jeopardy: Honor, Pain, and Truth-Telling in a Sixteenth-Century Italian Courtroom," *Sixteenth Century Journal* 29, no. 4 (1998): 3–29. Scott, in *Domination and the Arts of Resistance,* never discusses supplication. Carlo Ginzburg is more willing to explore gestures of submission. See his *Night Battles: Witchcraft and Agrarian Cults in the Sixteenth and Seventeenth Centuries,* tr. John Tedeschi and Anne Tedeschi (Harmondsworth: Penguin, 1985).
69. Fol. 11r, Francesca.
70. Fol. 11r–v, Francesca.
71. Fol. 10v, Francesca.
72. Fols. 11v–12r, Francesca.
73. Cavallo and Cerutti, "Female Honor," pp. 74–75.
74. Fol. 5r, Innocentia: "And when I was staying *here* in the house of my stepfather" (my italics).
75. Fol. 1r, Innocentia.
76. Fol. 6v, Innocentia. The timing of the remark suggests that she and her advisors had prepared her testimony carefully to be sure it included the usual evidence of bodily harm.
77. Ibid.
78. If so, to command the word was not to possess the language; Innocentia recognized her suitor's Latin but did not fathom it.
79. Elizabeth S. Cohen, "No Longer Virgins: Self-Presentation by Young Women of Late Renaissance Rome," in Marilyn Migiel and Juliana Schiesari, eds., *Refiguring Woman: Perspectives on Gender and the Italian Renaissance* (Ithaca: Cornell University Press, 1991), pp. 169–91; E. S. Cohen, "Artemisia Gentileschi," pp. 70–72.
80. For another attack on the maidservant for a betrayal causing seduction: E. S. Cohen, "Artemisia Gentileschi," p. 72.
81. Fol. 4v, Innocentia.
82. Fol. 8v, Francesca. Almost no judicial papers of the *vicario*'s court survive.
83. Fol. 13v, Vespasiano 3. I have found no trace of such testimony.
84. Fol. 13r, Vespasiano 2.
85. Fol. 13v, Vespasiano 2.
86. Ibid.
87. Nicole Castan, "The Arbitration of Disputes under the *Ancien Régime*," in John Bossy, ed., *Disputes and Settlements: Law and Human Relations in the West* (Cambridge: Cambridge University Press, 1983), pp. 219–60, charts the complex boundary between judicial and extrajudicial settlements; see

pp. 229–31 for seduction and abandonment. For the interplay of mediation and arbitration in one Mediterranean city: Daniel Lord Smail, "Common Violence: Vengeance and Inquisition in Fourteenth-Century Marseille," *Past and Present* 151 (May 1996): 28–59. For the role of courts in social disputes: Daniel Lord Smail, "Hatred as a Social Institution in Late Medieval Society," *Speculum* 76 (Jan. 2001): 90–126, esp. 120–26.

88. Fol. 15r, Vespasiano 3: "The father came to talk to me in jail and he reaffirmed in the presence of Your Lordship all the words he said to me when I asked him to give me Innocentia, his daughter, as wife."

89. Fol. 15r, Vespasiano 3.

90. Fol. 13v, Vespasiano 3. I have searched in vain in many documents to find a second trial. No trace of Vespasiano appears.

91. Fol. 15v, Vespasiano 4.

92. Pierre Bourdieu and Loïc Wacquant, *Towards a Reflexive Sociology* (Chicago: University of Chicago Press, 1992), p. 93 n. 40.

93. Ibid., pp. 20–21. For Bourdieu's opposition to the autobiographic self-fascination of Clifford Geertz and others: p. 72.

94. Ibid., p. 98.

95. For light punishments for rape: Guido Ruggiero, *Violence in Early Renaissance Venice* (New Brunswick: Rutgers University Press, 1980), pp. 156–59.

96. For this complex, controversial argument: E. S. Cohen, "Artemesia Gentileschi," esp. pp. 47–48, 55, 65–68.

97. Per Bak and Kan Chen, "Self-organized Criticality," *Scientific American* 264, no. 1 (Jan. 1991): 46–53.

INDEX

abortion, 156

adultery, 17, 20, 41, 166, 269n.131; law of murder and, 25, 231n.30

African (slave of Ascanio Giustini), 256n.165

agency, 122, 202; role play and, 13; moral conflicts and, 41; of women, 67, 75, 120, 227. *See also* women, agency of

Alberini, Marco (chronicler), 247n.39, 249n.66

Alberini, Rutilio (brother of Tiberio), 115

Alberini, Tiberio (husband of Cecilia Giustini), 84, 87, 91–92, 106, 115, 247n.39, 253n.135

Alberini family, 81, 95, 119

Alberto (lover of Lucretia Gramar), 150–51

Aldobrandini, Silvestro (papal secretary), 129, 131, 167

Aldrovandi, Ulissi, 278n.65

Alemanni, Alemanno (member of Santa Caterina confraternity), 56, 63

Alessandra (Bucchi neighbor), 203

Alessandro (young friend of the Bucchi), 203, 210, 283n.15

Alessio Lorenziano (beadle in love with Lucretia Casasanta), 12, 41, 52–69, 226

Amatrice (town), 160

Amayden, Theodoro (chronicler), 76, 240n.59, 241nn. 5, 7

amicitia, 268n.122

Amundsen, D., 280n.72

Ancona, 110–11

animals sacrificed to science, 192

binage, 141–46; as smuggler of his daughters' babies, 156, 161–62; testimony of, 145, 267n.100

Faustina (third daughter): birth, 138; concubinage, 155–59, 270n.153; first pregnancy, 155–56; jailed, 127; life story, 154–60; lodging in a nunnery, 158–59; protection of Livia from Pallantieri; 165, 272n.225; second pregnancy, 156–57, 160; seduction and rape by Pallantieri, 154–55; sexual history, 146; testimony of, 149, 154–55; torture, 159–60

Helena (Faustina's daughter by Pallantieri): birth, 157, 160; life story, 160–63; precarious baptism, 161–62

Livia (youngest daughter), 144, 149, 151; birth, 138, 163; character, 163; flirtations, 163–64; interrogation by Pallantieri, 164; life story, 163–65; literacy, 159; marriage, 158; shame for her family, 163; social awareness, 145–47; testimony of, 159, 163–65; as victim of Pallantieri's sexual advaces, 157–58, 164–65

Lucretia (eldest daughter): adulterous love affair, 150; assistance at sisters' childbirths, 157; birth, 138; concubinage with Pallantieri, 143–49; in court, 135, 147–48, 157; feelings expressed in court, 147–48, 150–51, 157; jailed, 127; marriage, 149–50; music lessons of, 138; pregnancy, 142, 146–48; relations with her son Orazio, 153; seduction and rape, 140–42;

testimony of, 136, 148–49, 155, 157; torture, 135–37, 147

Martia (second daughter): assistance at sisters' childbirths, 156; death, 154, 158; molestation by Pallantieri, 154, 158; presence at Faustina's rape, 154–55

Orazio (Lucretia's son by Pallantieri), 155; birth, 147–48; life story, 151–54

Stefano (son): patronized by Pallantieri, 153; still at liberty, 127

Grandi, Paolo (historian of Castel Bolognese, Pallantieri's town), 168, 262nn. 4, 7, 11, 263nn. 17, 21, 29, 31

Grieco, A., 268n.115

grief, 33

Grimani, Cardinal, 132

Groppi, A., 235n.6

Grubb, J., 255n.159

Gubbio, 96, 100, 109, 260n.226

Guicciardini, Francesco (historian and administrator), 174

habitus, 222

hair: uncovered, 89; washed, 55–56

Hairston, J., 284n.36

halberds, 102–3, 258n.184

Hamby, W., 278n.64

handkerchiefs, 41, 61–63, 186, 226

Hanlon, G., 258n.200

Harlan, D., 282n.7

heart, 180; dictates of, 61, 196; as surety, 196;

hermeneutic circle, and courtship, 282n.6

hierarchy, 168–69

Hippocrates, 192, 194, 196